CROWNS IN CONFLICT

Also by Theo Aronson

THE GOLDEN BEES
The Story of the Bonapartes

ROYAL VENDETTA
The Crown of Spain (1829–1965)

THE COBURGS OF BELGIUM

THE FALL OF THE THIRD NAPOLEON

THE KAISERS

QUEEN VICTORIA AND THE BONAPARTES

GRANDMAMA OF EUROPE
The Crowned Descendants of Queen Victoria

A FAMILY OF KINGS
The Descendants of Christian IX of Denmark

ROYAL AMBASSADORS
British Royalties in Southern Africa 1860–1947

VICTORIA AND DISRAELI
The Making of a Romantic Partnership

KINGS OVER THE WATER
The Saga of the Stuart Pretenders

MR RHODES AND THE PRINCESS: a play

PRINCESS ALICE
Countess of Athlone

ROYAL FAMILY
Years of Transition

CROWNS
IN CONFLICT

*The Triumph and the Tragedy
of European Monarchy
1910–1918*

THEO ARONSON

John Murray

© Theo Aronson 1986

First published 1986
by John Murray (Publishers) Ltd
50 Albemarle Street, London WIX 4BD

Typeset by Inforum Ltd, Portsmouth
Printed and bound in Great Britain
by Butler & Tanner Ltd, Frome

British Library Cataloguing in Publication Data
Aronson, Theo
Crowns in conflict : the triumph and the tragedy
of European monarchy 1910–1918.
1. Europe——Kings and rulers 2. Europe——
History——20th century
I. Title
940.2'88'0880621   D412.7
ISBN 0-7195-4279-0

Contents

Illustrations

Maps

ACKNOWLEDGEMENTS

1 From *George V* by John Gore, John Murray; 2 From *Recollections of
Three Kaisers* by ?, Herbert Jenkins 1929; 3, 15 Theo Aronson; 4, 13, 14,
16, 19, 20, 21, 22, 23, 24, 27, 28, 29, 30, 31, 32, 33 Imperial War Museum;
5, 6, 7, 8, 9, 10, 11, 17, 18, 25, 34 Reproduced by gracious permission of
Her Majesty The Queen; 12 From *The Life of the Emperor Joseph* by
Francis Gribble, Everleigh Nash 1914; 26 From *The Story of My Life* by
Marie Queen of Roumania, Cassell 1935

For
STELLA and COLLIE HILL
in memory of La Rimade

Simplified table showing the relationship between the First World War monarchs

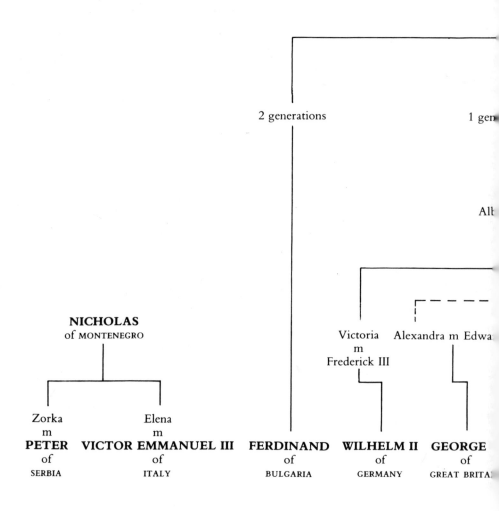

2 generations

1 gen

Alb

NICHOLAS
of MONTENEGRO

Victoria
m
Frederick III

Alexandra m Edwa

Zorka	Elena			
m	m			
PETER	**VICTOR EMMANUEL III**	**FERDINAND**	**WILHELM II**	**GEORGE**
of	of	of	of	of
SERBIA	ITALY	BULGARIA	GERMANY	GREAT BRITA

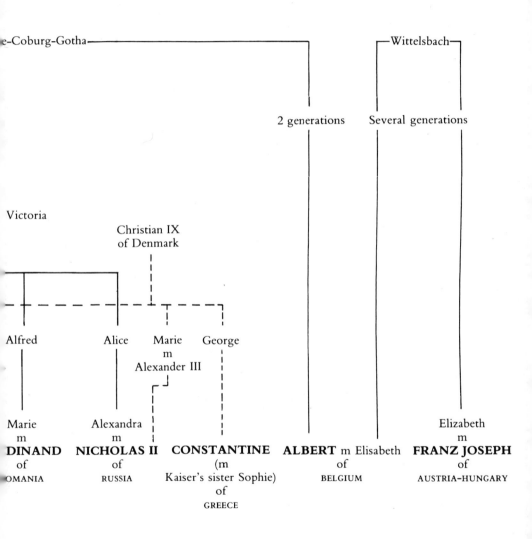

e-Coburg-Gotha   ⌐Wittelsbach⌐

2 generations   Several generations

Victoria

Christian IX
of Denmark

Alfred   Alice   Marie   George
                   m
           Alexander III

Marie   Alexandra   Elizabeth
m   m   m
DINAND   **NICHOLAS II**   **CONSTANTINE**   **ALBERT** m Elisabeth   **FRANZ JOSEPH**
of   of   (m   of   of
OMANIA   RUSSIA   Kaiser's sister Sophie)   BELGIUM   AUSTRIA–HUNGARY
                               of
                             GREECE

Author's Note

THIS BOOK is not a history of the First World War. Nor is it a political, economic and social survey of Europe from 1910 to 1918. It is a study of European monarchy in the final years of its last great flowering and, more particularly, of the twelve monarchs involved in the conflict of 1914–1918. The focus, throughout, is on the personal fortunes of these sovereigns; it is biography rather than history.

Whereas the falls of the Romanov, Habsburg and Hohenzollern dynasties have been dealt with before, this is the first time that the entire cast of embattled monarchs – including the lesser-known but no less interesting personalities such as the sovereigns of Bulgaria, Montenegro, Romania and Serbia – has been assembled in one book. It is the story of eight momentous years viewed, as it were, from the monarchical standpoint. The characters are dealt with in relation to each other, as members of an inter-related and international brotherhood, rather than as individual national sovereigns. It is an account of the passing, not only of their particular world, but of the entire monarchic and dynastic order of the Continent. It describes the brilliant sunset and the dramatic break-up of the Europe of the Kings.

I have received a great deal of help during the writing of this book. I am grateful to Queen Elizabeth The Queen Mother who very kindly gave me her impressions of Queen Marie of Romania; and to the late Princess Alice, Countess of Athlone, for her memories of so many of the characters portrayed in this book, particularly Kaiser Wilhelm II and King Albert and Queen Elisabeth of the Belgians.

Then I must thank those many people who, to a greater or lesser extent, have given me information and assistance. They are, in alphabetical order: Sir Alastair Aird; Dr Becker of the Staatsarchiv Sigmaringen; Dr Horst Brettner-Messler of the Haus- Hof- und Staatsarchiv, Vienna; Mr Gordon Brook-Shepherd; Dr Francesca Di Cesare, Director of the Biblioteca di Storia Moderna e Contemporanea, Rome; Mr S. Clout of the Imperial War Museum; Miss Frances Dimond, Royal Archives, Windsor Castle; Mr Oliver Everett, the Librarian, Windsor Castle; Mrs Irmgard Flett; Dr S.R. Foister; Dr E.G. Franz, Director of the Hessisches Staatsarchiv, Darmstadt; Angela Griffiths; Doreen and Malcolm Jones; Dr Letkemann, Director of the Geheimes Staatsarchiv, Berlin; the Countess of Longford; Mr Antonio

Spallone, Librarian at the Instituto Italiano di Cultura, London; Professor Norman Stone; Sir Roy Strong; Mr Emile Vandewoude, Archivist of the Palais Royal, Brussels; Mr R.I.B. Webster; Mr Peter Wilson.

As always, Brian Roberts has given me invaluable advice, encouragement and assistance.

I am grateful to the staffs of the British Library, the Newspaper Library at Colindale, the Bath Reference Library, the Bristol Reference Library, and the Department of Printed Books at the Imperial War Museum. To Mrs S. Bane and the staff of the Frome Library, I am, as always, deeply indebted for their unfailing patience and efficiency.

I must acknowledge the gracious permission of Her Majesty The Queen for the republication of material from the Royal Archives which is subject to copyright. Although I have listed all books consulted in the Bibliography, I am particularly grateful to the authors of the following books: *The Last Habsburg* by Gordon Brook-Shepherd, *Foxy Ferdinand, Tsar of Bulgaria* by Stephen Constant and *The Fall of the House of Savoy* by Robert Katz.

Prologue

'The Pomp of Kings'

OF ALL THE PAGEANTRY that marked the funeral of King Edward VII on 20 May 1910, nothing was more spectacular than the famous 'Parade of Kings'. This was the cavalcade, not only of kings and emperors but of crown princes, archdukes, grand-dukes and princes, that followed the slowly trundling coffin through the streets of London.

Never, declared *The Times*, had the British capital seen anything 'more splendid, more stately or more impressive'. Over fifty royal horsemen – nine monarchs, five heirs-apparent, forty imperial, royal and serene highnesses – rode through the densely packed streets. Three by three, with plumes fluttering, orders flashing, gold braid glinting and accoutrements all a-jingle, these 'visions', as *The Times* effusively put it, 'of gold and scarlet and blue and green' passed by in the bright spring sunshine. Behind, in twelve crimson and gold state carriages, came a galaxy of queens and princesses.

Here was a moment of supreme monarchical glory. Never before had such a concourse of royalty been gathered together in one place. What Queen Victoria used to call 'the Royal Mob' was out in force. Republican envoys, no matter how powerful the countries they represented, were firmly relegated to the end of the procession.

To the crowds lining the route from Westminster Hall to Paddington station, some of these royal figures were instantly recognisable. Beside the new British King, George V, rode the German Emperor, Wilhelm II. His features – the waxed moustache, the steely gaze, the aggressive bearing, the crippled left arm – were as familiar as were the warlike pronouncements by which he regularly sent shivers down the spines of Europe's diplomats. Behind, flanking old King George I of the Hellenes, came two younger sovereigns: King Haakon VII of Norway and King Alfonso XIII of Spain. Between Tsar Ferdinand I of Bulgaria and young King Manoel II of Portugal rode King Frederick VII of Denmark. Finally, with the heir to the Austro-Hungarian empire on his left hand and to the Ottoman empire on his right, came the Continent's newest sovereign, King Albert I of the Belgians.

Here and there, among the assorted royal and imperial highnesses that followed, could be spotted some particularly arresting figure: a Russian grand duke; a Japanese or Chinese prince; the brother of the Khedive of Egypt in a fez; a clutch of Balkan princes in their flat, round caps; a strikingly uniformed Italian duke; a honey-skinned prince of Siam and an olive-skinned prince of Persia; the Crown Prince of Bavaria in a scarlet sash; an Austrian archduke; the Dutch Prince Consort; Prince Danilo of Montenegro who, to the dismay of his British hosts, had arrived in London with an extremely attractive young woman whom he introduced as his absent wife's lady-in-waiting. When the harassed officials expressed grave doubts about the possibility of finding the lady a room in the crowded capital, Prince Danilo remained, they said, remarkably unperturbed.

In the twelve state carriages that followed drove no less than seven queens. With them were assorted princesses and royal duchesses, as well as the younger children of the new British sovereigns, King George and Queen Mary.

Who, seeing this collection of royalty clattering by, could doubt that the institution of kingship was flourishing? Indeed, nothing could better have symbolised the extraordinary early twentieth-century flowering of European monarchy than this swaggering cavalcade. And, with the exception of the more exotic eastern princes, most of these royals were related to each other. The late Edward VII had been known as the Uncle of Europe: and where he had not been the uncle of Europe's various kings and queens, they had been his cousins, or cousins-by-marriage, at several removes. There was hardly a Continental court that did not boast at least one of Edward VII's Coburg relations.

So Edward VII's grandiose funeral served both as a domestic occasion and as a public flourish. It was, as one of the late King's equerries put it, 'as much a family gathering as the mustering of a profession'. It marked, or seemed to mark, an apogee in the long history of Europe's reigning houses.

This famous 'Parade of Kings' illustrated something else. It was tangible proof of the tenacity of the ideal of monarchy. Who would have thought that well over a century after the French Revolution had threatened to sweep away the whole concept of kingship, the crowned heads of Europe would still be so firmly ensconced? Some thrones had fallen and others been shaken but the principle of monarchy had survived. And not only had it withstood the French Revolution and the revolutions that had followed it, but it had weathered the nineteenth-century spread of liberal, democratic, socialist and radical ideas.

How had this been achieved? Amazingly resilient, the reigning houses had come to terms with the liberal tenor of the times. It was as though they had an unspoken pact with liberalism. Because the burgeoning middle classes had persuaded themselves that the ruling dynasties had been converted to liberalism, the dynasties – by accomplishing some of the objects of liberalism – had contained it. When their subjects had demanded constitutions, they had granted them. Where there had been a clamour for extended suffrage, they had agreed to it. Nineteenth-century monarchs, as one historian has put it, 'excelled at selectively ingesting, adapting and assimilating new ideas and practices without seriously endangering their traditional status, temperament and outlook'.[1] The art which monarchy practised with more skill than any other was the art of self-preservation.

The monarchy, as one disgruntled British politician complained, 'has been sold to the democracy as the symbol of itself'.

Indeed, not only had monarchy ridden out the political storms of the nineteenth century, it had emerged from them with heightened prestige. Instead of diminishing, thrones had multiplied. The second half of the nineteenth century and the early years of the twentieth had seen the setting up of some half a dozen new thrones. Even as late as 1905, when Norway declared its independence from Sweden, it seemed inconceivable that the new head of state should be anything other than a king. The crowned heads of Europe lost no time in elevating a Danish prince, as King Haakon VII, to this 'revolutionary' throne.

By the year 1910, there were more monarchies than there had ever been. Without counting the sovereigns whose kingdoms and duchies went to make up the German empire, there were twenty reigning monarchs in Europe. Every country other than France and Switzerland (and even France had re-established the monarchy four times during the last century) was ruled by a sovereign.

Kings might no longer reign by divine right but, as hereditary monarchs, whether they be all-powerful autocrats as in Russia or virtually powerless constitutional monarchs as in Britain, their prestige and positions remained almost intact. A crowned and anointed sovereign was still generally regarded as someone mystical, unassailable, divinely guided.

Whatever their powers, the monarchs remained the glittering centrepieces of the hierarchical political systems of Europe. A reigning sovereign was the supreme national figure. He was the personification of the state, the symbol of continuity, the emblem of permanence, the magnet of all loyalties, the embodiment of the past history and the present identity of the nation. Laws were passed, orders issued, treaties signed and war declared in their names. Their portraits appeared, not only in all public offices and many private homes, but on banknotes, coins and stamps. So sacred was the image of the monarch that in certain areas of the Russian empire post office officials were said to be afraid to overstamp the Tsar's head.

The great ceremonies of state were all designed to exalt the monarchy. King, emperor or tsar was the focal point of meticulously stage-managed public appearances. No matter how wise or foolish, weak or strong, impressive or insignificant these sovereigns might be as individuals, the matrix of ceremonial ensured that they never appeared as anything less than demigods. There was nothing like a bemedalled uniform, a couple of handsome equerries and a row of obsequiously bowing officials to add lustre to even the most undistinguished-looking royal figure.

As commanders-in-chief of their armies, these soldier-kings could command an extraordinary degree of loyalty and adulation. They were forever reviewing troops, attending manoeuvres, taking part in military parades. Soldiers were invariably regarded as the sovereign's own men, and this was how many of the men regarded themselves. The Emperor Franz Joseph always referred to the Austro-Hungarian army as 'My Army'. In turn, his elegantly uniformed officers tended to walk with their heads thrust forward and their shoulders slumped in imitation of the ageing, round-shouldered Emperor.

'Don't think, officers,' declaimed one British general with more theatricality than accuracy, 'that I take orders from those swines of politicians! No, I only take orders from the Sovereign.'[2]

As well as being head of state, the monarch was head of society. During the first years of the twentieth century, reigning sovereigns remained the apex of a social pyramid, of a class structure that appeared fixed and immutable. Bolstered by the nobility, the aristocracy and a growing bourgeoisie increasingly anxious to emulate and identify itself with the upper classes, the monarchy seemed impregnable. Shrewdly, as the only institution that could legally confer titles and honours, the monarchy used this power to buy off any possible opposition. On the Continent, and in Germany especially, the rising middle classes were showered with orders and decorations. There was the Order of the Black Eagle, the Order of the Red Eagle, the Prussian Order of the Crown, the Order of the House of Hohenzollern and countless others.

'These orders, in turn,' noted one bemused American diplomat, 'are divided into numerous classes. For instance, a man can have the Red Eagle Order of the first, second, third or fourth class, and these may be complicated with a laurel crown, with swords, and with stars, and so on. Even domestic servants who have served a long time in one family receive orders . . .'[3]

The monarchs themselves were hardly less obsessed with decorations. Kaiser Wilhelm II, with all the audacity of the pot calling the kettle black, once described Tsar Ferdinand of Bulgaria as 'festooned with decorations like a Christmas tree'. And King Edward VII would be annoyed for hours if he spotted an order incorrectly worn or a uniform wrongly chosen.

Few things delighted these sovereigns more than the opportunity of wearing yet another uniform. Every state visit gave them the chance of buttoning themselves into the uniform of one of their host's regiments. 'What sort of dress for our meeting?' cabled an excited Wilhelm II to Nicholas II before their yachts dropped anchor for an informal get-together off the coast of Finland. No matter how outlandish a uniform the Tsar might suggest, the Kaiser's valets would be able to find it in one of his gleaming mahogany wardrobes.

But it was not only the political and social structures that ensured that the monarchy held the central position in national life. The very cities and palaces in which they lived emphasised the fact. Their capitals, which had burgeoned so spectacularly during the course of the nineteenth century, were monuments to traditionalism. The banks looked like Florentine *palazzi*, the museums like Greek temples, the railway stations like Gothic cathedrals. Every public building, whatever its style, recalled the glories of the past. And the focal point of these grandiose cities was the palace. More than the cathedral, more than the parliament house, these palaces dominated the capital. Reached by processional ways and triumphal arches, offset by vast squares and flamboyant statuary, built – for the most part – in the richly assertive Renaissance style, they were guaranteed to glorify and impress.

And where it was felt that yet more glorification was called for, there were additional civic tributes to the virtues and strengths of kings. Every other square boasted a statue of an elaborately helmeted monarch on a precariously rearing horse. In the Siegesallee in Berlin, Wilhelm II had erected thirty-two statues of past rulers as a memorial to the House of Hohenzollern from which he sprang. In Rome a white marble monument, looking like a giant wedding cake, was dedicated to the achievements of King Victor Emmanuel II. In London, plans had already been drawn up for the erection, outside Buckingham Palace, of a triumphant memorial to Queen Victoria.

In their portraits, by Fildes, Noster or Angeli, the sovereigns were depicted as the very personifications of power. Against backgrounds of swagged red velvet, they stood proud and masterful in their ermine-trimmed robes: one hand gripping a sceptre, the other the hilt of a sword, while on the gilded table beside them rested the supreme symbol of their office, a richly jewelled crown. These portraits could just as well have been painted in the *Grand Siècle*.

Within their palaces, everything was designed to overawe. 'With all their glitter and pageantry, their pomp and mise-en-scène,' writes Lord Frederic Hamilton, the courts of Europe emphasised the sovereign's direct link with the days of the divine right of kings. The state apartments were almost overwhelming in their magnificence. 'The throne room,' runs his breathless account of Wilhelm II's Berlin palace, 'was one of the most sumptuous in the world . . .'

Even more sumptuous were the Russian palaces. The Winter Palace in St Petersburg, with its *enfilade* of state rooms, gleaming with marble, porphyry and malachite and glittering with gold, glass and crystal, made an unrivalled royal setting, almost barbaric in its splendour. Yet the Dowager Tsaritsa of Russia could exclaim that she had no words to describe the beauty of Edward VII's embellishments to Buckingham Palace. 'It makes one's mouth water to see all this magnificence,' she reported to her son, Nicholas II.

Ceremonial within these lavish settings was formal to a degree. Everyone moved in strict order of precedence; everything was acted out according to long-established custom. Etiquette was particularly exacting at the courts of the three Continental empires – Germany, Russia and Austria-Hungary. It gave them an unreal air. Wilhelm II's court swarmed with pages dressed in the wigs, ruffles and knee-breeches of Frederick the Great's day. Four gigantic negroes in scarlet trousers, gold-embroidered jackets and white turbans stood guard at Tsar Nicholas II's door. 'They were not soldiers', explained the Tsaritsa's friend, Anna Vyrubova, 'and had no function except to open and close doors or to signal, by a sudden noiseless entrance into a room, that one of Their Majesties was about to appear.'

To be invited to a 'Ball at Court' (not to be confused with the less exclusive 'Court Ball') at the Emperor Franz Joseph's palace in Vienna, one had to lay claim to sixteen quarterings: to be able to prove, in other words, that one could trace one's ancestry back to eight male and eight female noble forebears. It was no wonder that the balls at the Hofburg were so deadly dull.

That these sovereigns saw themselves as a race of superior beings can hardly be wondered at. Even the more enlightened Edward VII remained acutely aware of the mystique that set kings apart from other mortals. When the German Crown Prince protested at having to give precedence at the British court to Kalakua, King of the Cannibal Islands, Edward VII had a perfectly reasonable explanation. 'Either the brute is a king,' he argued, 'or he is an ordinary black nigger. And if he is not a king, why is he here?'

Indeed, the profusion of imperial, royal, grand-ducal and most serene highnesses (not to mention imperial *and* royal highnesses) made for endless complications of precedence. Touchiest of all in these matters were the sovereigns themselves. Wilhelm II had once earned the sharp edge of his grandmother, Queen Victoria's tongue by suggesting that his Uncle Bertie, at that stage still Prince of Wales, treat him as an emperor in private as well as in public. And after Edward VII's funeral, the young King Alfonso XIII of Spain lodged a formal protest at being placed behind the older Kaiser, on the grounds that whereas he had succeeded at birth, in 1886, Wilhelm II had not succeeded until two years later. It was patiently explained that it was the Kaiser's close relationship to the late King, and not his seniority, that had earned him his place in the first row.

More heated still was the row between Tsar Ferdinand of Bulgaria and the

Archduke Franz Ferdinand of Austria as the Orient Express hurtled them across Europe towards London for Edward VII's funeral. With each wanting to have his private carriage ahead of the other, the Archduke had triumphed by having his carriage placed immediately after the engine. But Tsar Ferdinand had his revenge. As the Archduke needed to pass through the Tsar's carriage to reach the dining car, Ferdinand was able to refuse him permission to do so. The result was that the Archduke had to wait until the train reached a station, alight, hurry along the platform to the dining saloon and, having eaten, wait until the train stopped at another station before making his way back to his carriage.

Thorniest of all was the question of royal marriages. To maintain the illusion of a superior breed, royals intermarried. A *mésalliance* was regarded as little less than a mortal sin. The plainest of princesses who, in any other station, might have considered herself lucky to find a husband, frequently ended up a queen. For to marry outside the golden stockade of royalty was to court disaster.

When the Grand Duke Michael, brother of Tsar Nicholas II, married the twice-divorced daughter of a Moscow lawyer, his mother, the Dowager Tsaritsa, pronounced it 'so appalling in every way that it nearly *kills* me!' The marriage had to be kept, she instructed, '*absolutely secret*'. And when the Archduke Franz Ferdinand, heir to the Austro-Hungarian throne, married a mere countess, his transgression shook the meticulously structured Habsburg monarchy to its foundations. The union had to be morganatic, his wife had to give precedence to the least important of the archduchesses and his children were to be denied any rights as members of the imperial house. To this, the Archduke Franz Ferdinand had to swear a solemn oath.

Nor were these draconian prohibitions confined to the leading royal houses. One poor princess of Saxe-Weimar, on being told that she could not possibly, as a member of a royal family, marry a Jewish banker, promptly shot herself.

This same aura of exclusivity, of imperiousness, of grandeur surrounded these monarchs as they moved about their realms or paid state visits to their fellow sovereigns. They went bowling along beflagged boulevards in spectacular carriage processions; they cruised the Baltic or the Mediterranean in superbly appointed yachts; they drove to private appointments in highly polished motor cars. But, above all, they travelled by train. The opening years of the twentieth century saw the high summer of royal train travel. From Lisbon to St Petersburg, from London to Constantinople, these palaces-on-wheels carried the royal families of Europe to christenings, weddings, funerals, house-parties, private visits and public jamborees. The red carpet was forever being rolled out and the potted palms forever being set up for the arrival of yet another king or crown prince or dowager empress.

King George V's private carriages were as richly upholstered and as cluttered as any drawing-room at Sandringham. Kaiser Wilhelm II's dark blue and ivory coaches were decorated in ice-blue satin. The Tsar of Bulgaria's private train, with its green velvet walls in the drawing-room carriage and its turquoise silk hangings in the bedrooms, was described as '*un vrai bijou d'intimité voyageuse*'. Perhaps most luxurious of all was Tsar Nicholas II's train. Consisting of a string of royal blue saloon cars with the double-headed eagle coat of arms emblazoned in gold on the sides, it had everything – sitting-rooms, bedrooms, a study, a dining saloon, a kitchen equipped with all modern conveniences – to ensure the comfort of the imperial family as they journeyed across the interminable distances of the Russian empire. To confuse any potential assassin, two identical trains would make every journey. If nothing else, this halved the chances of the Tsar being blown to smithereens by revolutionaries.

The most important train journeys undertaken by the crowned heads were those which carried them on visits to each other. The meetings, both public and private, between the sovereigns of Europe, were generally regarded as momentous occasions. Who could doubt that by their exchange of showy state visits or by their informal talks in some Continental spa these crowned cousins were making history? Surely these plumed and bemedalled sovereigns were settling matters of international importance? Surely these queens and princesses, with their aigrettes, feather boas and pouter-pigeon silhouettes, were planning further dynastic aggrandisement? Could those mammoth family gatherings, on yachts or in country palaces, be anything other than occasions of great consequence?

The late Edward VII had certainly been regarded as a supreme royal diplomat. By his state visits to almost every capital in Europe, he had given the impression that he was a political force; that by his air of authority and astuteness of mind he was manipulating the affairs of Europe. His nephew, the Kaiser, had no doubt whatsoever that this was true. Edward VII might have been known as 'the Peacemaker' to some but to Wilhelm II he was 'the Encircler': a satanic schemer intent on ringing Germany with enemies. This was why, when, standing before the coffin of Edward VII, the Kaiser and the new British King ('the Encircler's' son, George V) clasped hands, their gesture was regarded – by the Kaiser at least – as one of deep international significance.

Even the most trivial incidents could have far-reaching repercussions. In 1909 Tsar Ferdinand of Bulgaria arrived on a state visit to Berlin with a valuable armaments contract which he intended to give to the German firm of Krupps. But while Ferdinand was leaning out of a window of the Neues Palais in Potsdam, on the occasion of a banquet in his honour, his fat bottom was stingingly slapped by his host, the exuberant Kaiser. When Wilhelm II refused to apologise for this bit of horseplay, Ferdinand left the palace in a huff. With him went his important armaments contract, to be placed with the rival French firm of Schneider-Creusot.

Enhancing still further the status of Europe's monarchs during this period was the growth of nationalism. Throughout the second half of the nineteenth century, as one after another of the populations of Europe were united into national groupings and people began to think of themselves primarily as Germans or Italians or Romanians, so did national pride become increasingly more militant. And who better to symbolise these ever more aggressive feelings of national identity than a national monarch? So gorgeously uniformed, so confidently mannered, so surrounded by pomp and deference, a king was much more impressive than any frock-coated president. Monarchs became, not only the representatives, but the personification of the state. As late as 1915 the Emperor Franz Joseph could announce that 'The King of Italy has declared was on Me' rather than that Italy had declared war on Austria–Hungary.

As well as personifying the state, these national sovereigns seemed, in a strange way, to mirror its characteristics. Who other than the sabre-rattling Wilhelm II could have headed the thrusting, aggressive Second Reich? Or than the courtly Franz Joseph the ageing, bureaucratic Austro-Hungarian empire? Even the irresolute Tsar Nicholas II somehow suited amorphous, mystical Holy Russia.

And if these monarchs had developed into the very symbols of nationalism, they had developed, no less, into the symbols of nationalism's natural successor, imperialism. For the early years of the twentieth century saw the golden age of imperialism. This was the era of world powers, of the spread of European civilisation, of high-flown theories of racial superiority, of land-hungry visionaries and exaggerated national pride. The great nations were expanding, trading, colonising, establishing spheres of influence and founding empires. Hard-headed realism walked hand-in-hand with high romance.

Until then, these kings had been monarchs on a European scale; now they were monarchs on a world scale. They found themselves reigning over vast areas of desert or jungle or grassland, over unscaled mountain ranges or unfathomed inland seas, over millions of Arabs and Africans and Indians. It was a time of extravagant imperial titles and extravagant imperial gestures. Britain's George V was a King-Emperor, holding sway over a quarter of the world's land mass and a quarter of the world's population. In 1911, at a huge durbar at Delhi, the capital of his Indian empire, George V stood beneath a golden-domed pavilion to receive the homage of his Indian subjects. 'The magnificent ceremonial among those millions of his peoples, many of whom felt for him and hailed him almost as a god,' wrote one of his biographers, 'convinced him finally and for his life of the majesty of his office . . .'[4]

Nicholas II, 'Autocrat of All the Russians', reigned over 130 million people in an empire so vast that as night was falling on its western borders, day was already breaking on its eastern shore. Not content with this, the Tsar fantasised about a 'Third Rome': a gigantic Russian successor to the Roman and Byzantine empires, which would stretch from the Balkans to the China Sea, incorporating Manchuria, Mongolia, Tibet, China and even India. 'The great task for the future of Russia', encouraged one of the Tsar's fellow sovereigns, 'is to cultivate the Asian continent.'

Kaiser Wilhelm II, as 'The All Highest', delivered thundering speeches on the subject of *Weltpolitik* and of the Reich's determination to claim its 'place in the sun'. His famous Berlin to Baghdad Railway, uniting the icy waters of the Baltic to the balmy waters of the Persian Gulf, was a typically imperialistic enterprise. King Victor Emmanuel III of Italy and King Alfonso XIII of Spain founded new empires in North Africa. The ambitious King Leopold II of the Belgians not only acquired but personally owned the vast Congo empire. From here, he planned to gain a foothold on the Nile and, moving north-wards into Egypt, to establish the Coburgs as latter-day pharaohs. More than one eastern European monarch, mesmerised by the domes and minarets of Constantinople, saw themselves being crowned in Saint Sophia as the new Emperor of Byzantium.

It was no wonder that to the majority of their subjects these flamboyant royal figures were regarded as a race apart. To ordinary people, the institu-tion of monarchy was bathed in an aura of mysticism and romance. Monarchs seemed more like creatures of mythology than men. Even the diseases which ran rife through their dynasties – melancholia in the Habs-burgs, madness in the Wittelsbachs, haemophilia in the Coburgs – tended to be *outré*, shrouded in secrecy. Many Spanish peasants believed the macabre rumour that a young soldier had to be sacrificed every day so that his warm blood might be used to keep Alfonso XIII's son, the haemophilic heir apparent, alive. Even the relatively matter-of-fact British royal family had a prince – King George V's youngest son – shut away from the public gaze.

Their deaths were often highly dramatic. Some of them were blown to bits by anarchists' bombs; others were killed by assassins' bullets; yet others were hacked to death by revolutionaries. Violent death came to be regarded as an occupational hazard. An assassinated sovereign became, in a way, a martyr to the cause of monarchy.

Was it any wonder that kings were considered hardly less than gods? That the dividing line between throne and altar had become increasingly blurred? Many believed monarchs had been especially ordained to rule over them; all knew that kings ranked first after God. In Germany, Wilhelm II used to refer to himself as 'The Instrument of the Almighty'. In Russia, peasants would fall to their knees in the fields as the imperial train thundered by and, in their conviction that the Tsar stood nearer to God than to the people, believed that he went to heaven once a week to confer with the Almighty. East African tribesmen, jolted out of their sleep by a violent earthquake, could only imagine that it signified the death of the King of England. To some, the fact that Halley's Comet had flashed its golden way across the skies on the night before Edward VII's funeral seemed like an omen of supernatural significance.

Could anyone doubt then, that this exclusive royal clan was a race of supermen? Who, seeing this self-confident parade of royalty through the streets of the world's greatest metropolis on the occasion of Edward VII's funeral, could imagine that their future was anything but assured?

How many, among the hundreds of thousands of overawed spectators would have guessed that this blaze of monarchical splendour marked, not a royal high noon, but a royal sunset?

For within a decade it would all – or almost all – have been swept away. Never again could such a multitude of kings and princes be gathered together. The most important of these apparently unassailable monarchs were about to be overthrown; such sovereigns as survived the First World War and its revolutionary aftermath were to be little more than figureheads. Against the military, political and social upheavals of these years, kings were to prove both powerless and irrelevant.

And, with the monarchs, would go a whole way of life. All the pageantry, all the pomp, all the panache with which they had diverted the world for so many centuries would disappear. 'I cannot, though,' wrote one diplomat after the war, 'help experiencing a feeling of regret that this prosaic, drab-coloured twentieth century should have lost so strong an element of the picturesque, and should have permanently severed a link which bound it to the traditions of the medieval days of chivalry and romance, with their glowing colour, their splendid spectacular displays, and the feeling of continuity with a vanished past which they inspired.'[5]

But something far more significant than this was to disappear. The entire monarchic and dynastic order of central Europe, as well as the civilisation built upon it, was about to dissolve. The First World War marked the passing of a social order; it constituted the last chapter of an age in history.

That great Armageddon signalled the end of the Europe of the Kings.

Part One

'THE OLD WORLD
IN ITS SUNSET'

1

The All Highest

WITH THE DEATH of King Edward VII, his nephew, Kaiser Wilhelm II, could at last lay claim to be Europe's leading monarch. While his assured and imposing uncle had been alive, Wilhelm II had always felt slightly overshadowed; now he was confident of having no close rival. King George V might reign over a larger empire, Tsar Nicholas II might wield more personal power, the Emperor Franz Joseph might have been on his throne for almost three times as long, but no one could deny that the Second Reich was the most powerful nation on the Continent and its Kaiser the most spectacular sovereign.

Fifty-one in the year 1910, Wilhelm II had been German Emperor for twenty-two years. During this time he had developed into one of the world's most recognisable figures. In that flood of official portraits and photographs with which he submerged the civilised world, he looked the very epitome of the warrior-king. Pictured in one of his four hundred uniforms, his eyes glaring, his chin jutting, his puffed-out chest glittering with orders, Kaiser Wilhelm II created an image at once heroic and intimidating. It was small wonder that a French general could describe the Kaiser's portrait on the wall of the German Embassy in Paris as 'a declaration of war'.

His public behaviour was hardly less aggressive. Here, too, he was rarely seen out of uniform. His speech was emphatic and his manner assertive. His handshake was like a grip of iron. His walk was an energetic strut. He was never happier than when sitting astride some great white charger acknowledging the cheers of the crowd. He was a tireless orator. In his loud and grating voice he would treat his long-suffering audiences to hours of what he considered to be his God-given eloquence. 'If Your Majesty would be a little more economical of such a gift', ventured one bold friend, 'it would be a hundred times more efficacious.'[1]

The advice came too late. From the day that he succeeded his father, the humane and moderate Frederick III, in 1888, Wilhelm II had been subjecting the world to his bellicose brand of oratory.

His egotism was notorious. He wanted, it was said, to be the bride at every wedding and the corpse at every funeral. He would always refer to 'my army' or 'my fortresses'; he never missed an opportunity to draw attention to 'my prowess' and 'my indefatigability'. Civic visitors' books and regimental bibles throughout Germany carried the sovereign's vainglorious inscriptions. *The Will of the King is the supreme law*, read one; and in the bible of the new Berlin garrison church he wrote, without quotation marks, *Ye shall walk in all the ways which I have commanded you, Wilhelm Imperator Rex.*

That he enjoyed some sort of special relationship with God, he never doubted. He was forever calling on his Celestial Ally to back him up in this or that project. With all the swagger of a parvenu emperor (the German Reich had been proclaimed in 1871, less than forty years before) he insisted that he reigned by divine right; that his sceptre had been handed to him by the King of Kings. Indeed, there were times when it was difficult to decide who ranked first: God or Kaiser.

His talents, he imagined, were exceptional. There were few things to which he did not turn his hand. He fancied himself as a poet, a novelist, a painter, a sculptor, an architect, a designer of ships, a sportsman, a strategist and a diplomat. He chose the Kaiserin's hats and put them on display once a year so that all could appreciate the excellence of his taste. He would assure his listeners that, in common with Frederick the Great, his Hohenzollern ancestor, he was an inspired composer.

To emphasise his manliness, the Kaiser would employ any device, however sadistic. The jewels of his many rings would be turned inwards so as to make his already vice-like handshake more painful. He would subject his entourage to crude practical jokes and punishing physical exercise. His conversation could be cruelly teasing or vehemently derogatory. He was often violent in his denunciation of the Jews or the Socialists.

Wilhelm II was a born showman. With his active encouragement, Berlin was transformed into one of the most impressive capitals in Europe: a city of massive gateways, triumphant statuary and colossal squares. His palaces – the Old Schloss in Berlin and the Neues Palais in Potsdam – were magnificent; his court the most lavish on the Continent. 'The rooms', wrote one enraptured guest, 'are very beautifully decorated. Their painted ceilings, encased in richly-gilt "coffered" work in high relief, have a Venetian effect, recalling some of the rooms in the Doge's Palace . . . Their silk-hung walls, their pictures, and the splendid pieces of old furniture they contain, redeem these rooms from the soulless, impersonal look most palaces wear . . .'[2]

In these ostentatious settings, the Kaiser behaved like the leading actor in a never-ending pageant. 'He did everything on the grandest possible scale; it was overwhelming,' remembered his British cousin, Princess Alice, afterwards Countess of Athlone. With his overdressed Kaiserin by his side and with one or two of his six strapping sons in attendance, he moved in a kaleidoscopic pattern of balls, receptions, parades and state visits. He had a costume for every occasion. For a gala performance of *The Flying Dutchman* he wore a grand admiral's uniform. For his state entrance into Jerusalem he draped himself in a white cloak emblazoned with a crusader's cross. To open the Reichstag he sported a crimson mantle and a gold, eagle-crowned helmet. Only with difficulty was he once dissuaded from dressing himself as a Roman general to inaugurate a museum of antiquities.

He had a passion for travel. Because of this he was known as *der Reise-Kaiser*. Well over half of each year was spent away from Berlin; indeed, a member of his household doubted if he were at home for one hundred days a year. His luxurious white and gold yacht, *Hohenzollern*, flying the imperial pennant with its braggardly message *Gott Mit Uns*, was forever cruising the Baltic or the North Sea; his blue and ivory train was forever criss-crossing the Continent. He visited the Sultan Abdul Hamid II in Constantinople; he rode through the specially widened Jaffa Gate into Jerusalem; he made one of his tactless speeches beside the tomb of Saladin of Damascus. There were few European capitals through which he had not ridden in glorious procession.

That so showy a personality should be surrounded by fawners and flatterers was only to be expected. He lived in an aura of adulation. His circle was as artificial and theatrical as himself. His officers saw themselves as a band of medieval knights devotedly serving their leige rather than as paid servants of the state; generals bent to kiss his hand; statesmen overwhelmed him with praise.

The Kaiser's relationship with his wife, the Kaiserin Augusta Victoria (known in the family as Dona) was generally regarded, in contemporary German terms, as exemplary. Born a princess of Schleswig-Holstein-Sonderburg-Augustenburg (Bismarck called her 'the cow from Holstein') Dona had married Wilhelm in 1881, when they were both aged twenty-two. Since then she had established a reputation as the perfect *Hausfrau*, confining her interests to *Küche, Kinderstube, Krankenstube und Kirche* – kitchen, nursery, sickroom and church. She had borne her husband seven children – six boys and a girl; and in the year 1910 their eldest son, the reactionary and frivolous Crown Prince Wilhelm, turned twenty-eight. The Kaiserin's public behaviour was no less satisfactory. With her full-blown figure and sumptuous dresses, she made a suitably imposing and dignified consort.

One of Wilhelm II's many cousins, the future Queen Marie of Romania, visiting Berlin in these years before the First World War, could not help being impressed by this theatrical Kaiser. He had invited her to accompany him to the official opening of some public building. 'I am grateful', she writes, 'that this occasion was offered me to see, I may even say *feel*, Kaiser Wilhelm in all his Prussian glory during a ceremony when he expanded in an atmosphere profoundly congenial to him and characteristic of truly German achievement . . .

'*Es ist erreicht*. It has been achieved! I felt that this was really Emperor

Wilhelm's Germany, something which had been moulded according to his taste and the ideal he was reaching out for. This colossal building stood for success: huge, solid, somewhat flashy, somewhat too splendid, too new, but an attainment, mighty, audacious, with a touch of aggressiveness about it, almost a challenge in fact . . .

'Luckily there are hours when occasionally some man touches his ideal, be it only for a fleeting instant. I could feel at that moment in my very bones Wilhelm's proud content, and because of this I was able to rejoice with him. In his own special, spectacular way, at that time Kaiser Wilhelm *was* a success.'

Such, then, was the façade. But when one looked behind the baroque grandeur of Wilhelm II's presentation of himself, things were rather different. Seldom, in fact, has the contrast between the fantasy and the reality of monarchy been more pronounced than in the person of Kaiser Wilhelm II.

Close to, with his greying hair, his sagging jowls, his spreading waist and his short stature, the Kaiser was not quite the warlord of popular imagination. He was always careful to keep his undersized left arm – rendered all but useless during his difficult birth – bent, so as to minimise its shortness. To make himself appear taller, he would sit on a cushion. If looked at too hard, he tended to shift that famous piercing gaze. In repose his face wore a sensitive, almost diffident expression. For the truth was that there lay, not far below that assured and brilliant surface, a sense of deep inferiority.

He was not nearly as warlike or as reactionary as he pretended. For all his arrogance, Wilhelm II did not mean any real harm. One of his sons afterwards admitted that, to avoid an appearance of 'softness', his father assumed a hearty toughness quite alien to his true nature. Wilhelm II was a sabre-rattler, not a fighter. He preferred military manoeuvres to actual battle; bloodthirsty words to bloodthirsty deeds. He wanted to be a Napoleon, said Winston Churchill, without fighting Napoleon's battles. He wanted victories without wars.

For all his apparent energy, he was lazy. For all his professed strength of will, he was ill-disciplined and capricious. For all his show of manliness, he was nervous, excitable, emotional. Any crisis, whether personal or political, tended to reduce him to a state of blind panic or nervous exhaustion.

The extravagant, romantic, sentimental atmosphere by which he was so often surrounded was not as innocent as it appeared. In 1907 several members of his entourage were publicly branded as homosexuals and his closest confidant, Count Philipp von Eulenburg (in whose circle the Kaiser was always referred to as *das Liebchen* – the little sweetheart) was actually tried for homosexual offences. Matters were hardly improved when, at the height of this scandal, the fifty-six-year-old General Hülsen-Haeseler, head of the

1 The nine sovereigns who attended the funeral of Edward VII, May 1910. Standing, from the left: Haakon VII of Norway, Ferdinand of Bulgaria, Manoel of Portugal, Wilhelm II of Germany, George I of Greece, Albert I of Belgium. Seated: Alfonso XIII of Spain, George V, Frederick VII of Denmark

2 The All Highest: Kaiser Wilhelm II in characteristically vainglorious pose

3 King Albert of the Belgians, a model constitutional monarch

military cabinet, collapsed and died after diverting the Kaiser and his guests by dancing – with considerable grace it is claimed – a *pas seul* in a ballerina's tutu.

Nor was Wilhelm's relationship with his wife quite what it seemed to outsiders. With the passing years, Dona had developed into the stronger personality. By now she not only saw it as her duty to protect him from his frequent indiscretions but she encouraged him, advised him and bolstered his often flagging resolve.

To his credit, Wilhelm II was sometimes aware of his own shortcomings. 'Do not hold me to my marginalia,' he once begged of his navy secretary, referring to the bellicose comments which he would scrawl in the margins of official documents. And to one long-suffering chancellor he exclaimed, 'I am what I am and I cannot change.'

Nor was the Kaiser quite as foolish as he sometimes sounded. His mind was lively, his memory excellent and his intelligence well above average. He had an insatiable appetite for information. There were times when his charm could be exceptional. More than one guest came away enchanted by the vivacity of his conversation and the warmth of his manner.

The fact was that the Kaiser was very much a product of his time and his environment. He had grown to manhood during those thrilling years in which Bismarck, by his 'blood and iron' methods, was forging the German empire; much of his militancy and absolutism was in direct reaction to the political moderation of his father, Crown Prince Frederick, and the outspoken liberalism of his mother, Crown Princess Victoria. In many ways, Wilhelm II had come to epitomise the Germany of the Second Reich – defiant, thrusting, power-conscious, ostentatious and ultra-sensitive.

King Edward VII was not far wrong in describing his nephew as 'the most brilliant failure in history'.

Wilhelm II, for all the strident authoritarianism of his public pronouncements, was a constitutional monarch. And so, by the year 1910, were all the sovereigns of Europe. Constitutional monarchy had been the royal answer to the liberalism of the age. By now every European country had the trappings of a democratic state: franchise, political parties, elected assemblies and representative governments. In theory, kings now owed their allegiance to the constitution rather than to God.

Yet the powers of these constitutional monarchs vis-à-vis their governments varied widely. In a country such as Britain, parliament was a sovereign body and George V virtually powerless. In a country like Belgium, King Albert sat in on ministerial meetings. In the less sophisticated Balkan states, monarchs like Carol of Romania or Ferdinand of Bulgaria exercised considerable personal control. And in the three Continental empires of Germany,

Russia and Austria–Hungary, the rulers – Wilhelm II, Nicholas II and Franz Joseph I – were all in a position to wield autocratic powers.

Of the three emperors, Wilhelm II was the one with the least well-defined status. The constitution of the Second Reich was extremely complicated, an uncomfortable blend of authoritarianism and democracy. It was, as Emil Ludwig has described it, 'a tissue of contradictions'.

The Kaiser held supreme executive power, governing through a chancellor who was not only appointed and dismissed by him but responsible to him alone. 'The Emperor', as one analyst has so graphically put it, 'regarded himself as being in the position of a landowner who had complete freedom in the choice of a bailiff to run his estates for him . . . The bailiff's job was to manage the estate to the general satisfaction, some people's views (and particularly the owner's) being entitled to more consideration than others.'[3]

There were two national assemblies in the Reich. The Bundesrat consisted of delegates from each of the states that went to make up the Confederation. The Reichstag – the more important of the two assemblies – was elected by universal male suffrage. The only practical limitation to the Kaiser's authority was the right of the Reichstag to refuse authorisation of certain expenditures. Through his chancellor, the Kaiser could appoint or dismiss ministers, propose legislation and summon and dissolve the assembly. Although the Kaiser could not always ignore these representatives of public opinion, an astute chancellor could usually play the three conservative parties off against each other; when he could not, and they continued to vote against him, he could usually ignore their vote. The Reichstag, as one disgruntled member once described it, was 'the figleaf of absolutism'.

But in spite of his potentially powerful position, Wilhelm II did not really take advantage of it. He was too indolent, too erratic, too irresolute to be an autocrat. He was quite content to leave the day-to-day running of the country to officials. And in his heart of hearts he realised that he could not really act in defiance of his chancellor, his ministers, his general staff or public opinion.

'When Germany made up its mind to go in a given direction', noted Theodore Roosevelt, '[the Kaiser] could only stay at the head of affairs by scampering to take the lead in going in that direction. Down at the bottom he realised this and he also knew that even this rather shorn power he possessed was not shared by the great majority of his fellow-sovereigns. But together with this underlying consciousness of the real facts of the situation went a curious make-believe to himself that each sovereign did represent his country in the sense that would have been true two or three centuries ago.'

Perhaps the most menacing cloud on Wilhelm's domestic horizon was the growth of socialism. By now the Social Democratic Party formed the main opposition group in the Reichstag. Steeped in the doctrines of Marx, Engels and Lassalle, the Social Democrats were republican and thus anti-monarchist in character. And not even Wilhelm II could ignore the fact that they were steadily improving their parliamentary position: in the elections of 1912 the Social Democrats emerged as the largest single party in Germany, polling over a third of the total votes.

Even so, republican socialism was not really a threat to the monarchy. Not yet, at any rate. Most German Social Democrats were less revolutionary than their leaders, and a somewhat paternalistic version of the welfare state, originally introduced by Bismarck, had tended to draw the teeth of the proletariat. Employment was high and wages adequate. Moreover, respect for authority was so ingrained in the German character, and the military cast – with its emphasis on unquestioning obedience – so powerful, that there seemed to be very little likelihood of the Kaiser losing his throne by either constitutional or revolutionary means.

For in spite of the fact that Germany harboured some of the most extreme radicals in Europe, it remained, above all, a *Militärstaat*: a country in the control of three powerful groups – the swashbuckling military, the rich industrialists and the old conservative landowning aristocracy known as the Junkers. Together, they supported the great patriotic movements such as the Pan German League and the Navy League, in the face of whose ever more clamorous nationalism the forces of the Left had very little chance of making themselves heard. Besides, there were few German workers who could resist the attractions of a more powerful and prosperous Reich.

As for the Kaiser, any fears that he might have had for the safety of his crown were disguised by his usual brand of bluster: the Reichstag was a 'madhouse', the deputies 'muttonheads', all agitators deserved to be locked up. 'The soldiers and the army, not parliamentary majorities and decisions, have welded the German Empire together,' he once declared. 'I put my trust in the army.'

'If it should ever come to pass that the city of Berlin revolts against its monarch,' runs another of his pronouncements, 'the Guards will avenge with their bayonets the disobedience of a people to its King.'

Whatever the limits of their constitutional positions at home, most Continental monarchs felt that when it came to foreign policy they were not only fully qualified but fully entitled to have the last word. So many things – their position as heads of state, their royal status, their family connections, their internationalism – gave them the right to a say. 'As long as it is a question of internal affairs, I must bow to the people's will,' declared King Constantine of the Hellenes, 'but in foreign affairs I must decide what shall or shall not be done, for I feel responsible before God.'[4]

Why God should have been more answerable to in foreign than in domestic policy is obscure, but Kaiser Wilhelm II would have well understood King Constantine's attitude. For of the many branches of government in which it pleased the Kaiser to imagine that he was an expert, foreign affairs were his especial province. 'I must be my own Bismarck,' he once declared and, without a vestige of the dismissed Bismarck's diplomatic skill, he pursued a foreign policy which he described, in another of those resounding phrases, as 'full steam ahead'. Exactly where he was steaming was not certain; particularly as he changed course with alarming frequency and suddenness.

Wilhelm II was a great believer in personal diplomacy. This he was just as happy to conduct in private – by letter or in conversation – as in public – by ranting speeches or frank newspaper interviews. He had very little time for the nuances of foreign policy; he saw it in heroic, almost medieval terms. His talk was all of 'mailed fists', 'unsheathed swords' and 'shining armour'. Foreign affairs gave him endless opportunity for those *grands gestes*, half-romantic, half-militant, in which he so delighted. In one of his more outrageous speeches, he urged his soldiers – about to take up arms against 'the Yellow Peril' – to make the name 'German' as feared in China as the name 'Hun' had once been in Europe.

When he felt that words were inadequate, or rather, that they needed additional embellishment, he would design vast allegorical paintings in which avenging angels with flaming swords encouraged buxom, helmeted and fiercy-eyed matrons towards deeds of national valour.

That foreign policy was the business of monarchs rather than of diplomats he had no doubts whatsoever. The peace of Europe, he firmly believed, was best kept in the hands of reigning sovereigns. When a German ambassador assured the Kaiser that one would need the gift of second sight to predict a certain result, Wilhelm was by no means put out. 'There *is* such a gift!' he exclaimed. 'Sovereigns often have it, statesmen seldom, diplomats never!' Always overestimating the ability of dynastic ties to influence power politics, he dashed off countless letters to his royal relations – Nicky in St Petersburg, Georgie in London, Sophie in Athens, Ferdy in Sofia, Missy in Bucharest – drenching them with unsolicited advice. That many of them were in no position to put his advice into effect even had they wanted to, bothered him not at all.

There was no diplomatic pie into which the Kaiser was not ready to plunge a finger; no area of the world free from his dramatic intervention; no subject on which he was not ready to air his views. Much given to snap decisions, changes of mind and unconsidered statements, he could ruin, in a moment, weeks of carefully constructed diplomatic policy. 'The other sovereigns', sighed one long-suffering politician, 'are so much *quieter*.' It was small wonder that Wilhelm II was the despair of his ministers; or that they so often jotted 'Not to be put before the Kaiser' on more controversial documents.

That Wilhelm II felt a need to exercise what he considered to be his diplomatic gifts is understandable. By now the Second Reich was in a dangerously isolated position. For during the course of Wilhelm II's reign there had been a momentous shift in the European balance of power.

One of Bismarck's chief boasts had been that, by a series of judicious alliances, he had kept the German empire safe and at peace for almost twenty years. To preserve the Continental *status quo*, to prevent what he called a nightmare of enemy coalitions and, above all, to avoid ever having to fight a war on two fronts, Bismarck had allied the Reich to the Russian, Austrian and Italian monarchies, leaving Germany's traditional enemy, republican France, out in the cold. For if one thing was certain, it was that France would never rest until she had avenged her defeat by Germany in 1870.

But Wilhelm II had seen all this change. On dismissing Bismarck in 1890, he and Bismarck's successor, Caprivi, had decided that Germany could no longer be allied to both Russia and Austria. With these two countries always at loggerheads in the Balkans, an alliance with both of them was not really practical politics. Germany must choose between them. Naturally, she chose Austria. The Russian alliance – the somewhat shaky cornerstone of Bismarck's foreign policy – was finished. Russia was henceforth obliged to look elsewhere for friends.

She looked, therefore, to France. An association between autocratic Russia and republican France seemed, on the face of it, unlikely, but the two countries had one very powerful factor in common: a fear of Wilhelm II's Germany. So, in the year 1893, an alliance was signed between them. Bismarck's great fear had been realised: Germany now faced the possibility of war on two fronts.

To counteract this threat, Wilhelm II had begun looking towards Britain. The Kaiser's attitude towards his mother's country had always been ambivalent: rather in the nature of a love–hate relationship. He admired Britain, he envied her, he was attracted to her, he feared her. He criticised her with characteristic vigour yet his criticism had never quite rung true. Although often seeming to go out of his way to antagonise Britain, the Kaiser appeared just as often to be thinking in terms of an alliance between these two great Teutonic nations. 'Not a mouse could stir in Europe without our permission' was how he at one stage visualised an Anglo-German agreement.

Yet as soon as Britain indicated that she, too, might be interested in some sort of closer co-operation, Germany backed off. Neither the Kaiser nor his ministers could quite bring themselves to respond to British overtures. Several times between the years 1898 and 1902, Britain had approached Germany; each time she had been rebuffed. Germany, assuming that Britain needed her more than she needed Britain, wanted her to offer something more concrete than just an understanding. Every British advance was met by a German evasion.

So Britain turned elsewhere. With the active encouragement of King Edward VII, she reached a series of understandings with several other Continental countries. Edward VII's celebrated state visit to Paris in 1903 paved the way for the Entente Cordiale between Britain and France. His meeting with his nephew-by-marriage, Alfonso XIII of Spain, in 1907 led to an agreement between their two countries. His 1908 visit to another nephew-by-marriage, Nicholas II, set the seal on the Anglo-Russian Convention, signed the year before. Indeed, the Triple Entente, by which Britain became loosely allied to France and Russia, was generally regarded as 'the triumph of King Edward's policy'.

The claim might have been exaggerated but it was certainly being taken seriously by Wilhelm II. The British King's main purpose, imagined his nephew, was the isolating of the Second Reich in a hostile Europe. That Germany had only itself to blame for this relative isolation was something that Wilhelm II refused to countenance. Yet the truth was that, as the most powerful nation on the Continent, Germany had become too self-confident and too militant for her own good. Fed on a diet of Nietzsche and Treitschke, the Germans felt themselves superior to 'lesser breeds'. No less than the Kaiser, did the politicians and diplomats behave in a manner guaranteed to insult and un-nerve their neighbours. The result was that while the other three great European nations – Britain, France and Russia – drew progressively closer, Germany was left with only decaying Austria–Hungary and second-rate Italy as friends.

By the year 1910, the great nations of Europe were ranged in two opposing camps. On the one hand was the Triple Entente of Britain, France and Russia; on the other the Triple Alliance of Germany, Austria–Hungary and Italy.

'Nations and Empires, crowned with princes and potentates,' reads Winston Churchill's honeyed view of Europe before the First World War, 'rose majestically on every side, lapped in the accumulated treasures of the long peace. All were fitted and fastened, it seemed securely, into an immense cantilever. The two mighty European systems faced each other glittering and clanking in their panoply, but with a tranquil gaze . . . the old world, in its sunset, was fair to see.'

Although not nearly as fair, or tranquil, as Churchill suggests, the old world was certainly locked in a system of alliances. And however much Wilhelm II might try to unlock this rigid system – at one stage he tried to revive the alliance with Russia, and he never ceased his flirtation with Britain – he found himself facing what Bismarck had always done his utmost to avoid: a nightmare of coalitions.

2

Constitutional King

FEW MONARCHS could have been less like the showy Kaiser Wilhelm II than his neighbour Albert I, King of the Belgians. Among Europe's more grandiose monarchs, King Albert was very much the odd-man-out.

Born in 1875, Albert was thirty-four when he succeeded to the throne on the death of his uncle, King Leopold II, in 1909. Abnormally tall, with a heavy body, a shambling walk, poor eyesight and unruly hair, he seemed more like an absent-minded professor than a king. He looked uncomfortable in uniform and untidy in civilian clothes. His faraway, abstracted air gave him the appearance, it was said, of someone who wanted to build something. By nature introvert and self-conscious, the King had no aptitude for the showier aspects of his calling. Embarrassed in crowds and tongue-tied with strangers, he could make neither rousing speeches nor interesting small talk. He seldom smiled. When he did, it was a wry, self-deprecating grin. Awkward himself, he was incapable of putting others at their ease. His preoccupied expression, magnified by his thick glasses, tended to make people even more inarticulate than he was. Excessive deference disconcerted him. 'My friend,' he said good-naturedly to a palace gardener who would not stop bowing, 'I am only a man like yourself.'

And not only did King Albert have very little taste or talent for courting popularity but he tended to regard it with some cynicism. A delighted equerry once remarked on the size of the crowds that had flocked to see the new King. They would be just as large, commented Albert drily, if he were being led to the scaffold.

It was away from the glare of public scrutiny that King Albert's qualities showed to better advantage. His compassion, his intelligence, his devotion to duty, his quiet strength, his capacity for leadership were far more apparent in the study or the council chamber than on the platform or in a procession. His ponderous manner and halting speech masked an astute mind. King Albert, his ministers were soon to learn, was no fool.

As King, Albert faced a formidable task. His uncle, Leopold II, from whom he had inherited the throne, had done nothing to enhance the popularity of the ruling Coburg dynasty. Indeed, by his licentiousness, avarice, hard-heartedness and ruthless exploitation in Central Africa which had earned him the title of 'Butcher of the Congo', Leopold II had stood condemned by all the world. Obsessed with the aggrandisement of his country and the enrichment of his dynasty, the autocratic old monarch had never set out to win the hearts of his subjects. If the monarchy were to survive the various pressures threatening the country, it would be up to King Albert to re-establish the popularity and respectability of the crown.

Fortunately, and in spite of his uninspiring appearance and manner, Albert had already won a certain amount of popular admiration. During his years as heir apparent (old King Leopold II's only son had predeceased him, and Albert's father, the studious Count of Flanders, had died in 1905) Albert had impressed his Belgian countrymen by his simple tastes and philanthropic activities. They had approved of his recreations: all that bicycling along the flat roads of Flanders and all that scaling of the jagged cliffs of the Ardennes. They had been no less approving of the seriousness with which he had devoted himself to social reform.

But what had impressed them most of all, perhaps, was the decorum of his private life. In 1900, at the age of twenty-five, Albert had married the twenty-three-year-old Princess Elisabeth, daughter of Charles Theodore, Duke *in* Bavaria (the dukes *of* Bavaria were the reigning branch of the dynasty), a member of the unconventional Wittelsbach family. In this warm-hearted and vivacious young woman, Albert, the dynasty and the country gained a personality of exceptional qualities.

The couple suited each other perfectly. Where he was solemn and self-doubting, she was extrovert and assured; where he was cynical and pessimistic, she was trusting and enthusiastic. What his character lacked, hers supplied. Unobtrusively and with great tact, Elisabeth smoothed his way and helped bring his complex personality to full flower.

During the closing years of Leopold II's reign, the couple had filled the ever-widening gap between king and people. At the birth of each of their three children – two boys and a girl – between the years 1901 and 1906, their popularity increased. After the depravity of Leopold II's private life (on his deathbed, the old King married the mistress whom he had first bedded when she was sixteen) the respectability of their home life made a refreshing change. There was something very touching in the unashamed devotion of the parents to their three children.

But it was for his impeccable constitutional behaviour that Albert was to win the most respect. Whereas Leopold II had often chaffed against, and on occasions circumvented, the restrictions imposed by the constitution, Albert's behaviour was always above reproach. 'Je suis un Roi con-sti-tu-tion-nel,' he would often remind his ministers in his slow, emphatic fashion.

In the struggle between the Catholic Party and its liberal and socialist opponents, he remained strictly neutral. Those who, because of the King's apparent diffidence, assumed that he would be a tool in the hands of the conservatives were to be proved as wrong as those who, because of his sympathy with the underprivileged, imagined that he would become a socialist king. Tolerant, adaptable and progressive, Albert steered a careful course between capital and labour.

'In the ministerial council', testifies one minister, 'he exerted the influence of a chief. This influence did not impose itself through the expression of some decisive and dictatorial opinion; it insinuated itself through his words, uttered somewhat slowly, as if he were in search of a more precise form, and accentuated by a few constructive gestures.'[1]

For in spite of constitutional limitations, Albert was in a far more influential position than some of his fellow constitutional monarchs. Sitting in on ministerial meetings, he was at least able to air his opinions. But he was also more vulnerable. For one thing, Belgium housed a strongly republican element. For another, the Belgian population was made up of two mutually antagonistic groups – the Flemings and the French-speaking Walloons. It was up to King Albert, almost entirely, to counteract the growing republican threat and to ensure that the crown remained the chief symbol uniting Flemings and Walloons.

These early years of Albert's reign saw an intensification of both the republican and the Flemish movements. An extension of the franchise, some fifteen years before, had greatly benefited the socialists. Now, by way of strikes and demonstrations, they were pressing for universal suffrage. And hand-in-hand with this spread of socialism went the spread of republicanism. 'Between Socialism and Monarchy', declared the chilling Socialist Manifesto published on the eve of the King's accession, 'there is no possible reconciliation, and when Belgium prepares itself to acclaim Albert I, a loud clamour of hope and defiance will rise from all the workers' breasts: *Vive la République Sociale!*'

King Albert would need all his skill to divorce this creed of republicanism from that of socialism.

The struggle between the Flemings and the Walloons – the Flemish-speaking, largely peasant population of the northwest and the French-speaking, more industrial population of the southeast – was causing King Albert equal concern. A late nineteenth-century movement, by a group of Flemish writers, to resurrect and champion the Flemish language, had by now been transformed into a political crusade. Hitherto confined to Flanders, this crusade had spread across the entire country: the *flamingants* were determined on nothing less than equal language rights.

King Albert, sympathetic to the Flemish struggle, gave his full support to linguistic reform. He encouraged the growth of Flemish culture, he used Flemish (which he spoke fluently) when addressing Flemish audiences, he was the first Belgian sovereign to take the oath of office in both languages. In speech after speech he would beg the Belgian people to cultivate the feelings which united them, rather than those which divided them.

This was easier said than done. An important section of the Flemish population remained discontented. It was a discontent which plagues Belgium to this day.

If Queen Elisabeth of the Belgians made the ideal wife and mother, she did not, at first glance, make the ideal queen. No more than King Albert did she seem fitted for her great task. She had neither beauty nor natural dignity. The calm, the hauteur, the commanding air of someone like the Kaiserin or Queen Mary, she lacked almost completely. She did not, in these early years, even dress particularly well. But when set against her remarkable force of character, these shortcomings were unimportant.

She had an alert face; her nose was sharp, her eyes bright, her smile dazzling. She was small and slender, with a quick, bird-like quality and boundless energy. Unlike her husband, she enjoyed her public duties. She delighted in her growing popularity and responded warmly to admiration and applause. Her manner, both in public and in private, was relaxed and confident; only in the company of the pretentious, the arrogant or the ostentatious was she ever less than charming. With empty ceremonial, with excessive protocol, with the activities of so-called society, she had very little patience. Rows of pompous dignitaries would often be held up while Queen Elisabeth chatted, with unfeigned vivacity, to some poet or musician or social worker. Her interests were wide-ranging and she brought to them an unflagging enthusiasm and a real intelligence. There was a professionalism, a complete absence of royal dilettantism, about everything she touched.

She shared, to the full, King Albert's concern for the health and well-being of their subjects. The knowledge gained, when Crown Princess, by tramping through working-class districts to acquaint herself with such matters as wages, amenities and living conditions, was now put to practical use. She founded various trusts, societies and associations to help the sick and needy.

Bohemian, rather than bourgeois, would be the word to describe the royal couple, wrote Charles d'Ydewalle. 'They were Bohemian in their unprejudiced outlook, their absolute lack of snobbishness, their unique position, their love of adventure, their indifference to danger, etiquette and criticism. They were nowise confined within the conventional limits of the bourgeois conception of life.'

Yet they could be regal when occasion demanded it. The state visits, the balls, the receptions, the banquets were magnificently staged affairs: the Queen could always be relied upon to bring a touch of theatricality to these occasions. Each May she held a garden party at Laeken, their elegant palace on the outskirts of Brussels. As there are few days in Belgium on which it does not rain, the reception would be held in those great conservatories in which the late Leopold II had taken so much pride. Dressed in white or pale blue, the Queen would move through these exotic, heavily scented glass galleries, impressing all with her ease and vivacity.

The annual state ball was another affair never to be forgotten. Brand Whitlock, the American ambassador, always remembered 'the dancers under the brilliant chandeliers, the jewels and the gleam of white shoulders, and the gold lace of the officers of the Guides – their trousers cherry red; and old generals whose breasts were heavy with orders; and suddenly the King, in black evening dress . . .'

More typical, though, is the vignette given by someone who was once received in audience by King Albert. As the King never knew how to bring an audience to a close, the two of them were making strained conversation when the guest, glancing up at a looking-glass behind the King's head, saw the reflected image of the Queen peeping through a doorway. She was making frantic signs to her husband to dismiss his guest.

'You must go,' said the King abruptly, and then added, as a means of softening the brusqueness of his order, 'but don't forget your handkerchief.'

As the guest, in complete bewilderment, looked down at the scrap of lace-trimmed fabric on a nearby table, a voice suddenly sounded from the doorway.

'It's *my* handkerchief,' said the Queen.[2]

Who would have thought that, in a few years time, this awkward monarch would have proved himself a hero, and that this spirited queen would have come to be regarded as little less than a saint?

The first important royal guest to be received by Albert and Elisabeth was Kaiser Wilhelm II. In October 1910 the Kaiser paid a state visit to Brussels to attend the *Exposition Universelle*.

Like his late uncle, Edward VII, Wilhelm II enjoyed few things more than a full-blown state visit. And Brussels, replanned and embellished by Leopold II to the point where it was known as 'Little Paris', made the perfect setting for those parades and processions in which the Kaiser took such delight. The buildings were gratifyingly a-flutter with German flags, the crowds were flatteringly enthusiastic, the speeches were suitably congratulatory. Wilhelm II rhapsodised over the glories of Belgian art and architecture and had a great deal to say about the country's commercial and industrial enterprise.

In his eagerness to win Belgian goodwill, the Kaiser laid frequent stress on the ties which united the royal houses of Belgium and Germany. King Albert's family, the Saxe-Coburgs, were German; Queen Elisabeth was a Bavarian; King Albert's mother, the Countess of Flanders, had been born a

Hohenzollern princess. So it was almost incomprehensible to the German Emperor that King Albert, through whose veins flowed the proud and autocratic blood of the Hohenzollerns, should pay so much attention to the opinions and aspirations of his subjects.

'Why grant so many audiences, and to men of no account?' he one day asked Albert. 'You have your policy – it is for them to follow it.'

'My country and I, we make our policy together,' explained the King.

'But we Hohenzollerns', protested the Kaiser, 'are the bailiffs of God.'

Such robust sentiments could have done little towards calming Albert's already considerable fears. For ever since his accession, the Belgian King had become increasingly apprehensive about the aggressive attitude of his powerful neighbour. He appreciated, to the full, how very vulnerable his country would be in the event of a future war between the great powers.

Wedged between those two implacable enemies, France and Germany, Belgium formed what was usually called 'the crossroads' or, more frighteningly, 'the cockpit' of Europe. Some years after the establishment of the kingdom of Belgium in 1831, the country's independence – and neutrality – had been guaranteed by the great powers. How much longer it could hope to maintain this neutrality was an open question.

With the countries of Europe becoming ever more firmly locked in alliances and sympathies, it seemed unlikely that strategically placed Belgium could remain unattached much longer. She was merely biding her time, it was assumed, until she saw which group of powers offered the best chance of victory in some future struggle. France suspected her of being in secret alliance with Germany, and Germany suspected her of being in secret alliance with France. In that golden age of clandestine diplomacy – of verbal agreements over the schnapps in gilded chancelleries, of secret clauses drawn up in the tilting saloons of royal yachts, of unofficial discussions under the linden trees of some elegant spa – few could believe that King Albert had not concluded some undercover alliance.

That Belgium was determined to maintain her neutrality was a simple truth that Europe's more Machiavellian politicians and diplomats refused to credit. To King Albert, neutrality was something positive, something to be cherished, protected and defended, not something to be bartered. Any Belgian approach to one of the rival power blocs, no matter how tentative, would give the other side all the excuse it needed to violate this neutrality. There is no doubt that an agreement with the Entente Powers – Britain and France – to whom Albert naturally inclined, would have benefited Belgium enormously, but the King remained stubbornly and meticulously impartial.

Nor was there any doubt that it was the braggardly Wilhelm II whom Albert feared most. Sceptical of Germany's intention of respecting Belgian neutrality, the King had begun, from the very outset of his reign, to urge the strengthening of Belgium's army and defences. Now, during the Kaiser's state visit, Albert was able to give voice to his apprehensions. In his speech of welcome, the Belgian King assured his royal guest that he had every confidence in the Kaiser's peaceful intentions. To this plain hint, Wilhelm II made a fulsome but noncommital reply.

But before leaving Belgium the Kaiser, flushed with the success of his visit, assured Baron van der Elst, of the Belgian Ministry of Foreign Affairs, that Belgium had nothing to fear from Germany. 'You will have no grounds of complaint against us,' he said expansively. 'I have a great affection for your King who, through his mother, belongs to our House. I will allow no one to do him harm. I understand your country's situation perfectly.'[3]

3

King Emperor

'A VERY NICE BOY' was how Kaiser Wilhelm II once described King George V to Theodore Roosevelt. The Kaiser was then fifty-one, the King forty-four. Yet always allowing for the German Emperor's tendency to patronise, there was something boyish about the new British King. Compared to his late father, the assured, urbane and cosmopolitan Edward VII, George V appeared diffident, unsophisticated, insular. He did not even have his father's commanding physical presence. Short, slender, with frank blue eyes and a neatly trimmed beard and moustache, George V looked what he was: an honest, unpretentious man of simple tastes and limited interests. His public manner was unsmiling; his conversation bluff.

The new King was singularly ill-educated. At his accession, admits one of his more well-disposed biographers, the forty-four-year-old George V had not yet attained 'the normal educational standard of the average public schoolboy at leaving age'.[1] He wrote with painful slowness; he was fluent in no foreign language. Incapable of philosophic or abstract thought, indifferent to the arts, science or even politics, the King shared the country interests and conservative outlook of those Norfolk squires among whom he had passed so much of his adult life. Shooting and stamp collecting were his chief recreations.

Yet George V was no fool. A youth spent in the Royal Navy (he was known as the Sailor King) had inculcated him with several valuable characteristics: self-discipline, orderliness and consistency. To these he brought his own fund of common sense. It was, and is, more important for a monarch to be dependable and dignified than clever or original. Unimaginative and unintellectual George V might have been, but he was a man with a strong character, an organised mind and a fully integrated nature. To the end of his life, he was to retain the unswerving sense of duty of a naval officer.

From the Navy too, had come the King's somewhat gruff, quarterdeck manner. In private, George V was known for his booming voice, his hearty laugh, his bantering tone and his salty turn of phrase. He had a quick temper and an impressive vocabulary of oaths. Yet all this naval bluster masked a compassionate nature and a kind heart. George V was a well-intentioned man whose innate shyness made him appear more brusque than he actually was.

His private life was eminently respectable. His marriage to Princess May of Teck in 1893 had been very successful. Although the match had been one of convenience rather than love, the couple had come to care for each other deeply and to suit each other admirably. Both were reserved and somewhat inarticulate, with a taste for domesticity and a belief in the bourgeois virtues of morality and industry. Queen Mary might have been more intellectually curious, more culturally aware and more socially enlightened than her husband, but she had long ago adapted her tastes and personality to his. By the year of George V's accession, the couple had six children – five boys and a girl – with ages ranging from fifteen to four. This, too, helped give the British throne a reassuringly domestic aura.

The same respectability characterised George V's court. The somewhat raffish air of Edward VII's day – the late-night card parties, the self-made men, the drifting cigar smoke, the mistresses – had been replaced by an almost middle-class decorum. 'The King's domesticity and simple life are charming,' wrote Lord Esher, that *éminence grise* of the previous reign. 'The King allows people to sit after dinner, whether he is sitting or not. There is no pomp . . . There is not a card in the house.'

The King's favourite home remained York Cottage – the cramped, unprepossessing house on the Sandringham estate in which he had lived as heir apparent; his favourite way of spending an evening was to dine at home with the Queen. An almost naval precision ordered his day. Punctual, methodical and punctilious, George V was happiest when bound by a set routine and surrounded by familiar faces. Compared to the restless glitter of the Edwardian court, it was all very wholesome, very peaceful, very correct.

But it was all still magnificent. George V might have had simple tastes but he was enough of a king to appreciate that he must maintain a certain standard of regal splendour. 'There are arguments', as the political analyst Walter Bagehot put it, 'for not having a Court, and there are arguments for having a splendid Court, but there are no arguments for having a mean Court.' This George V understood very well. Indeed, no capital in Europe – not the barbaric grandeur of St Petersburg, the showy militarism of Berlin nor the old-fashioned pageantry of Vienna or Madrid – could match the self-confident majesty of the British court.

'Nothing', wrote one of the King's Continental cousins, 'is more irreproachably perfect in every detail than the King of England's Court and Household, a sort of staid luxury without ostentation, a placid, aristocratic ease and opulence which has nothing showy about it. Everything is run on silent wheels that have been perfectly greased; everything fits in, there are no spaces between, no false note. From the polite, handsome and superlatively groomed gentleman-in-waiting who receives you in the hall, to the magni-

4 George V at the time of his accession to 'the greatest position there is'

5 George V and Wilhelm II drive through Berlin, May 1913

6 Kaiserin Augusta Victoria (Dona) and Queen Mary on the occasion of the unveiling of the Queen Victoria Memorial in 1911

ficently solemn and yet welcoming footman who walks before you down the corridor, everything pleases the eye, satisfies one's fastidiousness . . .'[2]

And if the King, in his somewhat old-fashioned clothes, never looked anything less than immaculate, the Queen, in her equally old-fashioned dresses, never looked anything less than majestic. Although no taller than her husband (each was five foot six inches tall) her upright carriage and towering hats gave an illusion of height. It was due, almost entirely, to her husband's conservative tastes that Queen Mary clung to the more opulent fashions of her early married life. Even with his untutored eye, says one of the King's secretaries, he could see that the dress which the Queen had chosen especially for her arrival in fashion-conscious Paris in 1914 was hopelessly out of date.

But this hardly mattered. Queens need not be fashionable any more than kings need to be intellectual. To see Queen Mary in one of her highly individual brocade dresses, blazing with diamonds was 'to understand the meaning of the word regal'.[3] The Queen might have been stiff, she might have been uncommunicative, she might even have been a little dull, but she looked every inch a queen.

So, if life within their private or at least semi-private homes – York Cottage and Balmoral Castle – was relatively unpretentious, life in their official homes – Buckingham Palace and Windsor Castle – was lived on the grandest of scales. The couple moved in a highly mannered world of private secretaries, lords-in-waiting, gentlemen ushers, equerries, ladies-in-waiting and hundreds upon hundreds of servants. Gradually the King and Queen mastered their natural shyness, their public nervousness and their preference for a quiet, countrified life, to play their parts with dignity and style. On all the great public occasions they stood out as the assured and unmistakable symbols of majesty.

King Emperor of the greatest empire the world had ever known, George V was yearly proving himself capable of filling what his grandmother, Queen Victoria, used to call 'the greatest position there is'.

One of the ways in which George V differed most fundamentally from his late father, Edward VII, was in his attitude to Continental Europe. Edward VII had been a European to his fingertips; George V was British through and through. The new King had very little interest in the politics, culture or way of life of the Continent; he detested foreigners. Lamentably insular, his poor command of French and German made him more insular still.

'It is hardly credible', wrote an astonished British consul-general from Berlin on the occasion of the King's visit in 1913, 'that Royal George cannot speak a solitary word of German, and his French is atrocious.'[4]

But the King did not mind. All his interests lay with Great Britain and her empire. His years in the navy and his subsequent journeys to various British dominions, colonies and dependencies had made him very conscious of his country's imperial, as opposed to its European, role. The King felt able to identify himself far more readily with Britons living abroad than he could with those Continentals so beloved of his father. George V saw himself, above all, as a British king.

It was ironic, then, that he should have reigned during the period when the Coburg dynasty, from which he sprang, reached its zenith; when his relations sat on almost every European throne. Among his first cousins he could count the German Kaiser, both the Tsar and the Tsaritsa of Russia, the King of Norway, the Queen of Spain, and the crown princesses of Sweden, Romania and Greece. The kings of Greece and Denmark were his uncles; their heirs were his cousins. The Dowager Tsaritsa of Russia was his aunt. The Queen of Norway was his sister. The kings of Belgium, Portugal and Bulgaria were all his cousins at various removes. Yet more of these cousins had married or would one day marry into the reigning houses of Austria, Italy and Yugoslavia. The kingdoms, principalities and duchies that went to make up the German empire were chock-a-block with his relations. And when they were not his, they were Queen Mary's. He was even related to that most outlandish of dynasties, the Bonapartes.

If, with his dislike of travel, his lack of diplomatic gifts, his mistrust of foreign foods and his want of foreign languages, George V did not relish the idea of following in his father's Continental footsteps, he did appreciate that he had a constitutional duty to pay some state visits. But when his foreign secretary, Sir Edward Grey, suggested that he visit Paris first, the King dug in his heels. With France being 'only a republic', he argued, it must come after the three leading Continental monarchies – Austria–Hungary, Germany and Russia.

In spite of George V's professed determination to dedicate himself to the affairs of the British empire, he was to become increasingly enmeshed in European politics. By the time of his accession, in 1910, Britain had finally abandoned her nineteenth-century position of 'splendid isolation' and, with the blessing of Edward VII, had come to understandings with both France and Russia. Whether King George V liked it or not, his country was now well and truly committed to Europe.

The first monarch to be received by George V was, inevitably, Wilhelm II. The King had invited the Kaiser to attend the unveiling of the memorial to their grandmother, Queen Victoria, erected outside Buckingham Palace, during the second week of May 1911.

Of all the Continental monarchs, his first cousin, Wilhelm II, was the one with whom George V was most closely involved. Both Edward VII and Queen Alexandra had disliked Wilhelm intensely: the King because he considered his nephew to be a conceited, bombastic, mischief-making mega-lomaniac; the Queen because she hated all Prussians. Although George V had tended, when younger, to echo his parents' opinion, the passing years – and his own accession – had made him more tolerant of the Kaiser's impetuosity.

For his part, the Kaiser was vastly relieved that his *bête noire*, his worldly Uncle Bertie, had been replaced by what he imagined to be his more pliable Cousin Georgie. 'He is a thorough Englishman and hates all foreigners,' explained the Kaiser good-naturedly to Theodore Roosevelt, 'but I do not mind that as long as he does not hate Germans more than other foreigners.'

Now, in his letter thanking his cousin Georgie for the invitation to the unveiling of the Queen Victoria Memorial, the Kaiser was at his most fulsome. 'You cannot imagine how overjoyed I am at the prospect of seeing you again so soon and making a nice stay with you,' he wrote. Never, he swore, would he forget the hours spent at the dying Queen Victoria's bedside; or that it was in his arms she had died.

'Those sacred hours have riveted my heart firmly to your house and family, of which I am proud to feel myself a member. And the fact that for the last hours I held the sacred burden of her – the creator of the greatness of Britain – in my arms, in my mind created an invincible special link between her country and its people and me, and one which I fondly nurse in my heart. This your invitation, so to say, sanctions these ideas of mine. You kindly refer to the fact of my being her eldest grandson; a fact I was always immensely proud of and never forgot.'[5]

George V's reaction to this effusion is not recorded.

The unveiling ceremony, on 16 May 1911, was a splendid occasion. Preceded by colourfully costumed Beefeaters and flanked by Gentlemen-at-Arms, King George and the Kaiserin, followed by the Kaiser and Queen Mary, walked in slow procession from Buckingham Palace towards Sir Thomas Brock's dazzlingly white monument. In bright spring sunshine, to the thunder of guns, the clash of military bands and the cheering of the crowd, the King pulled the cord which unveiled the statue of his redoubtable grandmother.

The Kaiser enjoyed it all immensely. In fact, he considered his three-day visit to London to have been a great success. The crowds were enthusiastic; the state occasions, including a ball at the palace, were superbly organised. Even the rumour of the engagement of his only daughter to the King's eldest son, although unfounded, would have given him some satisfaction. Never, Wilhelm was able to assure his chancellor, had he felt the atmosphere at Buckingham Palace to be so free, so open, or so friendly.

Yet it was on the occasion of this visit that Wilhelm II's tendency to take matters into his own hands led to one of his diplomatic gaffes.

Just before leaving for the railway station, the Kaiser brought up the question of Morocco with the King. To quell an insurrection in Fez, France, who was responsible for keeping the Moroccan peace, had very properly sent troops to restore order. The French move was hotly resented by a jealous Germany. She saw no reason why she, too, should not have a slice of the African cake. And so, in a casual conversation with the King before catching his train, the Kaiser told him that although Germany would never go to war for the sake of Morocco, she might claim compensation elsewhere in Africa.

To this suggestion, runs the German chancellor's subsequent report, the British King made no reply.

Notwithstanding the Kaiser's assurance that Germany would not interfere in the Moroccan business, she later despatched the cruiser *Panther* to lie off the Moroccan coast, at Agadir. This show of force was designed as a warning, not only to France, but to France's ally, Britain.

The incident caused a major crisis. For several weeks during the summer of 1911, until a diplomatic solution was reached, a European war seemed inevitable. And it was when the Agadir crisis was at its height that the Kaiser, in self-justification, blandly announced that he had warned the British King, during that talk at Buckingham Palace, that Germany intended sending a warship to Morocco. This George V denied.

The episode illustrates, not only Wilhelm II's unreliability, but how little he appreciated the limits of George V's constitutional powers. The days when a British monarch could agree important matters of foreign policy had long since gone.

But the question causing the greatest friction between Britain and Germany at this time was the expansion of the German navy. Jealous of British sea power, Wilhelm II was determined that Germany should have as magnificent a battle-fleet. In an atmosphere of almost hysterical chauvinism, two vast navy bills were passed in the Reichstag and the Kaiser's great shipbuilding programme put in hand. In a rousing speech in Hamburg in 1911, Wilhelm spoke of the need 'to strengthen our fleet further so as to make sure that nobody will dispute the place in the sun to which we are entitled.'

All this Britain, as Mistress of the Seas, resented. As a result, a frantic and expensive naval race had developed between the two great nations.

Yet the Kaiser's motives were not necessarily belligerent. Chancellor von Bülow was not far wrong when he claimed that, 'What Wilhelm II most desired was to see himself, at the head of a glorious German fleet, starting out on a peaceful visit to England. The English sovereign, with his fleet, would meet the German Kaiser in Portsmouth. The two fleets would file past each other, the two monarchs each wearing the naval uniform of the other's country, would then stand on the bridge of their flagships. Then, after they had embraced in the prescribed manner, a gala dinner with lovely speeches would be held in Cowes.'

But even the vainglorious Wilhelm II wanted something more tangible than this from his navy. A powerful German battle-fleet would deter any would-be aggressor. It would be a symbol of national greatness, ridding the upstart Reich of its inferiority complex and establishing it as a great maritime power. It might even induce Britain to forsake France and Russia and join the Triple Alliance of Germany, Austria and Italy.

So the shipbuilding continued. And so did the mutual distrust between these two great Teutonic nations.

If George V held what Queen Victoria had called 'the greatest position there is', he was, paradoxically, one of the world's least powerful monarchs. Compared with Europe's other leading sovereigns, the British King had very little personal control of national affairs.

The 'greatness' of his position was of prestige rather than power. He might have been the latest in a line of sovereigns stretching back almost a thousand years, he might have reigned over the world's greatest empire, but, politically, George V was all but impotent. For, in Britain, the theory of constitutional monarchy was to be seen in its most fully developed form. The ideal of George V's grandfather – Queen Victoria's husband, Prince Albert – that the monarchy should be some sort of supra-national institution, standing high above party and faction, had by now been realised.

In Britain, real political power was vested in parliament. 'A Republic', as Bagehot put it, 'has insinuated itself beneath the folds of a Monarchy.' To the disapproval of sovereigns such as Wilhelm II, George V dared not act in defiance of his government. To do so would be to force its resignation, with the subsequent general election being fought on the emotive issue of Crown versus People. This the monarchy could not risk. The King's role was purely advisory, limited to the right to be consulted, the right to encourage and the right to warn.

And in George V, Prince Albert's other dictum – that the monarch should be the symbol of all that was best in national life, the exemplar of the domestic virtues of morality, hard work and dignity – was also being realised.

It was these two characteristics – a lack of personal power and an abundance of personal prestige – that were to keep the British monarch afloat in the turbulent waters that lay just ahead.

4

Heir to the Caesars

IN THE SAME SPRING of 1911 in which George V unveiled the monument to his grandmother, Queen Victoria, Victor Emmanuel III of Italy unveiled an infinitely more ambitious monument to his grandfather Victor Emmanuel II – the monarch under whom Italy had been united a mere fifty years before.

No nineteenth-century king could have hoped for a more grandiose memorial. Dominating Rome's Capitoline Hill and designed with all the self-confident *bravura* of the age, it was a blindingly white confection of soaring columns, stepped terraces, winged angels, rearing horses, elaborate bas reliefs and, rising triumphantly at its centre, a forty-foot-high bronze statue of Victor Emmanuel II. Nothing could have spoken more grandiloquently of the achievements of nationalism or the glory of kings.

It was a pity, then, that this latest representative of the House of Savoy should have been so insignificant-looking a figure. Born on 11 November 1869, Victor Emmanuel III had become king on the assassination of his father, King Umberto I, in 1900. As an only, and worryingly puny, child, he was generally regarded as a regrettable result of inbreeding (his parents had been first cousins) and of a genetically exhausted family tree. The House of Savoy, having established itself as a powerful family in the foothills of the Alps in about the year 1000, could claim to be the oldest ruling house in Europe. So perhaps it was only to be expected that this successful dynasty, moving up from counts to dukes to princes to kings of Piedmont-Sardinia and finally, in 1861, to kings of a newly independent and united Italy, should appear to be dwindling away in the person of Victor Emmanuel III.

He was tiny. The most generous assessment of his height was five foot and not quite a quarter of an inch. There was nothing – not plumed helmets, clever tailoring, sweeping cloaks nor high-heeled boots – that could possibly compensate for so regrettable a lack of height. Kings must look, if nothing else, majestic: Victor Emmanuel merely looked ridiculous. When he sat on his specially low thrones, his feet did not quite touch the floor. When he appeared in the midst of his equerries and officers, he looked like the least important person present. On becoming commander-in-chief of the army, the standard had to be lowered to five feet. Standing beside his statuesque wife, Queen Elena, in her outsize *belle époque* hats, he seemed more like her son than her husband. He was the butt of numberless jokes; he was the object of considerable derision. It was said that he had all the characteristics of little creatures such as weasles or foxes; that he was cunning, selfish, not to be trusted.

Of that braggadocio so dear to the Italian heart, he had almost nothing. His manner could be chilling, his frugality was legendary, he was invariably to be seen in a shabby, even threadbare uniform. Court life, which under the late King Umberto and his forceful consort, Queen Margherita, had attained a certain splendour, had been simplified to the point of austerity. In the Quirinal Palace in Rome, the King and his family were content with a relatively small, sparsely furnished apartment. There was much less ceremonial, there were fewer liveried servants, state entertaining was cut down to a minimum.

'If I hadn't known we were going to the palace', complained one diplomat's wife, 'I should have thought we had made a mistake in the house. The square of the Quirinal was so quiet, almost deserted – no troops nor music, no crowd of people looking on and peering into carriages to see the dresses and jewels – no soldiers nor officials of any kind on the grand staircase . . . nothing like the glittering crowd of gold lace and uniforms one usually sees in the anteroom of a palace.'[1]

But much of the criticism of Victor Emmanuel III was unfair. There was a great deal more to him than was generally imagined. Although now remembered chiefly for the fact that he became Mussolini's cat's-paw, King Victor Emmanuel had many admirable qualities. In another country, at another time, he might have developed into an accomplished and popular monarch.

What he lacked in inches, he made up for in energy. He held himself erect, he moved briskly, his talk was rapid and to the point. His fellow sovereigns were often surprised by the breadth of his knowledge and the depth of his reading; he has been described as 'the single really learned monarch in Europe'. A visiting Hellenist was astonished at being able to talk to him about some abstruse point in Homer. A member of British Naval Intelligence was impressed by his intimate knowledge of the Royal Navy. Ambassadors found themselves disconcerted by his quick-fire, penetrating questions. More than one came away from an audience feeling drained and bemused.

He had a disarming naturalness. Although prepared to play his kingly role among the splendours of the Quirinal, he much preferred the rustic simplicity and cramped conditions of the Villa Savoia outside the city. Before long, he quit the palace altogether for permanent residence in the country: from there he would drive each morning to what he called his office in the Quirinal. His spare time was devoted to hunting and to the cataloguing and labelling of his famous coin collection. Like so many early twentieth-century monarchs, Victor Emmanuel was happiest in the almost bourgeois atmosphere of his domestic circle.

His marriage was very successful. Queen Elena was a daughter of that most picturesque of Balkan rulers, Prince Nicholas of Montenegro who, in 1910, proclaimed himself king of his mountainous little country. A tall, dark-skinned beauty (critics would refer to her as 'the shepherdess from Montenegro'; admirers as 'the black pearl') Princess Elena had been given a certain gloss at the Russian court. Since her marriage to Crown Prince Victor Emmanuel in 1896 and, more particularly, since becoming Queen of Italy four years later, Elena had developed into an impressive-looking woman. Yet she always retained something of the atmosphere of her native Montenegro.

As Theodore Roosevelt once wrote, 'She was a real peasant-queen, the Saga queen, the queen of the folk stories and fairy tales – the kind of queen whom the hero meets when he starts out with his wallet and staff and travels "far and far and farther than far", and finally comes to a palace up to which he strolls, and sees the King sitting in front of the door looking at the sheep or the chickens . . .'

The couple had five children: four girls and a boy who, for thirty-four days in 1946, would become Umberto II, the last King of Italy. Whereas Victor Emmanuel had been raised on somewhat Prussian lines (in his youth imitation of the new, Prussian-dominated German empire had been considered *de rigeur*) the children were being brought up in what was referred to as the Montenegrin fashion: that is, informally and with great freedom.

Lloyd Griscom, the United States ambassador of the time, was always impressed by the easy-going attitudes of the royal family. The same could not be said for their entourage. 'Afterwards', he once wrote of a hunting trip with the King on the royal estate at Castel Porziano, 'we drove to a pavilion over-looking the beach, where the Queen and the ladies-in-waiting joined us for lunch, a very stiff affair. The Court expected royalty to remain exclusive and live up to the accepted principle that they were in a class above and by themselves. In consequence the King and Queen could never relax, and always had to regulate their conduct to avoid shocking their own staff. It was hard on them, since by nature they hated formality and constraint . . .

'Directly the meal was over, we three sauntered towards the beach while the entourage disappeared in the other direction. Once they were out of sight, the most remarkable transformation came over the King and Queen. They began romping up and down on the sand, throwing shells, laughing and shouting, paying no attention to me. They both had cameras and now and then stopped long enough to snap pictures of each other.'

The royal couple carried out their many public duties – the state visits, the audiences, the tours of inspection, the launching of ships, the laying of foundation stones – conscientiously and uncomplainingly. Any national disaster, such as the terrible earthquake at Messina in 1908, revealed them at their best. Hurrying to the scene of devastation, they spent several days among the distressed and dying. The Queen worked on a hospital ship, tending to the injured. She was enough of a queen to appreciate that her presence brought immense comfort to the suffering. 'I am the Queen of Italy,' she said quietly to one severely crushed, bitterly sobbing old woman, 'and I tell you that you need have no fear.' Such is the potency of the royal mystique that the sobbing stopped immediately.

'There is no Italian worthy of the name, be he republican, socialist, or even anarchist who, however much he may be opposed to royalty as a system,' noted one contemporary, 'does not recognise their devotion and their personal courage in the face of national danger and distress.'[2]

But there was a more important way by which Victor Emmanuel III hoped to retain the loyalty of the various political groupings within his country. By keeping the monarchy free of controversy, by lifting it out of the political sphere, he intended to ensure the survival of his dynasty. For the crown to endure, it had to be the symbol of all Italians, and not only those natural monarchists, the conservatives. Over half a century before, Camillo Cavour, one of the architects of Italian unity, had preached that 'reforms carried out in time, instead of weakening authority, reinforce it: instead of precipitating revolution, they prevent it'.

This was a lesson which Victor Emmanuel had taken to heart. At the very start of his reign, in 1900, he had set a new tone by assuring the senate – the upper of the two chambers of the Italian parliament – that he not only supported the existing institution of constitutional monarchy, but that he favoured a 'liberal monarchy'.

Within months he had put his words into action. He replaced his late father's conservative prime minister with an undeniably liberal one who was, in turn, succeeded by the no less liberal Giovanni Giolitti. With Giolitti's appointment, the decade of the 'socialist monarchy' – the ten years leading up to the First World War – was under way.

As Giolitti's political reforms, including an extension of the franchise, coincided with an unprecedented economic boom (but always in the industrial north, at the expense of the impoverished south) the forces of revolutionary socialism were considerably weakened. Italian politics became less polarised; Marx, as Giolitti put it, was stored away in the attic. And however questionable his theories and methods might have been, Giolitti proved to be of considerable value to the House of Savoy: Victor Emmanuel III could not have hoped for a more loyal prime minister. These were to be the golden years of his reign. 'Liberal Italy' they called the country during this period and in few did this liberalism seem more strikingly personified than in the King.

The King's distaste for pompous ceremonial and lavish entertaining was well known; less appreciated was his strict adherence to the constitutional limits of his position. In spite of much wider personal powers, he aimed to be a monarch in the mould of Britain's George V or Belgium's Albert I; to distance himself from the everyday business of government. 'Does parliament make trouble for you?' asked one foreign ambassador. 'Oh, no, they don't make any for *me*,' he took pains to point out, 'but they do for the government.' And it was noticed that he seldom referred to himself as 'king' but rather to 'the position which I hold'.[3]

Yet this is not to claim that Victor Emmanuel was not fully conscious of the majesty of that position. Like all monarchs, he was very concerned with the importance of his kingly status and with the illustriousness of his dynasty. Modest in many things, he was never modest about the splendours and achievements of his house.

And it was in order to add still more lustre to his dynasty that Victor Emmanuel was so anxious to continue the task undertaken by his grandfather, Victor Emmanuel II. The *Risorgimento* – the unification of all Italians, under the House of Savoy – had still to be completed. It would be up to him to complete it.

In its determination to be taken seriously as a great power, Italy was fulfilling at least two of the classic qualifications: she was founding an empire and she was a member of one of the great European power blocs. The Libyan War of 1911–12 won her a vast tract of North African territory from the decaying Ottoman empire. And an alliance, concluded in 1882 by Victor Emmanuel's father, Umberto I, had linked her to the Central Powers, Germany and Austria–Hungary.

The House of Savoy – in spite of its long history – was at that stage so shallowly rooted in the soil of newly united Italy, so lacking in blood relations in the courts of Europe, so apprehensive of the spread of socialism within its realm, that it had imagined its position would be strengthened by allying itself to some long-established monarchical power. To this, the Hohenzollern and Habsburg empires, mastering their distaste for the brand-new kingdom of Italy, agreed. Austria hoped that the alliance would keep Italy out of its own happy Balkan hunting grounds, and Germany that it would secure another monarchist ally against republican France.

The Triple Alliance, signed in Vienna on 20 May 1882, bound Austria and Germany to support Italy in the unlikely event of her being attacked by France; and Italy to support Austria if she were attacked by two or more great powers, and to support Germany if she were attacked by France alone. It was not, in truth, much of a bargain for Italy.

In the years since then, the alliance had undergone various strains. Unlike his father, Umberto I, Victor Emmanuel had very little love for the Central Powers. To the liberal and self-effacing Victor Emmanuel, the Kaiser seemed ridiculously theatrical and his Reich dangerously authoritarian. His distaste for Wilhelm II's flamboyance was hardly diminished by the Kaiser's state visit to Rome in 1903. The German Emperor arrived with a suite of eighty, including a selection of hand-picked grenadiers whose height – intentionally or not – made the diminutive King of Italy appear even smaller. To the astonishment of the British ambassador, the Kaiser referred to Victor Emmanuel as 'the Dwarf' and to his Queen as 'a peasant girl'.[4] Nor were matters helped when, in his determination to improve the shining hour, the Kaiser, having laid the customary wreaths on the tombs of Italy's kings, plucked roses from the wreaths and handed them round to the Committee of Welcome.

The Emperor Franz Joseph, Victor Emmanuel liked even less. Not only did he consider him patronising and reactionary but he still regarded the Habsburg monarchy as the traditional enemy of a united Italy. After all, it was mainly from Austria that Italy had won its independence. So it was not really practical politics for Victor Emmanuel III to be allied to Franz Joseph when a completing of the *Risorgimento* depended on winning the Italian-speaking cities of Trieste and Trento and their hinterlands from Austria. Only by fighting Austria could Italy hope to reclaim her territory.

Inclining, far more naturally, towards the Triple Entente powers, and particularly towards democratic France and Britain, Victor Emmanuel's Italy began a secret flirtation with them. Never were the qualities of foxiness, of which the Italian King was so often accused, more in evidence than in the series of clandestine agreements drawn up during his reign. The most outrageous example of this Italian duplicity came in 1902 when Victor Emmanuel signed a secret agreement with France. In direct violation of the Triple Alliance, the two countries agreed on a policy of mutual neutrality. Seven years later he signed a secret agreement with that other Entente power, Russia, whereby the two nations agreed to co-ordinated action in the Balkans.

As an ally in war, Bismarck had once declared, Italy would be worth next to nothing. By now, she could not even be counted on as an ally at all.

5

Autocrat of All the Russias

OF ALL THE MONARCHS of twentieth-century Europe, the Tsar of Russia was, potentially, the most powerful. Not even those other autocratic emperors, Wilhelm II or Franz Joseph I, were in a position to wield as much personal power as Nicholas II. To the millions of peasants who made up the vast bulk of his subjects, this Autocrat of All the Russias was as a god.

The near-divinity of the Tsar was emphasised when, in the year 1913, Nicholas II celebrated the tercentenary of the Romanov dynasty. Throughout that summer, the imperial family took part in various national celebrations. The ceremonies began in March with a great choral *Te Deum* in the Cathedral of Our Lady of Kazan in St Petersburg. From the gigantic Winter Palace, stretching for a quarter of a mile along the River Neva, the imperial procession drove out through the streets of the city. Built, two centuries before, by Peter the Great on the marshes of the River Neva, St Petersburg was designed to be Russia's 'Window on Europe' – a spacious, Italianate, westernised city of baroque palaces, sweeping boulevards and ornamental gardens. With its pink granite quays, innumerable waterways and elegant bridges, it was known as 'the Venice of the North'. Its more barbaric splendours – and its undeniably northern climate – earned it the title of 'the Babylon of the Snows'. No sovereign in Europe could have wished for a more grandiose capital.

Yet for all the glories, both of the setting and the ceremonial, the tercentenary celebrations in St Petersburg were only a qualified success. The crowds lining the streets were lukewarm. Amongst the aristocratic audience at the state performance of Glinka's *A life for the Tsar* there was, says one observer, 'little real enthusiasm, little real loyalty'. The forty-five-year-old Nicholas II, so handsome in his uniform, looked disappointingly distant and dreamy. The forty-one-year-old Tsaritsa Alexandra, for all the magnificence of her clothes and jewels, appeared stiff and disdainful. Twice – once at a glittering reception at the Winter Palace and once at the Maryinsky Theatre – she left early. 'A little wave of resentment rippled over the theatre', noted one member of the audience.

Their four daughters, whose ages ranged from eighteen to twelve, were appealing enough but their only son, the nine-year-old Tsarevich, was apparently unable to walk. He had to be carried everywhere in the arms of a giant Cossack of the Guards. Only a handful of people knew what was wrong with him.

Things improved when, in May, the imperial family set off on a dynastic pilgrimage to Kostroma on the River Volga, where the first Romanov had been told of his elevation to the throne. As their luxurious steamer sailed up the river, peasants crowded the banks; some even plunged waist deep into the waters to get a closer look at the fabled Tsar. When he walked through the streets of provincial towns, workmen fell to the ground to kiss his shadow.

Climax to the celebrations came in Moscow where, in the great central square, Nicholas dismounted from his horse and walked, behind a row of chanting priests, into the Kremlin. At last, beneath the golden domes and among the twinkling icons of the Ouspensky Cathedral, in the ancient heart of Holy Russia, the Tsar could feel at one with his people. For here, he fervently believed, was the true Russia. St Petersburg, with its decadent aristocracy, its critical intellectuals, its bickering politicians and its discontented workers, was, as the Tsaritsa once put it, 'a rotten town, not one atom Russian'.

The authentic voice of the people, the imperial couple believed, could be heard in the address which the peasant delegation delivered to the Tsar. 'Be sure that our Lives belong to Thee,' ran the splendidly anachronistic phrases. 'Be sure that at the first call we shall place ourselves before Thee like a wall and sacrifice ourselves . . . for Thy dear life, Thy House and the glory of our country. Rule Tsar of the true faith to our glory and the terror of our foes.'

'Now you see for yourself what cowards those state ministers are,' remarked Alexandra to a lady-in-waiting at the height of the Moscow celebrations. 'They are constantly frightening the Tsar with threats of revolution, and here – you see it yourself – we need merely to show ourselves and at once all hearts are ours.'[1]

The Tsaritsa was being much too optimistic. No more than the Tsar did she understand the true nature of the web in which they had become enmeshed. For Nicholas and Alexandra were caught up in a personal and political situation of monumental significance.

Nicholas II, declared Wilhelm II on one occasion, was 'only fit to live in a country house and grow turnips'.[2] The Kaiser's judgement, for all its harshness, contained more than a grain of truth. Nicholas II was an unsophisticated and unintellectual man with a taste for family life and country living.

'He was not', says his cousin, Princess Marie of Romania, 'one of the giants, but the gentleness of his expression made him infinitely sympathetic;

something seemed to melt in one's heart when one looked at him, at his soft hazel eyes, at his gentle lips, when one watched his quiet movements, listened to his soft, low-toned voice.' With his affable manners and his considerable personal charm, the Tsar was frequently described as 'the most perfect type of English gentleman'.

Yet beneath that gentlemanly English exterior there lurked a profoundly Russian soul. And this despite the fact that, as a member of Europe's inter-married royal clan, almost no Russian blood flowed through his veins. Born on 18 May 1868, Nicholas had inherited neither the iron will of his father, Tsar Alexander III, nor the common sense of his mother – that lively Danish princess, sister to Britain's Queen Alexandra, who had become the Tsaritsa Marie Fedorovna. On the contrary, he was as stubborn, sentimental, superstitious, devious, secretive and fatalistic as any Russian *moujik* – peasant.

His duplicity was the despair of his ministers. 'Our Tsar', complained one of them, 'is an Oriental, a full-blooded Byzantine.' The minister went on to cite the occasion when, after a friendly, successful, two-hour-long meeting with the Tsar, he returned home to find the Tsar's written order for his dismissal lying on his desk.

Again, it was the Kaiser who supplied the explanation for his fellow sovereign's apparent shiftiness. 'The Tsar is not treacherous,' said Wilhelm, 'but he is weak. Weakness is not treachery, but it fulfils all its functions.' And Nicholas II's uncle, Edward VII, always maintained that his nephew was as weak as water.

It was this weakness, this inability to make up his mind, this avoidance of any open discussion, this lack of moral courage, that drove the Tsar's ministers to near distraction. They never knew where they stood. Once, after Nicholas had congratulated his prime minister on having drawn up a complicated programme of reform, the Tsar sent him a note cancelling the whole project. 'An inner voice', explained the Tsar, 'keeps on insisting that I do not accept responsibility for it. So far my conscience has not deceived me. Therefore I intend to follow its dictates. I know that you, too, believe that a Tsar's heart is in God's hands. Let it be so. For all laws established by me, I bear a great responsibility before God . . .'[3]

In other words, by leaving things to God, the Tsar could avoid having to make any firm decisions. That he was merely an instrument in God's hands, that it was to God alone that he was accountable, that he had been ordained by God to uphold Orthodoxy and autocracy, Nicholas II had no doubt at all. Only in this clinging to the theory of his God-given rights was he ever firm, or usually firm.

'The gentle but uneducated Emperor', sighed the British ambassador, Sir Arthur Nicolson, 'is afflicted with the misfortune of being weak on every point except his own autocracy.'

★

Backing up the Tsar, every inch of the way, was his wife, the Tsaritsa Alexandra Fedorovna. Born in 1872 as Princess Alix of Hesse-Darmstadt, a grand-daughter of Queen Victoria, Alexandra had long since forsaken her sensible Coburg background and her sober Lutheran upbringing. She had by now fully, even fervently, identified herself with her husband's country. But Russia had not taken to her with anything like the same ardour. In spite of her determination to dedicate herself to the welfare of the Russian people, the Tsaritsa was very unpopular. And she had been so from the start. Her hasty marriage to Nicholas, brought forward on the sudden death of his father, Alexander III, in 1894, had seemed somehow ill-omened. Their new Tsaritsa had come to them, whispered the superstitious Russians, behind a coffin.

In the twenty or so years since then, the Tsaritsa's luck had hardly improved. Although – with her firm features, sea-green eyes and red-gold hair – she was a woman of considerable beauty, her manner lacked all grace and charm. Painfully shy, she loathed all public appearances. Yet in no court in Europe were sovereigns on such merciless display. The magnificent Russian palaces, with their gigantic halls, their huge columns of jasper and malachite and their wealth of gold and silver ornamentation, were the setting for the most formal and exacting ceremonial in the world. The imperial couple were the central figures in a set piece of almost barbaric splendour. Yet through all this kaleidoscopic brilliance the Tsaritsa moved like an automaton. Incapable of saying a gracious word or of making a spontaneous gesture, she appeared cold, haughty, unapproachable.

And not only was Alexandra ill at ease in St Petersburg society, she thoroughly disapproved of it. To this withdrawn, intense and serious-minded woman, their decadence and frivolity were abhorrent. She was shocked by the happy-go-lucky way in which they practised their religion. Having been converted to Orthodoxy before her marriage, Alexandra had embraced it with all the fervour of her nature.

With equal ardour, she had embraced the principle of autocracy. No less than the Tsar – indeed even more, for she was more earnest, more passionate, more assertive than he – did she maintain that he was responsible to God alone. His autocratic powers must be preserved at all costs. She not only encouraged but strengthened her husband's distrust of all political reform. Her political creed was simple. The Russian people – and by the people she meant the humble, devout, unquestioning peasants – were devoted to the Tsar but, because of their childlike simplicity, they had to be ruled firmly and autocratically. Anyone wanting to destroy this autocracy was automatically an enemy, not only of the Russian people, but of God. The autocratic Tsar was God's anointed: thus the revolutionaries, or even the liberal reformers, were God's enemies.

In spite of these uncompromising beliefs, Alexandra was far from being the arrogant, power-hungry virago of her critics' imaginings. Among her

7 The diminutive Victor Emmanuel III of Italy

8 The ill-fated Russian imperial family in 1913. Standing, from the left: Grand Duchess Tatiana, Grand Duchess Olga. Seated: Grand Duchess Marie, Tsaritsa Alexandra, Tsarevich Alexis, Tsar Nicholas II, Grand Duchess Anastasia

family and her household, safe from the sneers of fashionable St Petersburg society, she revealed herself as a charming, compassionate and utterly unaffected woman.

Her marriage had been a brilliant success. Nicholas and Alexandra adored each other: they were as much in love after twenty years as they had been when they married. Together with their five children they formed a delightful family group, and since the unsociable Tsaritsa discouraged the children from mixing with others, the four young grand-duchesses and the little Tsarevich remained closely attached to each other and to their parents. At the very centre of national life, yet curiously cut off from it, the imperial family formed an island of domestic tranquillity.

Isolating the family still further from the realities of the Russian situation was their chosen way of life. For they lived, not in St Petersburg, but some fifteen miles south of the capital, at Tsarskoe Selo – the Tsar's village. The so-called village was, in fact, the very symbol of autocracy: an ornate, artificial, self-contained world of grandiose palaces, leafy parks, formal gardens, triumphal arches, heroic monuments and domed pavilions, all protected from the outside world by a high, ceaselessly patrolled circle of iron railings.

The imperial family lived in the Alexander Palace – the smaller of the two palaces – in an atmosphere which, in spite of the relative simplicity of their own tastes, was almost overwhelmingly lush, formal and, in the final analysis, unreal. Year after year slipped by, wrote one member of the household, 'and the little enchanted fairyland of Tsarskoe Selo slumbered peacefully on the brink of an abyss . . .'[4]

Their annual migrations in no way strengthened their contact with the real world. Spring and autumn took them, in their heavily guarded train, to the luxuriant scenery and mild climate of the Livadia Palace in the Crimea. In May they moved to the Peterhof Palace on the Baltic coast, an architectural extravagance created by Peter the Great to rival Versailles. June found them cruising the Gulf of Finland in the yacht *Standart* which, although as big as a small steamer and fuelled by coal, was as graceful as a sailing ship. In August they went to the imperial hunting lodge at Spala, deep in the Polish forest. In November they returned to Tsarskoe Selo for the winter and for their increasingly rare public appearances during the St Petersburg season. And wherever they moved, they were guarded, shielded, kept at arm's length from almost anyone other than their soft-footed servants, obsequiously bowing officials or respectful members of their households.

One cloud obscured their happiness. It was a cloud that, in the end, was to contribute to the destruction of them all. The Tsarevich, who turned nine in the year 1913, suffered from haemophilia.

On the Tsaritsa, the boy's illness had a particularly devastating effect. Appreciating that it was she who had passed the dreaded bleeding disease on to her son, that it was because of her that he had to suffer such terrible agonies, Alexandra dedicated herself, almost entirely, to his welfare. As there was nothing that the doctors could do to alleviate, let alone cure, her son's illness, she had turned, more and more, to God. Alexandra had always been drawn to the supernatural, to that particular Russian world of miracles, weeping statues, saintly relics, unaccountably glowing icons, faith healers and wandering Men of God. And, by the year 1913, she felt confident that, in this twilight world, she had found her link with the Almighty.

It had been in 1905 that the imperial couple had first met Gregory Rasputin – the dirty, uncouth, lank-haired, thirty-three-year-old *starets* or miracle worker, with his extraordinarily hypnotic eyes. There were several things, other than his reputation as a healer, that attracted the Tsaritsa to Rasputin. She liked his apparent simplicity. Never sycophantic, never grovelling, this plain-speaking *moujik* seemed the very personification of the loyal, devout, unchanging Russia of Alexandra's naïve imaginings.

But, more important than any of this, Rasputin was the one person who was able to relieve the Tsarevich's sufferings. Precisely how he achieved this is uncertain. One explanation is that Rasputin, with his hypnotic eyes and self-confident presence, was able to create the aura of tranquillity necessary to slow the blood through the boy's veins. Where the demented mother and the dithering doctors merely increased the tenseness of the atmosphere around the child, Rasputin calmed him and sent him to sleep.

Had Rasputin confined his activities to alleviating the Tsarevich's agony, things might have been different. But far from being a simple, pious *starets*, Rasputin was a man with a passionate lust for power. As his hold over the Tsaritsa and, through her, over the weak-willed Tsar increased, so did he come, ever more forcefully, to voice his political opinions and exercise his political influence.

Bolstering his position still further was the fact that his political creed confirmed the imperial couple's own view of Holy Russia: that the peasants and not the amoral aristocracy or the liberal intelligentsia or the industrial workers were the true people; and that autocracy was a divinely ordained institution.

In turn, Nicholas and Alexandra came to believe that for the dynasty to survive, for it to become stronger and reach the heights of glory, they must be guided, in all things, by this humble Man of God.

For all his belief in a divinely sanctioned autocracy, Tsar Nicholas II was, by the year 1913, a constitutional monarch or, at least, a semi-constitutional monarch. The change had been forced on him in 1905. Throughout that year

Russia had been torn by murders, bombings, strikes, riots, mutinies and uprisings. The Tsar's remedy – that terror must be met by terror – had solved nothing. So, in order to avert a full-scale revolution, Nicholas had been talked, very reluctantly, into granting a constitution. By the Imperial Manifesto of 30 October 1905, Russia was promised 'freedom of conscience, speech, assembly and association' and was granted an elected parliament – a Duma.

The experiment was hardly a success. Shocked by the rowdy scenes and revolutionary demands of its members, the Tsar – acting within his rights – dissolved the first two Dumas. The third Duma, elected on a revised roll favouring the country gentry, was a far more conservative body. A fourth Duma, elected in 1912 on very much the same lines, was equally amenable. Even Nicholas became reconciled to it. 'The Duma started too fast,' he explained to the British historian, Sir Bernard Pares. 'Now it is slower, but better. And more lasting.'

Not that the Tsar was unduly hampered by the deliberations of the Duma. The constitution had left him with considerable powers. Compared with other constitutional monarchs, such as George V, Victor Emmanuel III, Albert I or even Kaiser Wilhelm II, Nicholas was still very much the autocrat. Although no law could be passed without the consent of the Duma (and a built-in conservative majority usually ensured that it was) the Tsar retained his prerogative over defence and foreign affairs. Ministers remained servants of the crown, appointed and dismissed directly by the crown, with the crown free to accept or reject a minister's advice.

When one prime minister, feeling that he had lost the Tsar's confidence, threatened resignation, Nicholas would not hear of it. 'This is not a question of confidence or lack of it,' he said, 'it is my will. Remember that we live in Russia, not abroad . . .'[5]

In short, Nicholas II, in spite of his lack of any qualities of leadership, was still trying to run his empire like a latter-day Peter the Great. Trusting no one, he refused to delegate power. The result was that he was obliged to battle, almost single-handed, with all the complexities of his vast empire: its cumbersome bureaucracy, its burgeoning industry, its sensitive foreign relations, its widespread social unrest, its revolutionary violence, its powerful secret police, its complicated network of spies and informers and double agents.

When he did manage to find a man of the calibre of Peter Stolypin, who served as prime minister from 1906 to 1911, it was only to see him shot before his very eyes, at the Kiev Opera House. Yet such was the labyrinthine political structure of imperial Russia that, while Stolypin's assassin was known to be both a revolutionary *and* a police informer, he was suspected, with good reason, of being a tool in the hands of certain reactionaries.

In some ways, though, these years before the First World War were not entirely without their successes. Stolypin's celebrated 1906 land reform bill, by which millions of peasants were able to withdraw from unproductive village communes and to own their own land, was a deeply significant measure, drawing the teeth of much peasant dissatisfaction. What with half a dozen years of good harvests, a rapidly expanding industry and an increase in foreign trade, the economy boomed. The newly established Duma, for all its limitations, gave the country some semblance of democracy. Education was reformed, censorship was made less draconian, there was a blossoming in the worlds of the arts and the sciences. St Petersburg society attained new heights of brilliance and extravagance.

So eased was the political situation that Alexander Kerensky, a newly elected Labour deputy in the fourth Duma and an avowed anti-monarchist (in whose hands, moreover, the fate of the imperial family would one day rest) could claim that there was no longer any need for clandestine activity. 'The public was now accustomed to a free press, to political meetings, to political parties and clubs,' he declared. 'Trade unions, professional unions and co-operative societies were firmly rooted as part of daily life . . . freedom of speech for the deputies was absolute . . . the old secretive, underground, conspirative methods of revolutionary activity had passed into the limbo of history.'

It was no wonder that Lenin, the exiled and more militant revolutionary, often felt so despairing. Trailing disconsolately from one foreign city to another, consulting ever less hopefully with his dwindling band of supporters, he sometimes toyed with the idea of giving up his subversive activities altogether. With the improvement in both the political and economic climate of Russia, conditions were much less favourable for the sort of social upheaval on which he was pinning his hopes.

'I do not expect to live to see the revolution,' he wrote dolefully on one occasion.

Paradoxically, the Tsar benefited hardly more from this upturn in the national fortunes than did Lenin. The trouble was Rasputin. The new freedom, both of political discussion and of the press, meant that the activities of the *starets* soon became common knowledge. The capital seethed with stories: about his increasing arrogance, his outspoken conversation, his outrageous manners, his sexual appetites. It was claimed that he and the Tsaritsa were lovers. A series of letters, said to have been written by Alexandra to Rasputin, passed from hand to hand. Their fulsome phrases ('I only wish one thing: to fall asleep, to fall asleep for ever on your shoulders and in your arms . . . Come quickly, I am waiting for you and I am tormenting myself for you')[6] gave strength to the rumours. No story about the Tsaritsa and the *starets* was too scurrilous to be believed.

Nor were these comments confined to the gutter press. For Rasputin's political manoeuvrings were causing as much concern as his reported sexual exploits. Gradually, the *starets* had been turning his attention to distinctly more mundane political matters than the glorification of God and Tsar. Or rather, he set about achieving this by very dubious means. Working always through the Tsaritsa, Rasputin began organising jobs, contracts and honours for his protégés and backers. In time, his clique – or what was often referred to as 'the Tsaritsa's party' – would include bishops, generals, leading officials, ministers, even prime ministers. Ultimately, Rasputin was to become the most influential man in Russia.

One by one, in growing alarm, the various leading institutions and personalities of the empire began to speak out against Rasputin. The Church formally investigated his activities. The Duma debated his growing influence in national affairs. Two prime ministers drew up reports on his behaviour. Several members of the imperial family, including the Dowager Empress, voiced their concern.

It was all to no purpose. Alexandra refused to listen. She remained stubbornly convinced that the *starets* was a simple Man of God, sent to ease her 'long Calvary' and to ensure that her son lived to inherit the throne. Against anyone who dared criticise Rasputin, she moved with all the vigour of her nature. When the press attacked him, she talked the Tsar into ordering a ban on any mention of his name. When the Duma debated his political activities, she insisted that the prime minister put a stop to it. If anyone complained to the Tsar about him, she engineered their downfall. Even Kokovtsov, the prime minister, was dismissed because he had drawn up a damning report on the favourite.

The *starets* had only to drop a hint in Alexandra's ear for her to act. 'Our Friend's' advice, on every conceivable subject, became sacrosanct. The Tsaritsa would not rest until she had talked her complaisant husband into carrying out all Rasputin's wishes.

It would hardly be an exaggeration to say that by the year 1913 Rasputin, through the fervent Alexandra and her weak-willed husband, controlled the destiny of Russia.

6

Royal Meetings

'ONE SHOULD NEVER FORGET', the Kaiser's friend, Count Eulenburg, once remarked, 'that a discussion between two princes is propitious only when it confines itself to the weather.' Eulenburg's dry observation had been admirably borne out by the discussions which took place between Wilhelm II and Nicholas II in the summer of 1905. For in the same year that the Tsar had been forced into granting his subjects a constitution, he had been coerced, by the indefatigable Wilhelm II, into signing a treaty of alliance with Germany. The two monarchs – the Kaiser in his yacht *Hohenzollern* and the Tsar in his yacht *Stella Polaris* – had met at Bjorkoe, off the coast of Finland, that July, and it had been aboard the *Stella Polaris* that this extraordinary agreement had been concluded.

The incident had marked a climax in the relationship between Tsar and Kaiser. For several years before this Wilhelm II, who was not only nine years older than Nicholas II but an altogether more assertive personality, had taken it upon himself to act as the Tsar's mentor. In letter after letter he had bombarded Nicholas with advice on a limitless range of subjects. Indeed, it was in no small measure due to the Kaiser's urgings that Nicholas had embarked on a disastrous war against Japan in 1904.

For the truth was that in no field was the Tsar's weakness more apparent than in that of foreign affairs. Where Wilhelm II's foreign policy was conducted only too publicly, Nicholas II's was carried out with all the secrecy and duplicity of his nature; and of the nature of his state. Relying heavily on spies, secret police, undercover agents, clandestine treaties and verbal agreements, Tsarist diplomacy was of the most dangerous variety. And where the Tsar was as irresolute a man as Nicholas II, it was more dangerous still.

Determined to take full advantage of the Tsar's pliability, the Kaiser had come up with this latest idea: a historic treaty of friendship between their two empires that would serve as 'a cornerstone of European politics'. In this way, Wilhelm hoped to weaken the alliance between Russia and France (concluded in 1893 by Nicholas's father, Alexander III) and free the Second Reich from what he called 'the terrible Gallo-Russian pincers'.

It was for this reason that the Kaiser had arranged that secret meeting with the Tsar while they were cruising with their families off the Finnish coast that summer. Dressed in his admiral's uniform, Wilhelm crossed from the *Hohenzollern* to the *Stella Polaris*. In his pocket was a copy of the agreement. He was met by Nicholas, looking altogether less bellicose in the navy blazer and white trousers of an English yachtsman. It did not take the Kaiser long to interest the Tsar in his proposal. Having just suffered defeat in the Russo-Japanese War, Nicholas was feeling particularly friendless. The two monarchs went into what had been Alexander III's cabin and there, while Wilhelm 'sent up a fervent prayer to God', Nicholas read through the treaty.

'There was a dead calm,' reported the Kaiser in his inimitable fashion to Chancellor von Bülow, 'only the gentlest murmur from the sea, and the sun shone bright and clear into the cosy cabin, while right before my eyes lay the *Hohenzollern* in her dazzling whiteness, with the Imperial Standard fluttering high in the morning breeze. I was just reading, on its black cross, the words *Gott Mit Uns*, when I heard the Tsar's voice beside me say: "That is quite excellent. I agree!" . . . My heart beat so hard that I could hear it; but I pulled myself together and said with every appearance of casualness: "Should you like to sign it? It would be a very nice souvenir of our meeting!" '

Nicholas duly signed it and, in the certainty that the ghosts of 'Frederick Wilhelm III, Queen Louise, Grandpapa and Nicholas I' were looking on in approval, the Kaiser clasped the Tsar in his arms. That the treaty marked a significant turning point in the history of Europe, Wilhelm had no doubt whatsoever. No longer would Germany have to face the prospect of fighting a war on two fronts. His eyes, he tells us, were filled with 'tears of pure joy'.

The Tsar's ministers, when they came to hear about the treaty, were not anything like as joyful. Patiently, it was explained to Nicholas that he could not support France against Germany in one treaty, and Germany against France in another. The treaty would have to be repudiated. Yet when Nicholas tried to do this, in an embarrassed letter to Wilhelm, he was rewarded with one of the Kaiser's outraged telegrams.

'We have joined our hands together religiously,' wired Wilhelm. 'We have given our signatures before God, who has heard the promise we swore. I consider, therefore, that the treaty is still in force. If you desire some alterations of detail, propose them to me. But what is signed is signed! God is our witness!'

But the Kaiser was having trouble nearer home as well. Chancellor von Bülow wanted nothing to do with the treaty. For one thing, with Germany's long-standing friend, Austria–Hungary, often at odds with Russia in the Balkans, the agreement was not really practical. For another, the chancellor could not approve of his master acting without the advice, or even knowledge, of his ministers. In fact, the incident illustrated the limits of the Kaiser's powers. In theory, Wilhelm II had the right to form an alliance with whomsoever he pleased; in practice he could not do so without his chancellor's approval.

As Bülow did not approve, he threatened to resign. A more resolute monarch might have let him go and appointed a more sympathetic chancellor, but Wilhelm II was far from resolute. In an instant he changed from exultant diplomat into deflated neurotic.

'For the best and most intimate friend I have to treat me in this way without offering any adequate reason has given me such a terrible blow that I am quite broken down . . . I appeal to your friendship for me. Do not let us hear any more about resigning. Wire "all right" when you get this letter and I shall know you are going to stay. For the day after your request for release arrived there would no longer be a Kaiser alive! Think of my poor wife and children!'

Bülow did not resign; Wilhelm's poor wife and children were saved; and the treaty was dumped into the wastepaper basket of history. The Franco-Russian alliance remained firm.

Yet for all the importance of the Franco-Russian alliance, it was not in western Europe that Russia's emotions were most deeply involved. The marriage between autocratic Russia and republican France had been largely one of convenience: Alexander III had needed, not only to counterbalance the military might of Wilhelm II's Germany, but to take advantage of a French offer of enormous loans, at low rates of interest, in order to extend his railways and enlarge his army.

It was, rather, to the southeastern corner of Europe, to that conglomeration of little states known collectively as the Balkans, that Russian eyes were most longingly turned. With the Ottoman empire, which had until very recently held sway over the area, becoming yearly more decrepit, Russia's interest in the Balkans was once more beginning to quicken. Here, reckoned the Tsar, lay his empire's true sphere of interest. As a boy, Nicholas had been taught to believe, not only in a God-given Autocracy but in some future realisation of the age-old Russian dream of expansion southwards. By gaining control of the pinnacled city of Constantinople, Russia would dominate the Dardanelles and have access to the Mediterranean. And by establishing herself as protector of the largely Slav population of the Balkans, she would become the leading power in the area.

Nicholas would have been familiar with the writings of Nikolai Danilevski who, in his celebrated book *Russia and Europe*, argued that Russia was destined to defeat a decadent Europe and to form a great Slav federation with its capital in Constantinople.

In these imperial ambitions, Russia was brought face-to-face with the Austro-Hungarian empire. It, too, saw the Balkans as a legitimate sphere of interest. An ominous echo of Danilevski's arguments was sounded by

Crown Prince Rudolph of Austria–Hungary. 'I have always considered that Austria's mission in the east of Europe is a law of nature . . .' he once wrote, 'my conviction is stronger than ever that we have a great future in these regions.'[1]

The result was an intense rivalry between the empires of Nicholas II and Franz Joseph I. Conducted with all the intrigue, ambiguity and baroque complexity characteristic of the diplomacy of both regimes, this power-political game was a particularly dangerous one. Not without good reason were the Balkans known as 'the powder keg' of Europe.

In 1908, this Austro-Russian rivalry in the Balkans had brought Europe to the threshold of war. A highly complicated and utterly unscrupulous man-oeuvre, by which Austria annexed the Balkan provinces of Bosnia and Herzegovina, and left Russia – despite a secret agreement between the two countries – empty handed, led to talk of mobilisation of their armies. A flurry of letters between the emperors of Russia, Austria and Germany did nothing to calm the highly charged atmosphere.

War was averted only when Germany, coming to the aid of her Austrian ally, issued Russia with something very like an ultimatum. The Tsar, who was in no position to wage war, was obliged to back down.

The results of this Russian humiliation were far-reaching. The whole Bosnia–Herzegovina affair had been, in a way, a dress rehearsal for 1914. 'German action towards us has been simply brutal,' complained the Tsar to his mother, the Tsaritsa Marie, 'and we won't forget it.'

From now on, Russia not only began preparing for a future war against Austria and its German ally but she set about strengthening her alliance with France. At the same time Germany drew still closer to Austria, even to the extent of sanctioning its disastrous Balkan policies. The still-fluid situation was beginning to crystallise.

It was left to someone far removed from this almost eighteenth-century world of autocratic emperors, country house diplomacy and gold-laced ambassadors to give a chillingly realistic assessment of the situation. 'A war between Austria and Russia', wrote Lenin to his friend Maxim Gorky in 1913, 'would be a very useful thing for the revolution . . .'[2]

In May 1913 Wilhelm II played host to the last of the great royal family gatherings which had been such a feature of the European scene. To Berlin, for the marriage of the Kaiser's only daughter, Princess Victoria Louise, to the Duke of Brunswick-Lüneburg, came a galaxy of royal guests headed by George V and Nicholas II.

Although George V had been on the throne for three years, this was his first Continental visit. And even this was a private, not a state, one. In a letter to the apprehensive French government, Sir Edward Grey, the British foreign secretary, made it abundantly clear that the royal visit to Berlin was a purely family affair.

It was as a member of the family, too, that Nicholas II came to Berlin. And if, by now, the Tsar always felt slightly uneasy in the company of the Kaiser, he was delighted to see his cousin Georgie once more. As their mothers – the Dowager Tsaritsa Marie and Queen Alexandra – were sisters, the two men looked very alike. 'Only their uniforms', wrote the Kaiser's daughter, 'told the difference between them.'

The two monarchs were alike in other ways as well. Both were modest, well-intentioned men. In Britain, as one of the Tsar's biographers has put it, 'where a sovereign needed only to be a good man in order to be a good king, Nicholas II would have made an admirable monarch'.[3]

This great royal gathering in Berlin was a splendid example of what one observer has called 'those dynastic madrigals once thought to breathe harmony over discordant Europe'. For once the Kaiser refrained from giving his fellow sovereigns the benefit of his advice on international affairs (although their staffs were not similarly spared) and concentrated on impressing them with the brilliance of his court.

'The arrival of all the wedding guests turned Berlin into a magnificent showcase, a display of royalty rarely seen before,' enthused the bride-to-be. 'Masses of people gathered in the streets of the capital to witness the parade of princes. They had come from everywhere to line the route the wedding guests would pass, and the sight of the tremendous throng in Unter den Linden Opera Platz, and in front of the castle was indescribable.'

The Kaiser saw to it that everything – the colossal banquets, the military parades, the gala performance at the opera and the wedding itself – was superbly done.

Most memorable of all was the *Fackeltanz*, the Torch Dance traditional at German royal weddings, in which no one below the rank of royal highness was allowed to take part. It was danced in the *Weisse Saal* of the Old Palace in Berlin, a splendid hall in which the decoration was entirely white and silver. An inlay, in the shape of a crowned Prussian eagle, decorated the centre of the dance floor and was kept in a state of high polish, making it as slippery as ice. If, in his exuberance, an officer set foot on it and crashed to the floor, he would be barred from all court balls for a year. But no such boisterousness marred this occasion: the royal dancers behaved with exemplary dignity. Never before, writes one witness as these emperors and empresses, kings and queens, princes and princesses performed the elaborate ritual in the flickering torchlight, had royals been 'woven into so many family permutations, symbolic of regal accord'.

But it was not quite all accord. The neurotic Kaiser, always imagining that plots were being hatched behind his back, resented any time spent together by George V and Nicholas II. On the one occasion that the cousins did manage to have a private conversation ('Had a long and satisfactory talk with dear Nicky; he is just the same as always', runs the King's typically laconic report of the meeting) the Kaiser was greatly alarmed. George V suspected that 'William's ear was glued to the keyhole'[4] throughout the meeting.

For even at this late stage the Kaiser was hoping that Britain might be enticed out of the arms of Russia and France. Just a few years before, in one of his more than usually indiscreet conversations, held while on a visit to England and subsequently published in the *Daily Telegraph*, Wilhelm had claimed to be Britain's best friend. And as recently as 1912, with the naval race between the two countries at its height, the Kaiser was still hoping for a *rapprochement*. How, he demanded of George V's secretary, could Britain imagine that he – the grandson of Queen Victoria – could ever allow Britain to be threatened at sea? Surely it would be more sensible of Britain to ally herself to Teutonic Germany than to Latin France?

But it was not to be. Whatever the Kaiser's inclinations might have been (and, in truth, they changed from day to day) Germany's politicians and diplomats remained averse to any talk of an Anglo-German understanding.

In no way, though, did this affect the success of the British King's visit to Berlin. On the contrary, King George and Queen Mary enjoyed their stay immensely. The Queen, in gold and with pearls and diamonds sparkling at every turn, was far and away the most impressive figure at the wedding ceremony. She even, this most self-controlled of queens, indulged in a little traditional weeping as the bridal couple exchanged their vows.

'Later', wrote the bride, 'they used to say that she had sobbed because she had at that moment foreseen the forthcoming disaster of war the following year breaking over us. That is really out of the question. Queen Mary was very attached to the [bridegroom's] family and it was understandable that the ceremony should affect her.'

The King seemed equally oblivious to any 'forthcoming disasters'. 'Our visit to Berlin has, I think, been a great success in every way . . .' he wrote. 'Nothing could have exceeded the kindness of the [German] Emperor and Empress. He went out of his way to entertain us and to do everything in his power to make our visit a pleasant one.'

He trusted, he went on to say, that the visit would 'improve the relations between the two countries'.

A more cynical note was struck by Frederick Ponsonby, one of the King's private secretaries. 'On the whole the visit was a great success, but whether any real good is done, I have my doubts. The feeling in the two countries is too strong for a visit of this sort to alter.'

Where the German diplomats were doing precious little towards safeguarding the Reich against some future war, the generals were doing a great deal towards launching such a war. The Kaiser might confine himself to striking warlike attitudes and making bellicose speeches but his General Staff was treating it all far more seriously. Time and again they assured the Kaiser that a war against France and Russia was inevitable and that it would be as well for Germany to decide on the timing of it. Always the weathercock, Wilhelm II would sometimes agree with their calculations, sometimes not. Afraid of being accused of cowardice, he none the less shrank from giving the generals their heads.

German strategy for the envisaged war was contained in the Schlieffen Plan, drawn up by an earlier chief of staff and modified by the present chief, General Helmuth von Moltke. This involved a war on two fronts: a massive German offensive through Belgium against France (thus avoiding the forti-fied Franco-German frontier) and, once France had been defeated in a lightning campaign, a concentration of both the Germans and the Austro-Hungarian armies in the east to destroy the more lumberingly mobilised Russian army.

The success of this plan depended, very much, on the attitude of Belgium. The fact that Prussia had been one of the guarantors of Belgian neutrality in perpetuity was regarded as nothing more than a technicality. What was important for Germany was that Belgium should allow German troops to pass through her territory unhindered. At most, Germany expected Belgium to make some sort of token resistance and then fall back, leaving the German army to roll across Belgium, into northern France and on to Paris.

To judge Belgium's reaction to the plan, the Kaiser invited King Albert of the Belgians to visit Potsdam in November 1913. Moving awkwardly among the superbly uniformed German officers, King Albert very quickly realised what they were up to. On the occasion of a court ball the Kaiser pointed out General von Kluck as the man who was to 'lead the march on Paris'. On another evening, before a state dinner, Wilhelm launched into an impassioned harangue against France: because of continual French provoca-tion, he ranted, war had become inevitable. After dinner, General von Moltke returned to the subject. He had a great deal to say about the invincibility of the German army and the aggressive spirit of the German people.

'This time we must make an end of it,' he told the discomforted King Albert. 'Your Majesty cannot imagine the irresistible enthusiasm which will permeate the entire German nation on "The Day".'

King Albert could imagine it only too well. And to dispel any doubts about Belgium's attitude, he assured his hosts, in his quiet but emphatic way, that his country would remain neutral unless attacked. But if she were attacked, she would fight back. On returning to Brussels, Albert backed this up with an unequivocal statement to the effect that Belgium would declare war on any power that violated her territory.

If Wilhelm II found it necessary to strike terror into the hearts of his potential enemies, his tone was hardly less aggressive when reassuring his friends. In one of his verbose speeches at a banquet in Vienna, he assured his audience that he stood 'shoulder to shoulder . . . in shining armour' beside the 'august and venerable' Emperor Franz Joseph. And to his other ally, Victor Emmanuel III of Italy, he made a solemn if characteristically carping declaration. 'All the long years of my reign my colleagues, the monarchs of Europe, have paid no attention to what I have to say. Soon, with my great Navy to endorse my words, they will be more respectful.'[5]

Yet under all the bravado lurked a terrible apprehension. In the year 1913, the Kaiser celebrated the twenty-fifth anniversary of his accession. The occasion was marked by nationwide celebrations. All summer long Berlin was *en fête*. Along the new processional ways, transformed by flags, swags, banners and triumphal arches, tramped military parades or tradesmen's guilds. Kings and princes, rulers of the twenty-five states that went to make up the empire, flocked to the capital to pay homage to the Kaiser. At Leipzig Wilhelm unveiled a massive monument on 'the battlefield of the nations' to celebrate the centenary of the war against the French. The gesture was not lost on France. At a banquet in the *Weisse Saal* of his Berlin palace, he spoke of the confederation of the German states as 'an eternal union for the protection of the realm'.

To the perspicacious, though, the Kaiser was not quite as confident as he pretended. Bishop Boyd-Carpenter, in Berlin to offer congratulations on behalf of the British Council of Churches, sensed something very like despair behind that resolute façade.

'He was quite cordial,' wrote the Bishop, 'but he spoke with a note that was new to me . . . He seemed apprehensive; he spoke of the dangerous position in which Germany was placed, between two powers which understood one another and might prove hostile. When I left him, I felt he was under the influence of a great fear.'

7

His Imperial and Royal
Apostolic Majesty

'YOU SEE IN ME', the Emperor Franz Joseph once told Theodore Roosevelt, 'the last monarch of the old school.' This was true. By the year 1910 there was no crowned head in Europe who could match the courtliness, punctiliousness and self-confident majesty of the eighty-year-old Habsburg Emperor.

There was certainly no living monarch who had reigned longer. Having ascended the throne, at the age of eighteen, in 1848, Franz Joseph had been Emperor for over sixty years. At the time of his death, in 1916, he would have reigned for sixty-eight years; longer even than Queen Victoria. By now few of Franz Joseph's subjects could remember a time when this luxuriantly bewhiskered and impeccably uniformed old gentleman had not been their Emperor. Renowned for his unyielding standards and rigid self-discipline, he had become the very symbol of the old-fashioned values. On the ever-changing European scene, Franz Joseph remained the one constant feature.

His daily life functioned with all the precision of a well-oiled machine. In spite of being the representative of one of the grandest and oldest-established royal houses in Europe (the Habsburgs had reigned since the thirteenth century) the Emperor Franz Joseph was a man of modest manners and simple tastes. His private life was spartan in the extreme. He lived in two simply furnished rooms; he slept in an iron cot. When he wanted a bath, a tub was carried into his quarters. Rising at four, he would put on his uniform and be at his desk by five. That desk was a plain field-army table. His working day was divided between a mountain of paperwork, to which he gave meticulous attention, and the granting of audiences, conducted with stultifying formality.

With such new-fangled inventions as the typewriter and the telephone he would have no truck. At the age of eighty-four he climbed six flights of stairs rather than take the lift. Only once did he ride in a motor car; and then solely on the insistence of the more adventurous Edward VII.

Lunch would be eaten off a tray and washed down with a glass of beer.

Dinner was served at six in the evening and, in spite of the splendour of the scene – the rococo rooms, the gilt furniture, the glittering chandeliers, the liveried servants, the gold plate, the showy uniforms – the atmosphere was singularly cheerless. The Emperor ate fast and sparingly, hardly noticing what was put before him. No one ever addressed him first. In answer to his occasional questioning, guests were expected to reply as briefly as possible. The *cercle* after dinner, with the Emperor saying a word or two to each guest as he shuffled past, was tedious in the extreme. He always retired early.

Franz Joseph carried out his public duties faultlessly, conscientiously and, above all, punctually. Whether it be a court ball in the Hofburg Palace, a state visit to the opera, a diplomatic reception amid the glories of the country palace of Schönbrunn, or one of those military parades in which he took such a delight, Franz Joseph insisted that everything be done according to long-established tradition. Of the frivolous, decadent atmosphere of turn-of-the-century Vienna, there was no trace. Rules were there to be obeyed.

One night, for instance, the Emperor suffered a terrible choking fit and rang for help. His worried doctor, flinging on a dressing gown, hurried to his master's bedside. But the old Emperor was not quite so ill, apparently, as not to be able to choke out one word. It was 'Frack!' – 'Tail coat!' Even *in extremis* he demanded that the formalities be observed.

The Emperor's one relaxation was hunting. The mornings of those summer days spent in his undistinguished villa at Bad Ischl were devoted, almost entirely, to clambering about the mountainside in *lederhosen* in search of game. But by afternoon he was back at his desk. Work for him was more than a duty; it was a necessity.

His life had been a sad one, beset with personal and political problems. His marriage, to the beautiful Princess Elizabeth, a member of the unconventional Wittelsbach family of Bavaria (of whom Belgium's Queen Elisabeth was also a member) had been doomed from the start. As much as he adored her, this lack-lustre monarch could not long hold the interest of his capricious, temperamental, self-obsessed wife. Her absences from his stuffy court became progressively longer and in 1898, while on one of her restless wanderings, she was assassinated, for purely symbolic reasons, by an anarchist.

Their only son, the equally romantic and unstable Crown Prince Rudolph, had shot himself and his mistress at Mayerling, ten years earlier. Franz Joseph's brother, the Archduke Maximilian, having allowed himself misguidedly to be crowned Emperor of Mexico, was overthrown by revolutionaries and executed by a firing squad at Querètaro.

The only flame to warm this winter of Franz Joseph's life was his long-standing relationship with a retired actress, Katherina Schratt. More like a middle-aged, middle-class wife than a mistress, she suited her unexciting Emperor beautifully. They gave each other little gifts, they wrote each

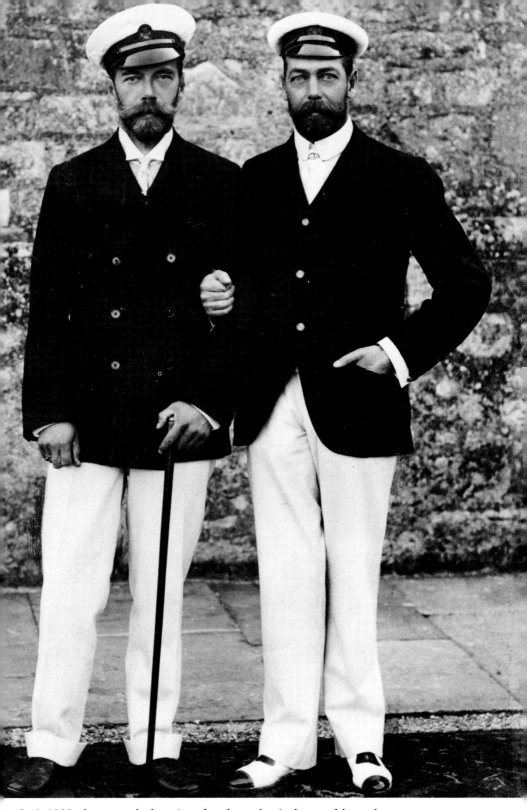

9 A 1909 photograph showing the close physical resemblance between the cousins Tsar Nicholas II and the future King George V

10 Wilhelm II and George V wearing uniforms of the regiments of each
other's armies, with the officers of the 1st Prussian Dragoon Guards,
Berlin 1913

other affectionate letters, they sat side by side drinking coffee and exchanging small-talk. Yet for all the *gemütlichkeit* of this relationship, the Emperor remained an arid, disillusioned, curiously luckless man. 'I am a *pechvogel*' – a bird of misfortune – he would sometimes sigh.

Never a man of much intellect or curiosity, Franz Joseph had become more mentally ossified with each passing year. Humourless, blinkered, conservative, obsessed with detail, he had the mind of a bureaucrat. 'For him', claimed one of the late Empress Elizabeth's ladies-in-waiting, 'only primitive concepts exist. Beautiful, ugly, dead, living, healthy, young, old, clever, stupid – these are all separate notions to him and he is unable to form a bridge leading from one to the other . . . His ideas know no nuances.'[1]

Oblivious to, indeed dismissive of, the extraordinary flowering of the cultural, intellectual and scientific life of turn-of-the-century Vienna, Franz Joseph presided over the most hidebound, parochial and fossilised court in Europe.

'In Vienna', said Tsar Ferdinand of Bulgaria to the French ambassador, Maurice Paléologue, 'one breathes in an atmosphere of death and decrepitude . . . I don't know if you have ever visited the Imperial necropolis, the *Kaisergruft* at the Capucin Church. It is airless, mouldy and decomposing. Well! The entire Austrian court is impregnated with this noisome smell . . . a smell which has spread from the court to all official circles . . . I know of nothing more lugubrious than dining at the Emperor's table: there one only comes across archaic countenances, shrivelled intellects, trembling heads, worn-out bladders. It is the exact image of Austria-Hungary.'

Distrusting the world of ideas, Franz Joseph felt deeply about only two things: his army and his dynasty. He delighted in parades, reviews and uniforms. These serried ranks, with their strict discipline and clockwork precision, were like some gigantic reflection of his own orderly lifestyle. The Emperor might not know much about modern strategy or modern weaponry, and might dislike too much talk of military reform, but he felt that the only institution on which his dynasty could depend was the army. And he was right. The Habsburg monarchy, as the historian A.J.P. Taylor has pointed out, 'lived only in the Austro-Hungarian army'. For the sad truth was that there was no such thing as an Austro-Hungarian Empire loyal to its Emperor.

To understand this, one needed to understand the composition of Franz Joseph's extraordinary realm.

Above the gateway into the Hofburg was carved the proud motto: *To Austria is the whole world subject.* Although things had changed a great deal since the Habsburgs had ruled the vast Holy Roman Empire, they still held sway over fifty million people of different nationalities – Germans, Magyars,

Czechs, Slovaks, Croats, Serbs, Slovenes, Italians, Romanians and Poles – artificially bound together by the accidents of history and the authority of the Habsburg dynasty. With the Habsburg lands stretching from the waters of the Adriatic in the south to the forests of Poland in the north, and from the Alps in the west to within two hundred miles of the Black Sea in the east, there was no such thing as a single Austrian nation. An earlier Habsburg emperor, on being assured that one of his subjects was an outstanding patriot, had very sensibly asked, 'But is he a patriot for *me*?'

The two dominant groups within this racial *mélange* were the Austrian Germans and the Hungarian Magyars. Since 1867 the empire had been divided into two semi-autonomous states of Austria and Hungary, linked by the person of a common ruler – the Emperor Franz Joseph. The arrangement did precious little towards solving the problems of this ramshackle structure: it remained a hotch-potch of inter-racial friction, unsatisfied political aspirations and strident nationalisms.

And this fragile edifice rested in the hands of a monarch who, despite his dignity, courtesy, authority and unquestioning sense of duty, was lacking in any of the qualities necessary to meet the challenges of his times.

Like his brother sovereigns, the emperors of Germany and Russia, Franz Joseph was an autocrat thinly disguised as a constitutional monarch. Obsessed with the preservation of his dynasty, he had, throughout his long reign, felt obliged to grant various political concessions: a little more autonomy here, a relaxation of an ordinance there, an extension of the suffrage somewhere else. But, in the final analysis, the empire was run by the Emperor and his vast army of bureaucrats. The Reichsrat, the Austrian parliament, for all the bombast of its speeches and the vigour of its resolutions, was virtually powerless. If the Reichsrat refused to pass a law, the Emperor would pass it by an 'emergency decree' instead. The members of the various parties were usually too busy bickering among themselves to present a serious challenge to the Emperor's powers.

What Franz Joseph exercised was 'absolute authority within a legal structure of constitutionalism'. His rule might have been described as 'latent absolutism' but it was absolutism none the less.

Yet it was never repressive in the way that the Tsarist regime in Russia was repressive. The Habsburg monarchy was not tyrannical or brutal: it was merely muddled, inefficient and ineffective. Far from being a tyrant, Franz Joseph was a glorified civil servant. It was, as A. J. P. Taylor has put it, 'a perpetual puzzle to him that he could not make his Empire work merely by sitting at his desk and signing documents for eight hours a day'. And, as he aged, so did effective power pass into the hands of those who drew up the documents: the sometimes well-meaning, sometimes corrupt but invariably irresponsible bureaucrats who governed the empire in his name.

In addition to the customary challenges of liberalism and socialism, the Emperor had to deal with the problems created by the multi-racial or multi-national nature of his empire. By a process of divide and rule, of playing off one group against another, by making concessions to more important nationalities at the expense of the less important ones, by allowing the Germans and the Magyars to dominate the Czechs, Slovaks, Croats and Serbs, he had hitherto managed to hold his patchwork domain together. He was astute enough to appreciate that the minority races would rather be dominated by him than by some larger minority race.

Yet the Emperor had never managed to create any sense of national unity, no feeling of loyalty towards the empire itself. By now the ageing Franz Joseph's empire had become hardly more than 'a fabric held up by a scaffolding of officialdom and by a precarious equipoise of national animosities'.[2]

Heir to this crumbling edifice, now that Franz Joseph's only son had committed suicide, was the old Emperor's nephew, the Archduke Franz Ferdinand. Forty-five years old in 1910, Franz Ferdinand was a corpulent, unsmiling, steely-eyed man with a pair of swooping, antler-like moustaches. Like his uncle, the Emperor, he was seldom seen out of uniform. Unlike his uncle, though, he had very little personal appeal. Humourless, impatient, energetic, given to black depressions and violent rages, he seemed more like a hard-headed Prussian than a light-hearted Viennese.

Yet this apparently unromantic man had made one supremely romantic gesture: he had married, most unsuitably, for love. His bride had been Countess Sophie Chotek, lady-in-waiting to his cousin, the Archduchess Isabella. In spite of all the Countess's advantages – her noble birth, her distinguished looks, her dignified manner, her agreeable nature – she lacked the one thing that counted in the Habsburg dynasty: royal blood. Only after protracted discussions would the old Emperor give his consent to their marriage. And then only on the condition that it was morganatic.

At a solemn meeting of the court and the privy council in the Hofburg on 28 June 1900, the Archduke Franz Ferdinand had been obliged to renounce all rights of rank and succession for his future children. His wife could never be his Empress; his children could never be regarded as members of the Imperial House; his eldest son could never inherit the throne.

Nor did the humiliations end there. Franz Ferdinand's morganatic wife, to whom the Emperor later accorded the title of Duchess of Hohenberg, was made to feel her inferior status in countless ways. Where, at court, both sides of the double doors would be flung open for even the least of the arch-duchesses, only one side was opened for her. She could sit neither in a royal carriage nor in the royal box at the opera. In fact, the couple would not be seen together in public in Vienna at all, not even on informal occasions. When Franz Ferdinand gave an official banquet for the German Crown Prince at his Belvedere Palace, his wife could not act as hostess. When he left her alone at the Belvedere, even for one night, the sentries would be withdrawn.

But beyond the empire, among Europe's less hidebound monarchs, the Duchess of Hohenberg was gradually being accorded recognition. Kaiser Wilhelm II, in his unpredictable way, had always been well-diposed towards Franz Ferdinand's wife. Regarding the Archduke as something of a soul mate, Wilhelm was on very friendly terms with the couple. He often visited them at their estate, Konopischt, where he shared Franz Ferdinand's two passions: the cultivation of roses and the slaughter of game. In 1909 the Archduke and his wife paid a state visit to Berlin where, much to their gratification, they were afforded full honours by the Kaiser. The question of precedence was neatly solved, at a state banquet at the Neues Palais, by seating all the guests at small tables, with the two royal couples at a table of their own.

The Kaiser's championship of the Archduke's wife had led directly to a measure of political accord between the two men. Working with an eye to the future, when Franz Ferdinand would be emperor, Wilhelm had set out to cultivate the younger man. Although the Kaiser's effusive, braggardly style would, in the ordinary way, have aroused his distrust, Franz Ferdinand was gratified by Wilhelm's attentiveness. The two of them needed each other. Wilhelm hoped, through their friendship, to strengthen the Austro-German alliance and to check future Austrian adventures in the Balkans. Franz Ferdinand was flattered by the prospect of one day standing as a friend and equal beside this powerful ruler.

An even more gratifying mark of recognition of the Archduke's wife came when the couple were received – privately but with Sophie being accorded proper status – by George V and Queen Mary at Windsor in November 1913. Although much of the time was spent shooting in atrocious weather, the couple made an excellent impression.

But it would need more than royal acceptance abroad to ensure a similar acceptance at home. The gulf between the Hofburg and the Belvedere remained as wide as ever. Neither personally nor politically did the Emperor Franz Joseph and the Archduke Franz Ferdinand see eye-to-eye.

This is not to say that Franz Ferdinand was some enlightened spirit setting himself up in opposition to his reactionary uncle. It was just that he considered the Emperor's rule to be too lax, too hesitant, too compromising. Far better informed than Franz Joseph about the affairs of the empire, Franz Ferdinand appreciated that *something* would have to be done if it were not to disintegrate entirely. What he favoured was more firmness. This firmness would be employed, not to stifle political life, but to reorganise it. He was particularly anxious to coerce the Hungarians, whom he hated, into adopting less feudalistic attitudes.

He realised, though, that something more than iron discipline was necessary to accommodate the clamorous nationalisms within the empire. At one stage Franz Ferdinand favoured 'Trialism', whereby the Dual Monarchy of Austria–Hungary would be converted into a union of three national states, the third being the restored Slav kingdom of Croatia. Later, he toyed with the idea of a federal solution, a sort of United States of Austria.

How seriously Franz Ferdinand had thought any of this through is uncertain; and, by this time, largely immaterial. For if the rotting carcase of the Habsburg Empire were not soon to be destroyed from within, it would almost certainly be destroyed from without.

The deepest thorn in Franz Joseph's side was the kingdom of Serbia. This wild and mountainous country, jutting into the southern borders of the Austro-Hungarian empire, had won its independence from Turkey in 1878. Since then, it had established itself as the most dynamic state in the Balkans. Fired with a poetic yearning to unite, not only all Serbs scattered throughout the Balkans into one greater Serbia, but all South Slav (Yugo Slav) peoples in a triumphant movement of national unification, little Serbia was becoming yearly more militant.

In this, she was being encouraged by Russia. Serbia's 'Slavonic Mission' accorded very well with Russia's no less fervent Pan-Slavism – that half-mystical, half-chauvinistic conviction of the superiority of the Slav peoples and of the Russian Orthodox Church. It was a conviction shared by Tsar Nicholas II.

It was most certainly not shared by his Catholic and Apostolic Majesty, the Emperor Franz Joseph. As most of the Serbs and other Slavs, whom Serbia was so anxious to unite, were his subjects, the Habsburg Emperor was determined to thwart Serbian ambitions. Already, by his annexation in 1908 of the largely Serb-populated provinces of Bosnia and Herzegovina, Franz Joseph had given his upstart neighbour a slap in the face. Serbia's determination to avenge this insult by declaring war on Austria had come to nothing. Without Russia's support, Serbia could not act. And Russia, backing down in the face of a stark German warning not to interfere, was unable to come to Serbia's aid. So Serbia was obliged to swallow her humiliation. And to bide her time.

But, in Franz Joseph's rheumy eyes, Serbia was more than just a troublesome neighbour. The Archduke Franz Ferdinand might dismiss it as a country of 'rascals, fools and prune trees' and the Emperor himself might regard the Serbs as little more than brigands, but there is no doubt that Franz Joseph considered them to be a real threat to Habsburg power. Twice, in the course of his long reign, had he seen his dynasty humbled by nationalist movements. In 1859 Italian unification, spearheaded by Victor Emmanuel II's Piedmont, had cost him his Italian possessions. In 1866 German unification, led by Wilhelm I's Prussia, had put paid to his ascendancy in Germany. He was determined that it would not happen a third time. Serbia's ambition, to unite all South Slavs at Austrian expense, must be checked before it was too late.

In his stand, the old Emperor was being backed up by his powerful ally, Wilhelm II. Both in public speeches and in private correspondence, Wilhelm II assured Franz Joseph of German support against Serbia and, through Serbia, against Russia. In a letter to the Archduke Franz Ferdinand, the Kaiser was equally adamant. 'I hold myself prepared for everything that God may ordain,' wrote Wilhelm. 'I keep my powder dry and I am on my guard. You know that you may count on us.'

It was left to the British ambassador in Vienna to strike a less histrionic, more realistic note. 'Serbia', wrote Sir Arthur Nicolson at this time, 'will one day set Europe by the ears, and bring about a universal war on the Continent.'

Part Two

THE BALKAN POWDER KEG

AUSTRIA – HUNGARY

TRANSYLVANIA

Belgrade

ROMANIA

Bucharest

BOSNIA

Sarajevo

SERBIA

MONTE-
NEGRO

BULGARIA

Sofia

MACEDONIA

THRACE

Constantinople

Salonika

GREECE

TURKEY

Athens

THE BALKANS

at the outbreak
of the First Balkan war

Turkish territory

8

League of the Balkan Kings

IN THE WINTER of 1912–13, a *frisson* of fear passed through the ranks of Europe's leading monarchs. Their Balkan colleagues, whom these more sophisticated sovereigns considered only just worthy of their kingly titles, suddenly plunged their countries into a war against Turkey. With the Balkans always in a dangerously inflammable state, there was no knowing where such a conflict might lead. It needed only 'some damned foolish thing in the Balkans', as Bismarck had once warned, to set Europe ablaze. Would this ganging-up of the Balkan kings against the Turkish sultan be that damned foolish thing?

If these Balkan rulers were only just kings, their kingdoms were only just countries. Almost a century before, Count Metternich had said, with pardonable exaggeration, that the East began at the Landstrasse. But even in his day the East – in the form of the Ottoman empire – had receded a good way from the outskirts of Vienna. Since then, it had receded even further. One by one, during the course of the nineteenth century, the various Balkan countries had won their independence, or semi-independence, from the Turks; by the early years of the twentieth century, all that remained of the European possessions of the once-mighty Ottoman empire was the area around Constantinople and, beyond it, the central Balkan territory known as Macedonia. How much longer the 'Sick Man of Europe' could remain alive was an open question.

Five independent Balkan states had emerged, or re-emerged, from this gradual shrinking of the Ottoman empire. They were Greece, Romania, Bulgaria, Serbia and Montenegro. And, as each country won its independence, so did monarchical Europe ensure that a sovereign was provided to rule over it. Greece, Romania and Bulgaria were given scions of reigning European houses; Serbia and Montenegro provided their own home-grown rulers.

Different from each other in many ways – and no two men could have been less alike than the rough-hewn Nicholas of Montenegro and the effete Ferdinand of Bulgaria – these Balkan rulers had certain things in common.

All reigned over simple, turbulent, largely peasant populations. All, whatever their own religions, had to respect the Orthodoxy of their subjects. All needed to be strong, astute and infinitely patient men in order to work with the faction-forming politicians who made up their parliaments. All had to overcome that lethargy and corruption which, no less than the domes, minarets and latticed balconies of their towns and villages, was a legacy of many centuries of Turkish domination.

Paternalistic rather than autocratic, these Balkan kings exercised considerable personal power. They kept foreign affairs and defence firmly in their own hands and it is doubtful that there would have been much economic growth – whether roads, railways, hospitals, factories or schools would have been built – had it not been for the unstinting efforts and international contacts of their sovereigns. Almost single-handed, they had been obliged to drag their backward states into the twentieth century. Whatever their individual failings might have been, these Balkan kings were all energetic, conscientious men, dedicated to the advancement of their countries and the welfare of their subjects.

They were also dedicated to the aggrandisement of their kingdoms. With the exception of the Greeks and the largely Latin population of Romania, the Balkan peoples were Slavs. But as these Slavs were made up of different nationalities – Serbs, Montenegrins, Bulgarians and others – there were various movements aimed at uniting each national grouping. This meant that each monarch had his eye on those of his nationals living in his neighbour's kingdom: the King of Serbia on the Serbs living in Bulgaria and Bosnia, the Tsar of Bulgaria on the Bulgarians living in Thrace and Macedonia, the King of Romania on the Romanians living in Bulgaria and Transylvania.

Every state had its 'unredeemed' territory, its national expansionist dream. In Greece it was the 'Great Idea', in Romania 'Romania Mare', in Serbia the 'Serbian Dream', in Bulgaria 'Greater Bulgaria'. The result was that these kingdoms were always at odds with each other. It also explained why they proved such fertile ground for Russian and Austro-Hungarian ambitions.

There was, though, one territory on which these bickering monarchs could lay claim without treading on each other's toes (not initially, at any rate) and this was the last sizeable Turkish outpost in Europe – Macedonia. Fringed by the Balkan states of Greece, Montenegro, Serbia and Bulgaria, Macedonia had a predominantly Slav population, a mixture of national minorities of all its neighbours. Indeed, its very name inspired the French culinary term – *macédoine*. As such, and because its Turkish masters ruled it with great harshness, Macedonia was in an almost continuous state of ferment. It was a ferment which its Balkan neighbours were only too happy to encourage: a break-up of Macedonia would mean an enlargement of their own countries.

It was this prospect of rich territorial pickings, allied to a genuine concern about Turkish misrule, that in 1912 achieved the near-impossible: an alliance of four Balkan monarchs – King Peter of Serbia, King Nicholas of Montenegro, King George of the Hellenes and Tsar Ferdinand of Bulgaria. By the winter of 1911–12 secret talks had opened between the four states.

In February 1912 the coming-of-age of Prince Boris, heir to the Bulgarian throne, provided his father, the flamboyant Tsar Ferdinand, with an excellent opportunity for demonstrating this new Balkan accord. Ferdinand staged a three-day-long series of festivities in his capital, Sofia, to which the heirs apparent of Romania, Serbia, Greece and Montenegro were invited. Also present were the royal representatives of the Tsar of Russia, the Emperor of Austria–Hungary and the German Kaiser. Highlight of this royal jamboree was a *Te Deum* in the Cathedral of St Alexander Nevski, recently built in the neo-Byzantine style so dear to the hearts of Balkan royalty. According to the Orthodox ritual and among the multi-coloured mosaics and twinkling icons, this next generation of Balkan rulers gave thanks.

By that summer the four monarchs had announced the formation of the Balkan League. Secretly, it was agreed that their combined armies would launch an attack on Turkey later that year. War was to be declared by the least of the four sovereigns – King Nicholas of Montenegro.

Born in 1841, King Nicholas of Montenegro had ruled his mountainous country since the age of nineteen, in 1860. He was the latest representative of the long line of Vladikas, or Prince-Bishops, in whom civil and ecclesiastical power had been combined for several centuries. His youthful accession was due – as was only to be expected in as volatile a country as Montenegro – to the assassination of his predecessor, an uncle. Yet not until the fiftieth anniversary of his accession, in August 1910, had Nicholas assumed the title of King. Until then, he had been a reigning prince.

In his seventy-second year, at the time of the formation of the Balkan League, King Nicholas was generally regarded as a highly romantic figure: the very personification of a poetic, picturesque and warlike people. He certainly looked like everyone's idea of a Montenegrin ruler. Tall, heavily built, luxuriantly bewhiskered and eagle-eyed, he invariably wore his country's colourful national dress. With his military reputation and commanding presence Nicholas was able to play the role of simple patriach for all that it was worth.

But he was not quite as simple as he liked to make out. As a young man Nicholas had been educated abroad. He could speak French, German, Italian, Russian and some English. In a country where, on his accession, not even the President of the Council could read or write, his literacy was a distinct advantage. It contributed to his reputation as a poet and playwright or, as contemporary writers preferred it, a 'warrior-bard'. It certainly encouraged him in the conviction that his subjects were utterly unfitted to manage their own affairs. As a result, Nicholas had always ruled his country as a fairly benevolent despot. And this in spite of the fact that, in 1905, he had granted his subjects a constitution.

Yet for all his despotism, Nicholas was never unapproachable. Instead of using the council chamber or the audience room, he conducted much of his official business under a huge oak that stood opposite his palace in the little capital, Cetinje. Here, in mid-morning or late afternoon, the old monarch would sit, gossiping, advising or even judging civil and criminal cases. A shrewd as well as an able man, Nicholas was very much alive to the advantages to be gained from the guise of a genial father-figure; particularly to those western statesmen or diplomats to whom all things Montenegrin were suffused in an oriental glamour. Politicians, who would have been shocked by such authoritarianism in London or Paris, were charmed by it in Cetinje. 'He carried well into the twentieth century', wrote one Englishman, 'the essence of Balkan medievalism at its best.'

His fellow royals were hardly less approving. 'I liked his air of jovial bonhomie, the firm grip of his hand, his keen, dark eyes and rugged bronzed face,' enthused Prince Nicholas of Greece. He also enjoyed the old monarch's fund of anecdotes. King Nicholas unfailingly recounted the one about the visit to Montenegro of the British King, George V, in the days when he was still a midshipman. Unable to make the servants at Nicholas's primitive court understand that he wanted an egg for breakfast, Prince George was reduced to miming a hen laying an egg. He did it so convincingly that the servants brought him his egg.

By the time Nicholas came to power, the centuries-old tradition, whereby the reigning – and celibate – Prince-Bishops named their nephews as their successors, had happily come to an end. In 1860, he had married a dark-haired beauty by the name of Milena Vukotić, by whom he had no less than twelve children. In the palace, which was a simple, two-storied villa on the dusty main street of the capital (itself hardly more than an overgrown village) the royal family lived an almost bourgeois life. The equerries might be dashingly uniformed, the furnishings ornate and the walls covered with portraits of foreign monarchs, but the atmosphere was anything but regal. Younger members of the family were quite likely to be found leaping from chair to chair in competition to see who could travel furthest without touching the floor. The garden was hardly more than an area of hard-packed earth, to allow the children to use it as a playground.

Yet most members of this exuberant tribe made very advantageous marriages. When a foreign visitor once regretted that Montenegro had no exports, the old King countered with a smiling, 'Ah, but you forget my daughters.' Known as 'the black pearls', several of these Montenegrin princesses had been packed off to the Russian court to be groomed and educated. Far from giving these girls ideas above their station, this foreign polishing made them appreciate their father's mountain kingdom all the more.

Most married well. Princess Elena married the future King Victor Emmanuel III of Italy; Princess Zorka the future King Peter I of Serbia. Two others married Russian grand dukes, cousins to Tsar Nicholas II; yet another married a Battenberg prince, the brother-in-law of one of Queen Victoria's daughters. It was the two Montenegrin princesses Grand Duchess Militsa and Grand Duchess Anastasia who first introduced the infamous Rasputin to the Tsaritsa Alexandra of Russia.

With the majority of his daughters so gratifyingly well placed, and with him being a key figure in Balkan politics, Nicholas came to enjoy considerable international prestige. He found himself in the happy position of being courted by the great powers. Fellow sovereigns showered him with decorations and orders, foreign governments were always ready to lend him money, every second house in his capital was a legation.

Although, as a nation of Slavs, Montenegro felt a close kinship with Russia, Nicholas was not above indulging in traditional Balkan diplomatic practices. He is said to have 'approached diplomacy in the spirit of a farmer playing off the cattle dealers one against the other at a market'.[1] *Ich bin ein alter Fechter* was one of his boasts, using *Fechter* in its old-fashioned slang sense of 'borrower'; and a borrower – of subsidies from whatever country was ready to pay them and with which he is rumoured to have lined his own pockets – he certainly was. He was astute enough, though, even at the risk of his popularity, to prevent his hot-headed subjects from precipitately taking up arms to avenge any insult – real or imagined – from the country's traditional enemies, Turkey and Austria–Hungary.

It was this national hatred of the Turks that made Nicholas's carefully planned declaration of war against the Ottoman empire in October 1912 so popular. Wilhelm II, regarding the formation of the Balkan League as a triumph for Russian ambitions, might denounce Nicholas as 'a cattle thief', but to his exultant subjects gathered round his palace in Cetinje, their old monarch was nothing less than a hero.

The crowds that gathered around the Belgrade palace of Nicholas's ally, neighbour and son-in-law, King Peter of Serbia, that October night, were equally enthusiastic. To the Serbs, their King was no less of a hero, and the Turks no less of an enemy.

Unlike Nicholas I, Peter I had ruled his country for a mere decade. But if the assassination of an uncle had brought Nicholas to the throne of Montenegro in 1860, a far more horrific murder had brought Peter to the throne of Serbia in 1903.

The rivalry between two Serbian families, Obrenović and Karadjordjević, who had ruled the country in turn for almost a century, came to one of its bloodiest climaxes on a sultry night in 1903. The Obrenović King and Queen, Alexander and Draga, were hacked to death by a party of rebellious, pro-Karadjordjević officers, and their bodies flung out of the palace window. That successfully accomplished, Peter Karadjordjević, then living in exile in Geneva, was elected King by the Serbian National Assembly.

'Nothing', as one observer drily remarked, 'succeeds like success, especially in the East, and the triumphant extirpation of the Obrenović dynasty has conveniently won all hearts to the cause of Karadjordjević.'[2]

A fortnight or so after the murders, King Peter I of Serbia entered Belgrade in triumph.

The message of welcome from the new Serbian King's neighbour and father-in-law, Nicholas of Montenegro, was particularly fulsome. But King Peter was the last man to be impressed by this flowery rhetoric. For one thing, there was not much *rapport* between him and his father-in-law; for another, he was a man of few words. Indeed, the only similarity between these two mountain kings was of age and status. Peter certainly did not have Nicholas's piratical appearance or swashbuckling manner. In his late sixties at the time of the First Balkan War, Peter I was a small, slightly built man whose vigorously curling silver moustache did not really compensate for the frailty of his appearance. 'His features, though somewhat emaciated, wear an agreeable and intellectual expression,' wrote one observer, 'but are scarcely suggestive of native force of character.' Stricken with rheumatism, he walked with a limp.

But King Peter was more forceful than he looked. In younger days he had proved himself a brave and resilient soldier and he was still capable of much physical endurance. His will was like iron. Until his family had been forced by their rivals to flee Serbia, he had been raised in almost peasant-like simplicity; in the forty-five-year-long exile which followed, much of it spent in Geneva, simplicity had become his dominant characteristic. That, and the particularly Swiss traits of honesty, industry, conscientiousness and puritanism. He had also imbibed a measure of liberalism. Sitting in his bleak rooms in Geneva, he had translated John Stuart Mill's *Essay on Liberty* into Serb.

So it did not take the King long to realise that he would need all his strength of character to deal with his new subjects. Like all the Balkan people, the Serbs were a proud, touchy, militant race, not easily tamed or regimented. And, like all the Balkan monarchs, it was left, very largely, to King Peter to revitalise his country. By the time that he allied it to the Balkan League, Serbia was, if not the strongest, certainly the most aggressive state in the area.

If King Peter did not exactly live like one of those peasants whom he professed to admire, his private life was undeniably spartan. After the raffishness of the previous regime, where the Queen had once been the King's mistress, the new Serbian court was austere, respectable and run on the simplest lines. 'Menus! Menus!' King Peter exclaimed to a startled major-domo who, on the day of the new King's arrival, had asked what sort of menus he preferred. 'I have no time for menus. Never speak of such things to me again.' The palace in Belgrade – the very one out of whose windows the bodies of the previous King and Queen had been tossed – was an undistin-guished building standing on a busy street. All day long the trams hurtled past the front door; all night the crowds jabbered at the pavement café on the corner.

Within the palace, with its small, dark rooms a-clutter with furniture from previous reigns, the atmosphere was uncompromisingly masculine. King Peter's wife, Princess Zorka of Montenegro, had died in 1890. His eldest son, Prince Djordje or George, was a violent, unbalanced creature who was eventually struck off the line of succession for kicking his valet to death. Not even in Serbia could he hope to get away with that. His younger son, Prince Alexander, was the opposite: a highly disciplined and imperturb-able young man with a passion for the somewhat monastic quality of army life.

Where King Peter (and his sons) differed most radically from his rival predecessors was in his aggressive patriotism. While the Obrenovićs had been prepared to come to terms with Franz Joseph's empire from time to time, King Peter remained hostile. And it was during his reign that the 'Serbian Dream' – the determination to unite, not only all Serbs, but all South Slavs under the Serbian crown – began to take on the air of an almost sacred mission. King Peter's accession promise, that he would realise the 'traditional aspirations of the Serbian people' had not been mere rhetoric: he aimed to preside over the freeing of his fellow Slavs from Turkish and Austro-Hungarian domination and to unite them all in a Greater Serbia.

With the outbreak of the First Balkan War, the fulfilment of the dream seemed to come closer. Not only would those Serbs living under Turkish rule in Macedonia be delivered but their territory would be annexed to Serbia. It was no wonder that the Serbian troops set out for war 'as radiant', as one chronicler has put it, 'as lovers'.[3]

That this outbreak of trouble in the Balkans could be contained was the best that the great powers could hope for. This was certainly the Kaiser's view. 'Let them get on with their war undisturbed,' he wrote. 'Then the Balkan states will show what they can do, and whether they can justify their existence. If they smash the Turks, then they will have right on their side and are entitled to some reward. If they are beaten, they will sing small: we shall have peace and quiet for a long time and the question of territorial changes will vanish. The Great Powers must keep the ring around the battlefield in which this fight will be conducted and to which it must be confined: we ourselves should keep cool and avoid overhasty action.'[4]

It was sound reasoning, but not even the Kaiser was able to stick to it for long. This was because of the initial and quite unexpected successes of one of those four monarchs who made up the Balkan League: Tsar Ferdinand of Bulgaria. Almost overnight he was to reveal himself as the most ambitious of conquerors.

Ferdinand of Bulgaria could hardly have differed more radically from his allies, the kings of Serbia and Montenegro. No one would ever have described him as an unpretentious mountain patriarch. On the contrary, he was the most *outré* crowned head in Europe.

Tsar Ferdinand was fond of referring to himself as the latest Bourbon King. That was a characteristic piece of self-dramatisation. His mother had indeed been a Bourbon or, more precisely, a Bourbon–Orleans: her father had been the last Bourbon to reign in France – Louis Philippe, the Citizen King. But Ferdinand's father had been a Coburg: one of that tribe of princes of the house of Saxe-Coburg and Gotha who, by their judicious marriages into the leading royal families, had prompted Bismarck to refer scathingly to Coburg as 'the stud farm of Europe'.

Whatever else Ferdinand might have inherited from the Coburgs, it was not their good looks. In appearance, he was almost all Bourbon. His doting and ambitious mother, Princess Clementine of Bourbon–Orleans, always maintained that not one of the living descendants of King Louis XIV resembled the Sun King more closely than did Ferdinand. Fifty-one in 1912, Ferdinand was a tall, portly, straight-backed, regally moustached and bearded figure whose most prominent feature was his huge Bourbon nose. *Der Naseferdinand* – the Nose-Ferdinand – was Wilhelm II's nickname for him.

'An ardent lover of beauty,' says Crown Princess Marie of Romania, 'Uncle Ferdinand was well aware that his nose was too prominent a feature.' Did she not think, he once asked her, that with his tiny eyes and his nose like a trunk, he looked like an elephant? 'But, my dear niece,' he hastened to add, 'I also have all the sagacity of that venerable animal.'

If Tsar Ferdinand had the nose, and the sagacity, of an elephant, he certainly had none of an elephant's ponderousness. On the contrary, he was the most amusing, irreverent and sarcastic coversationalist in any court in Europe. He dressed with great panache. No monarch, not even Wilhelm II, could cram more medals and orders on to a tunic. With his passion for precious stones, he covered his pale, long-nailed fingers with exotically jewelled rings; about his neck he always wore a gem-encrusted cross on a silver chain. His whole air was artistic, affected, sybaritic, decadent.

11 The Emperor Franz Joseph of Austria–Hungary: 'the last monarch of
the old school'

12 The Archduke Franz Ferdinand, heir to the Austro-Hungarian Empire

13 King Peter of Serbia, after a hospital inspection during the Balkan wars

'If I ever feel tired or depressed, I have only to look at a bunch of violets to become myself again,' was the sort of remark guaranteed to startle his less worldly listeners.

The choice, by the Bulgarian government, in 1887, of this foppish prince as ruler of the recently created but still Turkish-dominated state of Bulgaria had sent a ripple of astonishment through the courts of Europe. 'He is totally unfit,' telegraphed an agitated Queen Victoria to her prime minister, 'delicate, eccentric and effeminate . . . Should be stopped at once.' And Lady Paget, wife of the British ambassador in Vienna, reported that 'his affectations are innumerable. He wears bracelets and powders his face. He sleeps in pink surah nightgowns trimmed with Valenciennes lace. His constitution is so delicate and his nerves so finely strung, that he only consults ladies' doctors.'

Yet to the amazement of everyone – other than his redoubtable mother, the widowed Princess Clementine – the effete Prince Ferdinand not only accepted the Bulgarian challenge but made a brilliant success of his reign. For the truth was that behind that decorative façade lay a very shrewd mind. Ferdinand of Bulgaria proved himself to be far more intelligent, astute, unscrupulous and tenacious than he had ever been given credit for. That languid manner masked an iron resolve. Before many years had passed, he was being hailed as 'the new Machiavelli'. It was a description that pleased him inordinately. He would probably not even have minded that other, even less complimentary nickname, 'Foxy Ferdy'.

Gradually, from being the mere reigning prince of an impoverished and barely recognised country, Ferdinand won the official acceptance and grudging respect of Europe's leading monarchs. And finally, in 1908, taking advantage of the fact that the rest of Europe was about to be distracted by Austria's annexation of Bosnia and Herzegovina, he boldly threw off Turkish suzerainty and proclaimed himself Tsar of a fully independent Bulgaria.

His *coup* infuriated many of his fellow sovereigns. Nicholas II of Russia bitterly resented the fact that Ferdinand had styled himself 'Tsar': he called it 'the act of a megalomaniac'. Wilhelm II was no less resentful. How dare Ferdinand elevate himself to the same plane as the rest of Europe's major sovereigns?

But however much Ferdinand might be resented or scoffed at abroad, he was generally appreciated at home. And the growing political and material stature of his country was reflected in his way of life. Convinced of the international advantages of a brilliant court, Ferdinand indulged his taste for luxury, splendour and ceremonial to the full. Always obsessed with such things as rank, precedence, titles, orders and decorations, he organised his court along the most punctilious lines.

What he was hoping to recreate was the elegance and ritual, not of other contemporary European courts, but of the courts of his illustrious Bourbon ancestors. Before long, the palace in Sofia had become renowned for its stylishness.

'Entering the Palace,' writes Meriel Buchanan, daughter of the British minister in Sofia, 'one was greeted by a company of the [Tsar's] bodyguard, who stood on every step of the wide staircase, gorgeous in their scarlet, silver-braided uniforms, with the grey astrakan cap and the eagle's feather held in a jewelled clasp. Ushered into the white and gold room, one waited for the Tsar's entry before going on to the enormous dining-hall with its big horseshoe table covered with wonderful flowers. One ate off priceless china, gold and silver plates; the service was faultless, the food perfect; a concealed band played loud enough to cover any lull in the conversation, but never too loud to drown it. The glitter of decorations, the medley of uniforms . . . all these made a picture that was full of colour, a little unreal and fantastic, and gave one the feeling that one was on a stage, taking part in a musical comedy or a romance of Ruritania . . .'

To the lushness of this royal setting, Ferdinand could always be relied upon to provide a few more bizarre touches. The entrance hall to the palace was sprayed with pine essence. His study was decorated in that most modish of *fin de siècle* colours, mauve. The palace chapel, heavy with the scent of massed flowers and sweet incense, was kept at hot-house temperature. The holy water stoop was filled with violets.

In spite of being the ruler of an Orthodox country, Ferdinand had remained a Catholic. But his Catholicism, like that of the Tsaritsa Alexandra of Russia's Orthodoxy, was of a particularly flamboyant variety. He, too, was only too ready to steep himself in the shadowy fringes of religion: to merge it with all the manifestations of the Decadent Movement – spiritualism, clairvoyance, the occult. To him, religion and superstition were intertwined.

His country palaces and houses, whether overlooking the Black Sea or set among Bulgaria's spectacular mountains, were surrounded by beautiful gardens. Ferdinand was a passionate and knowledgeable gardener; few things gave him more pleasure than to stroll, stick in hand, among those banks of rhododendrons or terraces of roses or through his conservatories, stocked with exotic plants from all over the world. Seriously interested in the natural sciences, he wrote learned studies on birds and animals. 'The tiniest rock plant could thrill him for hours,' claims one of his mother's ladies-in-waiting.

Not all his pursuits were quite so erudite. Ferdinand had a taste for handsome young men, provided they were blond. Any muscular young soldier who happened to catch the Tsar's gimlet eye was quite likely to be appointed a palace orderly; any square-jawed chauffeur ('goodness, all those *chauffeurs!*' sighed one palace intimate) would find himself driving his monarch into the woods for a little dalliance on the pine needles. Ferdinand was said to have been a frequent visitor to that paradise for rich turn-of-the-century homosexuals, the island of Capri.

Yet, a Coburg to his fingertips, Ferdinand did not allow sexual preferences to stand in the way of royal obligations. For the sake of his dynasty and his country he married, not only once, but twice. His first wife, Princess Marie Louise of Bourbon-Parma, on whom he had never set eyes until the day they became engaged, was a long-nosed creature with quiet manners and a kindly nature. Having dutifully borne her husband four children, including an heir, Prince Boris, Marie Louise died, at the age of twenty-nine, in 1899.

Ferdinand did not think of marrying again until his adored mother, Princess Clementine, died in 1907. His second wife was chosen in a no more romantic manner than his first. He did not, he explained frankly to the friend whom he had commissioned to find him a consort, 'want a wife who would expect affection or even get attention'.[5] Princess Eleonore von Reuss-Köstritz, whom he married in 1908, certainly got neither. A plain but practical woman, Princess Eleonore seems to have been fully informed about what were delicately referred to as her husband's 'foibles'. Even so, she must have been acutely embarrassed when, on being entertained by King Carol of Romania on the way back to Sofia after their wedding, her outraged husband insisted that the double bedroom assigned to them be exchanged for separate quarters.

All in all, by the period immediately preceding the First World War, Tsar Ferdinand had established himself as both the most fascinating and important monarch in the Balkans. Since assuming the title of Tsar in 1908, he had been received as an equal by almost every sovereign in Europe. In 1911, the aged Emperor Franz Joseph presented him with the most coveted order in Christendom and one after which he had long hankered: the Golden Fleece. Never one to pass up an opportunity of drawing attention to his own importance on the international stage, Ferdinand declared that 'the highest order of Christianity for the first time sheds its radiance this side of the Balkans: it is an auspicious omen for the future!'

The formation of the Balkan League in the summer of 1912 was a step towards the realisation of this radiant future. For no less than any other Balkan ruler was Ferdinand determined on the aggrandisement of his realm.

Until now, his main concern had been for the continued existence of Bulgaria as an independent state. This had depended, very largely, on his ability to play off Russia against Austria–Hungary. With both powers regarding a strong, independent and prosperous Bulgaria as a bar to their hopes of expansion in the Balkans, Ferdinand had to keep them sweet without seeming to favour one at the expense of the other. It was a game at which he had always excelled.

In time, this was to become magnified into a balancing act between the Triple Alliance and the Triple Entente. Either group would have been happy to welcome Tsar Ferdinand as a fully committed ally. But it had suited him better to remain uncommitted.

Ferdinand's machinations were aimed at more than just the preservation of his country and his crown. Not even the fact that he, this least military of men, had built up his army into the most effective fighting force in the Balkans, was enough to satisfy his ambitions. His wish was to see his country extended south into Turkish-owned Thrace and Macedonia, so that his southern border would be the sparkling waters of the Aegean sea. By overcoming his distaste for his Balkan neighbours and by joining them in their war against Turkey, he hoped to achieve this.

But Ferdinand had a still more fervent wish. This was to claim the greatest prize of all – Constantinople.

For many years now, Tsar Ferdinand had been obsessed with a 'dream of Byzantium'. 'Think of me,' he would murmur meaningfully to anyone about to visit Constantinople. Maurice Paléologue, the French minister, once found himself left, deliberately, in a room in Ferdinand's palace in which the most prominent feature was a vast allegorical painting of a triumphant Ferdinand riding a charger high above the domes and minarets of this fabled city. Another painting, elsewhere in the palace, was a full-length portrait of Ferdinand dressed in the robes of a Byzantine emperor.

For the strongest ambition of this strange, complex and highly romantic monarch was to have himself crowned, as the new Emperor of Byzantium, beneath the great dome of Saint Sophia.

It was an ambition that was to come astonishingly close to realisation with the outbreak of the First Balkan War.

9

The Balkan Wars

'THERE HAS BEEN no fighting in our time', writes Rebecca West, 'that has the romantic quality of the Balkan wars that broke out in 1912.' Compared with the war which loomed just ahead, these Balkan campaigns had an almost amateur air. Everyone – the officers in their lavishly braided tunics and aigrette-sprouting fur caps, the mustachioed and bandoliered men, even the peasant women who helped haul the heavy guns – was fired with enthusiasm for the cause. Resolutely they marched beside the lumbering bullock carts and loaded mule trains, singing as they went.

And few aspects of this first Balkan war were more romantic than the advance of Tsar Ferdinand of Bulgaria towards Constantinople. While the armies of his allies, the kings of Serbia, Montenegro and Greece, crossed the northwestern and southern borders of Macedonia, his troops poured into neighbouring Thrace and headed towards Constantinople.

To the histrionic Ferdinand, this was more than just a war. It was a crusade. He had always been proud of the fact that through his veins ran the blood of St Louis – the canonised King Louis IX of France who had died while leading the last Crusade to the Holy Land. Ferdinand now declared that this, too, was a crusade: 'a just, great and sacred struggle of the Cross against the Crescent'.[1] Whether or not he really believed this is another matter.

The campaign was extraordinarily successful. Within two weeks every Turkish army in Europe had been defeated. Ferdinand's troops proved especially efficient. Although pockets of Turkish resistance remained, the armies of all four members of the Balkan League made rapid advances. By 23 October 1912, the victorious Bulgarians had driven the Turks back to their last line of defence, a mere twenty miles from Constantinople.

Ferdinand was jubilant. In a matter of days, the effeminate *bon viveur* had been transformed into an all-conquering hero. His fellow sovereigns stood amazed. The excitable Kaiser, quite forgetting that the defeated Turks had been German-trained, claimed that here was the new 'blood and spirits' that Europe needed. 'Perhaps we shall see Ferdinand as Tsar of Byzantium? Or as supreme leader of the Balkan Confederation?'

Europe's other leading monarchs were distinctly less ecstatic. George V muttered about Ferdinand's 'vanity' and 'theatricality'. If the vainglorious Bulgarian sovereign were to carry out his promise of setting up the cross on the dome of Saint Sophia, there would be repercussions throughout the Moslem world. 'I have eighty million Mohammedan subjects,' grumbled the worried British King.

The old Emperor Franz Joseph was even more put out. At an earlier stage he had favoured the formation of a Balkan alliance. He imagined that an alignment of Bulgaria, Romania and Greece (but excluding Austria's *bête noire*, Serbia) would be a shot in the eye for Russian Pan-Slav ambitions. But by now the victories of the Balkan League and the deliverance of the Macedonians had merely led to an increased restlessness among the nationalist minorities of Franz Joseph's polyglot empire.

Most worried of all was Tsar Nicholas II. Although his support for his fellow Slavs – and particularly the Serbs – in the Balkan League was unquestioned, he did not relish the idea of Constantinople falling into the hands of Tsar Ferdinand. For control of Constantinople meant control of the Dardanelles. In a conversation with Prince Henry of Prussia, Wilhelm II's brother, Nicholas II, pretended that the matter of whether or not Ferdinand entered Constantinople was of supreme indifference to him. In the meantime, though, his diplomats were scurrying about the foreign ministries of his Entente allies, begging them to stop the Bulgarian advance.

But nothing, it seems, was going to stop Ferdinand. His moment was at hand. He was determined to enter Constantinople in triumph and to celebrate mass in Saint Sophia. To this end he sent an order from his headquarters to the capital for the state coach and six white horses, the parade uniforms of the royal guard and, it was claimed, his Byzantine emperor's costume. To a Turkish request for an armistice, he gave a ringingly blunt refusal.

'We shall dictate the peace', he declared, 'in Constantinople.'

But it was not to be. Rain, cholera and a sudden stiffening of the Turkish resistance checked the Bulgarian advance. With his troops bogged down in the mud and muddle of the defences outside Constantinople, Ferdinand's dream of Byzantium began to fade. In the meantime, though, his allies had been making rapid advances into Macedonia. The Serbs proved especially successful. To the consternation, not only of Tsar Ferdinand but of the Emperor Franz Joseph, Serbia was soon occupying great areas of Turkish territory. And, in spite of her pre-war agreements with Bulgaria, she clearly intended to hang on to them.

To prevent the no less victorious Greeks from likewise laying claim to territory which he coveted, Ferdinand hurried some of his forces southwards to take the Aegean port of Salonika. But the Greeks beat him to it. When, on

19 December 1912, Tsar Ferdinand arrived in Salonika by train, it was to find his ally, King George of the Hellenes, already established there.

But Ferdinand was equal to the occasion. Determined that he should not be received by the Greek King in the humbling position of a guest, Ferdinand left his train just before it steamed into Salonika and drove swiftly, and in secret, to the Bulgarian consulate in the city. The Greek royal family, lined up in triumph at the station to greet the Bulgarian ruler, were greatly put out to discover that their guest was not on the train. They were obliged to drive to the Bulgarian consulate where, to their annoyance, they found the Tsar calmly reviewing a detachment of Bulgarian troops.

Kaiser Wilhelm II, his initial admiration for the victorious Ferdinand having by now cooled, had become seriously alarmed at the success of the Russian-backed Balkan League. He felt sure that it would lead to a conflict between Russia and Austria–Hungary which, in turn, would mean a general European war. In the course of a meeting with his friend, the Archduke Franz Ferdinand, Wilhelm assured him of German support in any such eventuality.

Two weeks later he convoked a 'war council' at the Neues Palais at Potsdam, to which various members of the army and navy staff, but no civilian members of the government, were invited. At this meeting, they discussed their London ambassador's report that Britain would definitely side with France in the event of some future European war.

But in his conviction that princes were better diplomats than ambassadors, the Kaiser sent his brother, Prince Henry, to England to sound out George V on the matter. If Germany and Austria were to go to war against Russia and France, asked Henry, would Britain come to the aid of the two latter powers? Yes, answered George V, 'under certain circumstances'.[2]

This answer Prince Henry, never the most reliable of emissaries, interpreted as a half-promise of British neutrality. It was an interpretation which the Kaiser was only too ready to accept. That it was not up to the British monarch to decide whether or not his country went to war was something which Wilhelm II seemed unable to appreciate.

As it happened, that particular war scare blew over. In December 1912 an armistice was signed between the Balkan League and the Ottoman empire. While the various armies retained their respective positions, a peace conference opened in London. Not unexpectedly, it very soon degenerated into a squabble between the Balkan allies over their spoils. The peace treaty, signed in May 1913, was hardly worthy of the name.

On the very day after it was signed, Serbia and Greece concluded a secret alliance whereby they would act against their recent Bulgarian ally and divide Macedonia between themselves.

On the afternoon of 18 March 1913, the sixty-eight-year-old King George of the Hellenes was enjoying his daily walk through the streets of Salonika. He had been living there ever since the city had been won from Turkey four months before. As he and his equerry passed a squalid café near the harbour, a raggedly dressed man drew out a revolver and shot the King dead.

The assassin turned out to be mentally deranged. While awaiting trial, he committed suicide.

King George's eldest son, Crown Prince Constantine, was at Janina, another city which had recently fallen to the Greeks, when he heard the news of his father's death. He immediately set out for Athens to assume the crown.

Few monarchs were to prove more popular than King Constantine of the Hellenes during the early years of his reign. For one thing, he ascended the throne at a time when Greece was flushed with its victories during the First Balkan War; for another, he was a man of impressive appearance and exceptional qualities.

Born in 1868, Constantine was forty-four at the time of his accession. His father, one of the sons of King Christian IX of Denmark, had been invited to accept the Greek throne in 1863. His mother, Queen Olga, had been a Russian grand duchess. That no Greek blood flowed in Constantine's veins was only too apparent: he was a blond giant of a man, towering head and shoulders above most of his subjects. In earlier days he had been described as 'a young Hercules' and with his balding head, broad shoulders and great height, King Constantine was still an imposing-looking man.

With this rugged appearance went a rugged manner. Constantine was an honest man – open, straightforward, incapable of insincerity or dissimulation. There were times when his frankness could lead to misunderstandings: he was often outspoken and intolerant. Yet he was never autocratic. King Constantine had a way of making people feel thoroughly at ease; his good nature was one of his most outstanding characteristics. In Greece, which at this time was still a relatively unsophisticated country, these qualities were greatly appreciated.

Constantine's years as *Diadoch*, or Crown Prince, had been devoted, largely, to the army. Educated in Germany (Greece, in the late nineteenth century, had boasted no suitable university) he had served in the 2nd Prussian Guards. In 1897 he had become Commander-in-Chief of the Greek army. And although his military career had often been subjected to the caprices of Greek politics (at one stage he had even had to resign his position) Constantine had proved to be an inspiring commander. Not only was he a man of considerable military ability who introduced many reforms, but he was extremely popular with the troops. His bluntness, even his occasional bursts of temper, were things which the men appreciated. His vocabulary of Greek oaths had to be heard, they said, to be believed.

And the fact that their *Diadoch*, unlike his Danish father, had been born in Greece and was a member of the Orthodox faith, counted for a great deal with the Greek soldiers. It imbued him with an almost mystical prestige. That their Commander-in-Chief should have become King at the very time that the Greek army had finally triumphed over the hated Turks, gave his accession an added significance.

Internationally, Constantine enjoyed an importance far in excess of his status as the King of humble Greece. For both he and his wife, Queen Sophie, were closely related to Europe's more illustrious monarchs. As Constantine's father, King George I, had been the brother of both Britain's Queen Alexandra and Russia's Empress Marie, the new Greek King was first cousin to George V and Nicholas II. Queen Sophie, one of that great tribe of Queen Victoria's grand-daughters who sat, or would one day sit, on European thrones, was sister to Kaiser Wilhelm II. Indeed, Constantine and Sophie's wedding, in Athens in 1889, had been one of those splendid late nineteenth-century royal jamborees: a coming together of that inter-related crowd that Queen Victoria always referred to as 'the Royal Mob' (than which, she would add, she disliked *nothing* more).

Although Constantine, Sophie and their six children, born between 1890 and 1913, lived a charmingly simple life in their palace in Athens or in their country place at Tatoi, they remained very much part of that royal clan. But gratifying as such grand and influential connections were in peacetime, they were to prove, in the years ahead, to be little short of disastrous.

King Constantine had hardly had time to swear allegiance to the constitution before the Second Balkan War broke out. This time, instead of attacking the Turks, the erstwhile allies turned on each other. An offer by Tsar Nicholas II to arbitrate between King Peter of Serbia and Tsar Ferdinand of Bulgaria on the basis of the pre-war treaty was politely but firmly rejected by the Serbian King. The Serbs had no intention of handing over their recently acquired Macedonian spoils to Bulgaria, whatever their pre-war arrangements might have been. So there remained little for Ferdinand to do other than to launch an attack on the Serbian forces in Macedonia. By the beginning of July 1913, the Second Balkan War was under way.

This time King Peter of Serbia was allied, not only to the kings of Greece and Montenegro, but to King Carol of Romania. Deciding that he might as well get what he could out of the fracas, King Carol ordered his troops to attack Bulgaria from the north. Ringed by enemies, the Bulgarians were soundly beaten. By the terms of a second peace treaty, signed in August 1913, Ferdinand was obliged to sit helplessly by while vast tracts of territory were doled out to Serbia, Greece, Romania and even Turkey.

Tsar Ferdinand's humiliation was complete. Not only had he seen his dream of Byzantium dissolve but almost all his plans for a Greater Bulgaria had been frustrated. Nevertheless, the steely resilience which lay at the heart of that apparently effete personality did not fail him, not even in this moment of black despair.

'My hour will come,' declared Ferdinand to young King Alfonso XIII of Spain. 'I shall have my revenge; I shall set fire to the four corners of Europe!'[3]

King Constantine emerged from the Second Balkan War with an even greater reputation. By the terms of the Treaty of Bucharest, Greece now controlled all southern Macedonia, Thrace and the Epirus, the Aegean Archipelago and Crete. The size of the country had more than doubled. It was undoubtedly a moment of national glory.

On 5 August 1913, the triumphant King returned to Athens from the front. Under a blazing summer sun, the battle cruiser *Averoff*, escorted by the entire Greek fleet, dropped anchor in Phaleron Bay. Dressed in plain service khaki and wearing no decorations, Constantine disembarked, to be met by Queen Sophie. Together, in an open landau, the couple drove through the hysterically cheering crowds towards the capital.

At Hadrian's Arch, where a special stand had been erected for disabled war veterans, Constantine suddenly ordered his coachman to stop. Alighting from the carriage, he walked over to the stand and solemnly saluted the wounded men. In a completely spontaneous gesture, one crippled soldier picked up a laurel branch from the ground and, hobbling over to the King, handed it to him. In silence, Constantine carried it back to the landau.

In some ways, the little incident symbolised the almost mystical relationship which had developed between the Soldier-King and his men. The troops were devoted to this unaffected giant who had led them to such magnificent victories and had won for them such widespread territory. To them, he was now known as the 'Son of the Eagle'. This close communion between Constantine and his soldiers was to influence much of his thinking in the months ahead and, in the end, lead to an agonising personal and political dilemma.

But no such foreboding clouded this brilliant homecoming. As the King and Queen drove through the roaring crowds – he so tall and soldierly and she so erect and proud – it was not difficult to believe that an old prophecy was being fulfilled. Throughout the centuries of Turkish domination, the flame of Hellenism had been kept flickering by the legend that Byzantium would rise again when another Constantine and Sophie sat upon the Greek throne. This new Constantine would reconquer Constantinople and make it the capital of a great Hellenic empire. It was, in short, the Greek version of the dream that obsessed so many Balkan monarchs.

Before leaving the front, the King had given each soldier who had served under him a photograph of himself. It showed him in plain khaki uniform and dusty boots, smoking a cigarette. Each picture carried the hand-written inscription: 'To my gallant fellow soldiers of two glorious wars.' It was signed CONSTANTINE B. (B, standing for King, always followed the royal name.) Yet, to many of its enraptured recipients, this scrawled B looked more like IB, which in Greek numerals stood for XII. The last Emperor of Byzantium had been Constantine XI; had the new King, inadvertently or intentionally, signed himself Constantine XII? Was he destined to lead his people back to Constantinople and there, under the great dome of Saint Sophia, to wear again the imperial crown of Byzantium?

Not long after his return to Athens, Constantine set off on a tour of various European capitals. The journey, traditional for most monarchs, both confirmed his accession and allowed him to visit his many relations. In Berlin he was entertained by his brother-in-law, Wilhelm II, at a state banquet. In his characteristically fulsome way – for he dearly loved the idea of a warrior-king – the Kaiser paid tribute to Constantine's military prowess and then, quite unexpectedly, presented him with a field marshal's baton. Taken by surprise, Constantine blurted out an impromptu speech of thanks in which he made mention of the fact that he had received his military training in Germany.

The Kaiser, in drawing up a draft of the Greek King's reply for publication, slightly altered the emphasis. Out of politeness, Constantine made no objection.

The subsequent publication of the speech, together with a photograph of Constantine in his German field marshal's uniform complete with spiked helmet, caused a furore, especially in Germany's most implacable enemy, France. Constantine was astounded. When chided by his secretary for having agreed to the Kaiser's slanted version, the King's answer was typically artless.

'How was I supposed to know that the thing would be telegraphed all over Europe?' he protested.

He could, with more justification, have pointed out that his cousin, George V, was also a German field marshal, and that the Kaiser was a British field marshal.

But the harm had been done. From now on it was firmly believed, by the Entente powers, that the Greek King was pro-German.

No sovereign, not even King Constantine of the Hellenes, won more acclaim in the Balkan wars than old King Peter of Serbia. Although he, and King Nicholas of Montenegro, had been too old to play an active part in the fighting, King Peter had presided over a glorious chapter in his country's history. Not only had his kingdom doubled in size but it had increased, enormously, in self-confidence. In a matter of months, the dream of Greater Serbia was being realised.

That Serbia's next target would be the deliverance of the Serbs living in the Austro-Hungarian empire there was very little doubt. 'The first round is won,' crowed the Serbian prime minister, 'now we must prepare for the second round, against Austria.'[4]

Of this, Austria was very well aware. As the Serbs hailed their aged King in his moment of glory, the even older Franz Joseph was thinking in terms of snuffing out that glory. Yet the Emperor realised that any attempt to crush Serbia would be regarded as a move against Serbia's powerful protector, Russia.

For by this stage Russia was deeply involved in Serbian affairs. The country had become a key factor in Nicholas II's anti-Austrian policy. King Peter, as a democrat and an ascetic, might have disapproved of the absolutism and extravagance of the Romanovs but he realised that his country would have to accept the help and protection of Russia. When his son, the austere Crown Prince Alexander, travelled to St Petersburg to thank the Tsar for his support of the Serb cause during the recent Balkan wars, Nicholas II replied that he had simply been doing his 'Slav duty'.

By now the Russian minister in Belgrade was busily encouraging Serbian expansionist ambitions, both officially through King Peter and his government and through clandestine support of various patriotic organisations. Chief of these Russian-backed secret societies was the Black Hand. With its cells, its sinister initiation ceremony, its oath of allegiance and its preference for 'terrorist action' rather than 'intellectual propaganda', the Black Hand attracted the support of a variety of extremists. At one time even Crown Prince Alexander gave it his support.

But the average member of the Black Hand was a far less temperate, far more explosive type than the Crown Prince. That sooner or later one of these hot-headed young patriots would commit some violent act in the sacred cause of a Greater Serbia was only to be expected.

From out of the imbroglio of the Balkan wars came an opportunity for the Russian Tsar, Nicholas II, to form yet another friendship: this time with King Carol of Romania.

On the face of it, it seemed an unlikely partnership. The iron-willed King Carol, who had ruled Romania since it had been created in 1866, had been born a prince of Hohenzollern-Sigmaringen, a Catholic branch of the Prussian ruling dynasty. And since 1883, Romania had been tied, by secret treaty, to the Triple Alliance of Germany, Austria–Hungary and Italy. The Romanians, moreover, were not Slavs but Latins. By a trick of history, Latin culture and language had survived in the mountains of Transylvania long after the Roman Empire had fallen. The very name, Romania, harked back to the days when the country had been part of Roman civilisation. So the

Romanians felt no affinity with the Russian Slavs.

On the other hand, King Carol's sympathies for his native Germany and his high regard for the old Emperor Franz Joseph were not shared by the majority of his subjects. In fact, they regarded the Austro-Hungarian Empire as their enemy. The chief reason for this was that many Romanians still lived under Austro-Hungarian rule. Indeed, the heart of ancient Romania lay in Hungarian-occupied Transylvania. And, no less than all the Balkan states, did Romania have a national dream of uniting all Romanians in one state: *Romania Mare*.

With precious little chance of this dream being realised by peaceful means, certain Romanian politicians began to think in terms of a closer understanding with Austria–Hungary's great enemy – Russia. By 1913 relations, which had never been particularly good between Russia and Romania, suddenly improved. The Russians, appreciating that Romania's friendship would be very useful in some future war against Austria–Hungary, began paying her court. Perhaps Romania could be persuaded to leave the Triple Alliance and join the Entente powers – Russia, France and Britain?

Although there seemed little likelihood of the ageing King Carol forsaking Germany and Austria–Hungary, the chances of his heir being encouraged to do so were rather more promising. In time, the childless Carol would be succeeded by his nephew, Crown Prince Ferdinand. And if the Crown Prince was a somewhat ineffectual personality, his wife, Crown Princess Marie, was an altogether more assertive type. Beautiful, theatrical and self-regarding, Marie of Romania was a woman of considerable intelligence. Like those other consorts – Queen Elisabeth of the Belgians, the Tsaritsa Alexandra of Russia and Queen Sophie of the Hellenes – she was destined to make her mark in the coming conflict.

As her father had been Queen Victoria's second son, Alfred, Duke of Edinburgh, and her mother the only daughter of Tsar Alexander II, Crown Princess Marie was first cousin to George V, Wilhelm II and Nicholas II. A woman of passionate feelings and outspoken loyalties, Marie made no secret of her pro-British and pro-Russian sympathies. The Austrian ambassador in Bucharest had recently warned his government that Crown Princess Marie's 'character and mentality is one of the most important reasons for putting relations with Romania on quite another basis'.[5] In other words, once Marie had become Queen, Austria would not always be able to take Romanian friendship for granted.

This, Russia appreciated. And what better way of encouraging Crown Princess Marie's pro-Russian sympathies than by that classic diplomatic manoeuvre: a royal marriage? With a royal alliance still being regarded as a significant instrument of foreign policy, the Russian foreign ministry began to think in terms of a match between the eighteen-year-old Grand Duchess Olga, eldest daughter of Tsar Nicholas II, and the twenty-two-year-old

Prince Carol, eldest son of Crown Prince Ferdinand and, more important, Crown Princess Marie of Romania. What better way of bringing Romania into the Entente camp than by a marriage between the Tsar's daughter and Romania's future king?

Although flattered by the proposal, Crown Princess Marie was not very well disposed towards the idea. Her reasons were personal rather than political. She was afraid that Olga, like her mother, might be a transmitter of haemophilia. She did not want the dreaded disease carried into the Romanian royal family. Nevertheless, not wanting to dismiss the idea entirely, the Crown Prince and Princess, with their son Carol in tow, accepted an invitation to visit the Tsar in the spring of 1914.

The visit was not a great success. 'The outward pomp and show of power was still there, glittering palaces, guards-regiments, wild-looking Cossacks on constant patrol,' wrote Marie of Tsarskoe Selo. 'But all this ended at the front door, and stepping over the threshold you entered suddenly into a quiet family life, uniform, exclusive and rather dull.'

First cousins as both the Tsar and the Tsaritsa were to Marie, she could not get close to them. Nicholas II, for all his habitual charm and courtesy, seemed to be living, she says, 'in a sort of imperial mist'. Alexandra she found as reserved, inarticulate and awkward as ever. 'She managed to put an insuperable distance between her world and yours, her experiences and yours, her thoughts, her opinions, her principles, rights and privileges. She made you, in fact, feel an intruding outsider, which is of all sensations the most chilling and uncomfortable.'

And as for Prince Carol and Grand Duchess Olga, neither showed the slightest desire to become better acquainted.

'Much had changed in Russia,' concluded Marie, 'and a feeling of dissatisfaction lay over all things. Tsarskoe Selo seemed to sleep, but beneath that sleep lay something uncanny which we sensed without being able to explain it.'

To her, Tsarskoe Selo seemed 'that mysterious centre where somewhere in the shade Rasputin held his fatal sway'.

The visit was returned that summer. The Russian imperial family paid a formal, day-long visit to the Romanian Black Sea port of Constanza. They were met on the sunlit, gaily beflagged pier by King Carol, his Queen, the Crown Prince and Princess and their children. For the old King it was a significant day. No monarch had paid him a state visit since the Emperor Franz Joseph had come eighteen years before. To many of his subjects, the occasion seemed to accentuate the growing rapport between Russia and Romania.

While the ministers of their respective countries held talks, the two royal families carried out the customary engagements: a *Te Deum* in the cathedral, a drive through the town, a military parade, an official luncheon, a state banquet. It was all judged a brilliant success. Even Alexandra made 'brave efforts to be as gracious as possible'.

But whatever else the imperial visit might have achieved (an alliance was to be concluded two years later) it brought the proposed marriage between Prince Carol and Grand Duchess Olga no nearer. The couple were simply not interested in each other. 'I don't want it to happen,' the young Grand Duchess had told her tutor, Pierre Gilliard, on board the imperial yacht that morning. 'Papa has promised not to make me, and I don't want to leave Russia. I am a Russian and I mean to remain a Russian.'

By this decision, Olga turned her back on the one certain way that could have saved her from her fate in that cellar in Ekaterinburg.

That evening the imperial family sailed back to Russia. Crown Princess Marie, who was never to see any of them again, ran along the pier to watch the departing ships. 'It was a gorgeous night,' she wrote in her inimitable fashion, 'the heavens a mighty map of stars. For a long time I stood there at the very end of the pier; the ships were now mere specks of light. A lump rose in my throat; the great day was ended, had slipped over into Eternity like so much else . . .'

14 The Warrior-Bard: the brigandly Nicholas of Montenegro

15 Foxy Ferdinand, the *outré* Tsar of Bulgaria

16 Constantine of the Hellenes, during the Second Balkan War

10

Regicide

ON SUNDAY, 28 June 1914, the Archduke Franz Ferdinand, heir to the Habsburg throne, with his morganatic wife Sophie, Duchess of Hohenberg, drove into Sarajevo.

Like two pouter pigeons, the couple sat side by side in their open car as it was driven through the beflagged and sunlit streets of the little Balkan capital. Tightly buttoned into his field marshal's uniform and with a fountain of green peacock feathers sprouting from his peaked hat, Franz Ferdinand was looking uncharacteristically benign. Beside him, in her lavish hat and lace dress, Sophie was her usual, dignified self. Both appeared highly gratified by the warmth of their reception.

Why, in spite of repeated warnings that it would be dangerous for the heir to visit the capital of Bosnia, did Franz Ferdinand insist on carrying out his engagement? After all, as recently appointed Inspector-General of the Austro-Hungarian armed forces, Franz Ferdinand had come to Bosnia to attend military manoeuvres close to the Serbian border: surely this was a highly provocative act? And was this official visit to Sarajevo not equally provocative? Franz Ferdinand knew that Bosnia and its capital were aflame with Slav nationalism and terrorism.

In the decades since the assassinations at Sarajevo, many reasons have been propounded for Franz Ferdinand's apparent pigheadedness. It has been claimed that his visit was designed as a shot in the eye for upstart Serbia; that it would serve as a warning that the Habsburg empire would tolerate no trouble, neither from the Serbs beyond its borders nor from the Slav seccessionists within. Even the date chosen for the visit was said to be significant. June 28 – or June 15 by the Serbian Orthodox calendar – was Vidov-Dan, a Serbian anniversary commemorating the fourteenth-century defeat of Serbia by the Turks and therefore an especially emotional day for Serb nationalists.

Others claim that, in a convoluted way, the Archduke's visit was meant to demonstrate his sympathy for the Slavs. His appearance among them would illustrate his concern for them: it would give them an opportunity to appreciate their future Emperor better. Franz Ferdinand was known to loathe that other dominant group within the Empire – the Hungarians – and to have some understanding of the legitimate aspirations of the Slavs. Was he not planning one day to grant them some measure of autonomy within the framework of a federated Habsburg empire?

There were said to have been more personal reasons as well. The visit would bolster Franz Ferdinand's self-esteem. Cut off from the centres of Austro-Hungarian power, the Archduke craved the recognition which an official visit such as this would bestow. And he craved it, even more, for his wife. For fourteen years, because of the morganatic nature of their marriage, Franz Ferdinand had been obliged to see his wife suffer in a hundred little ways. He therefore welcomed an opportunity for her to be received, by his side, as an equal.

But the explanation was simpler than this. Franz Ferdinand went to Bosnia because it was his duty to do so. If the manoeuvres had indeed been planned as a warning to Serbia, it was not he who had planned them. Nor, having already been received in state – with his wife – by Kaiser Wilhelm II, King George V and King Carol of Romania, did he really need a visit to a small Balkan capital in order to assert himself and elevate Sophia. In fact, far from wanting to go to Bosnia, Franz Ferdinand had tried to get the trip cancelled. Filled with an unaccountable apprehension, he had approached the Emperor about it. But Franz Joseph had held firm and, dedicated soldier that he was, Franz Ferdinand had felt duty-bound to carry out the Emperor's wishes. In the final analysis, Franz Ferdinand went to Sarajevo because he was commanded to do so.

Two attempts were made on the couple's lives in the streets of Sarajevo that day. As their procession neared the city hall, a bomb narrowly missed their car. 'I come here on a visit,' shouted the badly shaken Archduke to the agitated officials gathered for the civic reception, 'and you throw bombs at me! It's an outrage!'

To avoid the possibility of another such outrage, it was decided that the procession would make the return journey by a different route. Apparently – and incredibly – the only person not to have been told of the change of plan was the driver of the leading car. Yet had he been allowed to continue along the wrong route, the couple might yet have escaped assassination: it was when the procession was held up in order to allow the leading car to reverse and change direction that the assassin struck. A slim, nineteen-year-old boy aimed a pistol and fired twice. The first shot hit Franz Ferdinand, the second Sophie. While he remained upright, she slumped against him.

'Sopherl, Sopherl, don't die. Stay alive for our children,' murmured Franz Ferdinand as the car sped on towards the governor's palace.

In the meantime, the assassin had been arrested. His name was Gabriel Princip, a Bosnian of Serbian extraction and one of six young fanatics who had conspired to kill Franz Ferdinand that day. It was by the merest chance that Princip had suddenly found himself face to face with his victim as the procession halted to allow the leading car to change direction.

'I am a South Slav nationalist,' he later explained at his trial. 'My aim is the union of all Yugoslavs, under whatever political regime, and their liberation from Austria.' He could hardly have put it more succinctly.

Since then, there have been several theories about the true originators of the Sarajevo murders. That the young conspirators were acting alone seems unlikely. The most plausible theory is that they were organised by the chief of the Serbian military intelligence, a bull-like patriot known as Colonel 'Apis', who happened to be the chief of the notorious Black Hand as well. Fearing that Franz Ferdinand's intention of granting reforms to the Slavs within the empire might weaken the cause of South Slav nationalism, Apis had decided that the heir must be killed before becoming Emperor. It has also been suggested that he was hoping to provoke a general war, in the cause of Greater Serbia, and that he was being encouraged by the Russians.

But whoever the originators of the murders might have been, their efforts were successful. Fifteen minutes after the shooting, Franz Ferdinand and Sophie died, side by side, in a room in the governor's palace.

Franz Ferdinand's last words could hardly have been less appropriate.

'It is nothing,' he muttered feebly.

Only gradually did the monarchs of Europe come to a full realisation of the implications of the murder of the Archduke Franz Ferdinand. At first they were more appalled by the crime of regicide than by the possible consequences of that crime.

Wilhelm II was racing his yacht *Meteor* off Kiel when the news was shouted to him from an Admiralty launch coming alongside. He immediately cancelled the regatta and returned to Potsdam. 'The cowardly detestable crime . . .' he wired to his chancellor, Bethmann-Hollweg, 'has shaken me to the depths of my soul.' But his plan to attend Franz Ferdinand's funeral was firmly scotched by the Emperor Franz Joseph. In the hope of keeping King Peter of Serbia away from the funeral, explained the Austrian ambassador to the astonished Kaiser, no other monarchs would be allowed to attend.

Tsar Nicholas II was also at sea, aboard his yacht *Standart* off the coast of Finland, when he heard the news. But no more than most sovereigns did he appreciate its significance. Unlike the Kaiser, he did not even feel it necessary to return home. In any case, the Russian imperial family was facing what seemed like far more serious concerns at the time. On boarding the *Standart*, three days before, the haemophilic Tsarevich had twisted his ankle. By now he was in the most agonising pain. And this time there was no appealing to Rasputin to alleviate the boy's suffering. For, on the day before Franz

Ferdinand's assassination, an attempt had been made on the *starets*'s life. Yelling 'I have killed the Anti-Christ!', a woman plunged a knife into his stomach as he walked the streets of his home village, Pokrovskoe. For a fortnight Rasputin was gravely ill. But, blessed with a powerful constitution, he pulled through. To Nicholas and Alexandra, the assassination attempt at Pokrovskoe far outweighed in importance that of Sarejevo.

Britain's George V proved no more perceptive than the rest. 'Terrible shock for the dear old Emperor,' he noted in his diary on the night of the murder. Queen Mary, too, saw it as yet one more cross to be borne by 'the poor Emperor' and as yet one more crime to be committed by anarchists. But, implacable monarchist that she was, the Queen was not quite so distressed as not to consider it 'a great blessing' that *both* the Archduke and his morganatic wife had been killed: it made 'the future less complicated with regard to the position of their children', she noted.

The object of all this solicitude – the old Emperor Franz Joseph himself – was not nearly as upset as was generally imagined. 'I found Papa amazingly fresh,' noted his daughter, the Archduchess Marie Valerie on the day after Sarajevo. 'He was certainly shocked . . . but, as I had imagined in advance, he was not personally stricken.' And when an official letter was being drafted in which the Emperor was to thank the Grand Master of the Imperial Court for arranging the various ceremonies connected with the Archduke's death, Franz Joseph crossed out the words which read 'a death painful to me'.

But lack of personal grief for the victim did not denote any lack of strong reaction to the crime itself. That Franz Joseph had not liked his nephew was neither here nor there. The heir to the Habsburg throne – a sacrosanct being, chosen by God to continue the six-century-long rule of the Habsburg dynasty – had been struck down. To preserve the pride of his House, Franz Joseph was obliged to punish the perpetrators of this outrage. The Emperor might have been old and tired and peace-loving but he was enough of a monarch to insist that the crime of regicide be avenged.

That the guilt lay with Serbia, the Emperor had no doubt at all. 'The bloody deed was not the work of a single individual but a well-organised plot whose threads extend to Belgrade,' wrote Franz Joseph to Wilhelm II. 'Although it may be impossible to establish the complicity of the Serbian government, no one can doubt that its policy of uniting all Southern Slavs under the Serbian flag encourages such crimes and that the constitution of this situation is a chronic peril for my House and my territories.'[1] Serbia, he concluded, must be eliminated as a political factor in the Balkans.

And even if Franz Joseph had not been so intent on 'eliminating' Serbia, his more warlike associates, particularly his foreign minister, Count Berchtold, and his chief of staff, General Conrad von Hotzendorff, would have egged him on. No less than the monarch himself were the political and military authorities convinced that the preservation of the monarchy depended on the subjugation of Serbia.

The first thing for Franz Joseph to do was to make sure of Wilhelm II's support. Without it, he dare not make a move against Serbia. This was obtained, by the Austrian ambassador, during the course of one of those elegant and leisurely luncheon parties at which so much of the diplomacy of the period was conducted. The Kaiser, without waiting for his chancellor's concurrence, assured the Austrian ambassador that the Emperor could count on his full support, whatever happened. His armour was ready for buckling on, his sword for unsheathing, his banner for unfurling. No less than Franz Joseph did Wilhelm feel that the Serbs must be crushed, even at the risk of a general war.

But he doubted that it would come to that. 'I do not believe in any serious warlike developments,' he said to one senior military man the following day. 'The Tsar will not place himself on the side of regicides.'

Having delivered this wildly inaccurate prediction, the Kaiser set out on his annual cruise off the coast of Norway. The Wilhelmstrasse and the General Staff heaved a collective sigh of relief. For at least three weeks they would be safe from their master's weathercock changes of policy direction.

From this point on, things began gathering momentum. Assured of German support, or given the Kaiser's 'blank cheque', Austria drew up an ultimatum to be presented to Serbia. 'We must confront Serbia with the sharpest kind of ultimatum,' declared Franz Joseph. 'If they do not knuckle under we will go to war.'

Indeed, the ultimatum was so deliberately sharp that no self-respecting country could possibly have accepted its terms. Wilhelm II, on receiving a copy on board the *Hohenzollern*, called it 'a spirited note', while Sir Edward Grey, the British foreign secretary, declared that he had never known one state address another in such formidable terms.

The Austrian ultimatum was delivered on 23 July 1914; that is, twenty-five days after the assassination of the Archduke Franz Ferdinand. It could have been presented four days earlier, but as Raymond Poincaré, the French President, was paying a state visit to his ally, Tsar Nicholas II, the Austrians delayed its delivery until the French had sailed from St Petersburg. The Entente allies must be allowed no opportunity for consultation.

During the following ten days, Europe was drawn inextricably into war.

Yet at the time it seemed – at least to the monarchs most immediately concerned – that war was not necessarily inevitable. Serbia's reply to the Austrian ultimatum was abject; but not abject enough for Vienna. So diplomatic relations between the two states were broken off. '*Also doch*' – So, after all – muttered Franz Joseph on hearing the news, but went on to comfort himself with the observation that 'the breaking off of diplomatic relations still does not mean war'.

The Kaiser was even more optimistic. Or he may simply have been more realistic. By now back from his cruise, Wilhelm had been warned, by his ambassador in London, that British neutrality could not be taken for granted in the event of a European war. This unnerved him. Switching abruptly from war lord to man of peace, he expressed his delight at the conciliatory tone of the Serbian reply. 'A great moral victory for Vienna,' he wrote, 'and with it every reason for war disappears.' This last phrase he underlined.

In his determination to keep the peace, he dashed off a telegram to the Tsar – in the English which the two sovereigns always used in their personal exchanges – asking 'Nicky' in the name of 'the hearty and tender friendship which binds us both from long ago with firm ties', to help him in his 'efforts to smooth over difficulties that may still arise'. He signed it 'Willy'.

Nicholas II was just as worried. 'Everything possible must be done to save peace,' he said to a member of his entourage. 'I will not become responsible for a monstrous slaughter.'

But, of course, Russia was obliged to come to Serbia's aid. Not only was she the traditional protector of the Slavs but, as a great power, she dare not again suffer the sort of humiliation she had suffered at the time of Austria's annexation of Bosnia and Herzegovina in 1908. Already, on hearing of Austria's ultimatum to Serbia, Nicholas II had promised Crown Prince Alexander of Serbia that 'Your Royal Highness may rest assured that Russia will in no case remain indifferent to the fate of Serbia.'

Yet the Tsar could assure the French ambassador that 'notwithstanding appearances, the Emperor Wilhelm is too cautious to launch his country on some wild adventure and the Emperor Franz Joseph's only wish is to die in peace.'

But it was not, apparently, the Emperor Franz Joseph's only wish. On 28 July he rejected the reply to his ultimatum and declared war on Serbia. On the following day Nicholas II, after some characteristic shilly-shallying, ordered a partial mobilisation of the Russian forces – along the Austrian border only.

This led to a positive snowstorm of telegrams between Nicky and Willy. It was all to no purpose. On the afternoon of 30 July the Tsar's foreign minister, Sazonov, convinced Nicholas that the order for a general – as opposed to a partial – mobilisation could no longer be delayed.

'Think of the responsibility you are advising me to take,' protested Nicholas. 'Remember, it would mean sending hundreds of thousands of Russian people to their deaths.'

But eventually, he gave in. 'The Tsar,' wrote Sazonov later, 'remained silent and his face showed the traces of a terrible inner struggle. At last, speaking with difficulty, he said "You are right. There is nothing left for us to do but get ready for an attack upon us. Give . . . my order for [general] mobilisation." '

With this order, Tsar Nicholas II set off a chain reaction that nothing could stop. The monarchs, and the diplomats, might assure themselves that mobilisation did not necessarily mean war, but the generals knew better. Once the cumbersome process of mobilisation had started, war became almost inevitable.

The Kaiser, on hearing of the Tsar's mobilisation order, proclaimed a state of 'imminent war' and drew up an ultimatum in which Russia was required to halt all military preparations by a certain time. Another ultimatum was sent to Russia's ally France, demanding that she remain neutral in the event of a Russo-German war. A third ultimatum went to Belgium in which it was made clear that, with or without permission, German troops would cross Belgium into France.

With Russia ignoring the ultimatum, Germany declared war. The date was 1 August 1914 and the time was just after seven in the evening.

Even at this late stage the Kaiser was hoping that the conflict could be confined to the eastern front. A few days before, on 26 July, his brother Henry, who had been yachting at Cowes, had called on their cousin, George V, at Buckingham Palace. In the course of an eight-minute talk, the King had expressed the hope that Britain might be able to stay neutral in the coming struggle. 'But if Germany declared war on Russia, then I am afraid we shall be dragged into it,' explained the King.

Prince Henry, having first gone to see his sister, Queen Sophie of the Hellenes, who was holidaying with her children in Eastbourne, returned to Germany. There he blandly assured the Kaiser, as he had done the year before, that the King had said that Britain would remain neutral. This the Kaiser, with that unshakable belief in the powers of crowned heads, interpreted as an official assurance of British neutrality. When Admiral von Tirpitz expressed his doubts about Britain staying out of the war, the Kaiser gave a crushing reply.

'I have the word of a King and that is enough for me,' declared Wilhelm.

This was why, when it finally became clear that Britain would not remain neutral, the Kaiser lost his temper. In a flurry of marginal notes, he abused the British as 'a mean crew of shopkeepers', their foreign secretary as 'a common cur', and George V as 'a liar'. He even lashed out against his late uncle, Edward VII, whom he held responsible for encircling Germany with enemies. 'Edward VII is stronger after his death than I, who am still alive,' railed the Kaiser. His uncle's nefarious work had been 'finally completed and put into operation by George V'.

But even after he had reluctantly signed the order for general mobilisation, Wilhelm held out hopes of a war on the Russian front only. Patiently, it was explained to him that the redeployment of the million men who were already moving towards the Belgian frontier was impossible. Once the military machine had begun to roll, once the famous Schlieffen Plan had been put into operation, there was no way of stopping it.

Yet the worried Kaiser could still send a telegram to George V, explaining that for 'technical reasons' mobilisation could not be countermanded but that 'if France offers me neutrality which must be guaranteed by the British fleet and army, I shall of course refrain from attacking France and employ my troops elsewhere.'

The no less worried King Albert of the Belgians was also in touch with the Kaiser. On the day before receiving the German ultimatum, he had written Wilhelm II a personal appeal. Albert had hoped that the Kaiser might be able to give him some sort of private reassurance: a reassurance which Wilhelm could not, for political reasons, make public. With the help of Queen Elisabeth, King Albert drafted the letter.

'All her remarks', says Baron van der Elst, who was with them on the occasion, 'were sound and betrayed a sure judgement and that particular tact which often makes women better psychologists than men.' She spoke softly, he says, almost timidly, putting her views in the form of questions. Every word, every phrase of the important letter was carefully considered. When it was finished, the Queen suggested that she translate it from French into German. To ensure that it was done with the utmost accuracy, she fetched a dictionary from an adjoining room and, placing it on an armchair beside her, knelt in front of a low table and began to write. Behind her, bent anxiously over her shoulder, stood Albert. Only when the couple were completely satisfied, was the letter despatched.

The Kaiser's answering telegram, received on the same day as the German ultimatum, was merely another attempt to get the Belgian King to accept the Kaiser's terms. 'As the conditions laid down made clear,' telegraphed Wilhelm blandly, 'the possibility of maintaining our former and present relations still lies in the hands of Your Majesty.' In other words, Albert was to agree to the passage of the German army through Belgium.

'What does he take me for?' exclaimed Albert in a rare show of anger. With that he gave orders for the blowing up of the bridges across the River Meuse.

And so, inexorably, the alliances locked into place. On 1 August Germany had declared war on Russia. On 3 August she declared war on France and Belgium. On 4 August, with the Germans having invaded Belgium, Britain honoured her long-standing commitment to defend Belgian neutrality and declared war on Germany. On 5 August Austria declared war on Russia. On

12 August Britain declared war on Austria. The third member of the Triple Alliance, Italy, remained for the moment uncommitted.

By the flood of martial elation which now surged through the German Reich, the Kaiser alone remained unaffected. All those warlike posturings, by which he had helped create a climate for war, were suddenly revealed for what they were. 'I have never seen a more tragic, a more ravaged face than that of our Emperor during those days,' declared Admiral von Tirpitz. On the day that he sat down in the Berlin Schloss to sign the order that would start his armies moving towards the frontiers, the Kaiser wore an almost doomed expression.

'Gentlemen,' he said to the military and naval chiefs gathered around his desk, 'you will live to regret this.'

And later, because in Wilhelm II pathos and bathos were always intertwined, he declared indignantly, 'To think that Georgie and Nicky should have played me false. If my grandmother [Queen Victoria] had been alive, she would never have allowed it.'[2]

Of the twelve monarchs who were to be buffeted by the winds of the First World War, only three could be claimed to have borne some responsibility for it. They were Franz Joseph I, Nicholas II and Wilhelm II. But to what extent were they responsible?

In theory, they might have been able to prevent it. Franz Joseph could have accepted the conciliatory Serbian answer to his ultimatum. Nicholas II could have stuck to his order of only partial mobilisation in the hope of confining the war to the Austrian front. Even Wilhelm II could have refused to order general mobilisation. But in practice, there was very little they could do. Autocratic or semi-autocratic sovereigns they might have been, but they were very much at the mercy of the military cliques within their countries. They had become the servants rather than the masters of the generals, the politicians and the armaments manufacturers.

Perhaps, if the three emperors had been more resolute or more astute characters, they might – given the strength of their constitutional positions – have been able to shape or control matters more effectively. But, in their different ways, all three were ineffectual men: Franz Joseph too hidebound, Nicholas II too vacillating, Wilhelm II too insecure.

In all three empires there was a feeling that internal problems – political, social and economic – could be solved by a victorious war; that this was the only way to rally the entire populace behind the monarchy. For the survival of their dynasties, for the prestige of their countries, these monarchs allowed themselves to be convinced that war was not only necessary but imperative. In the face of the urgings of their general staffs, who were determined not to be caught at a military disadvantage, the sovereigns were all but helpless.

Most anxious for war was Germany. Alarmed by the growing might of Russia and, to a lesser extent, France, German statesmen and generals were set on fighting a war sooner rather than later. The murder of the Archduke Franz Ferdinand had given them exactly the sort of excuse they were waiting for: while appearing to be the aggrieved party they could launch their attack. 'If I hadn't done it,' said Franz Ferdinand's assassin in his prison cell, 'the Germans would have found another excuse.'

So while the Kaiser, in his erratic way, was trying his best to prevent or at least contain the war, his politicians and generals were busily fostering it. All his frantic efforts, all his emphatic instructions and scrawled marginalia, all those wordy telegrams to Nicky and Georgie counted for nothing. What the Kaiser thought or did was largely immaterial. His mind was being made up for him; not least by his more tenacious Empress and by his fear of being accused of cowardice by his bellicose heir, Crown Prince Wilhelm.

'I don't believe the Kaiser wanted war,' confided George V to the departing German ambassador, 'but he was afraid of his son's popularity. His son and his party made the war.' It might have been simplistic reasoning but it did contain a grain of truth.

Immaterial, too, was the fact that the Kaiser was related to both Nicholas II and George V. When set against the forces of nationalism and militarism, these dynastic relationships counted for nothing.

The truth was that by 1914 Europe had developed into a series of rival power blocs, all competing with each other, all striving to be larger, stronger, more magnificent than each other. Each wanted a bigger navy, a stronger army, a more lucrative market, a greater empire than the others; each was anxious to score diplomatic victories over its neighbours. An explosion had become almost inevitable.

On such giant waves, on such mountainous seas, the sovereigns could only bob about like so many corks. As the historian, Golo Mann, has put it, 'The men who to the world appeared as the ruthless authors of the war did not know what had happened to them.'

But what they did know, or rather, what they were coming to suspect, was that they had helped unleash something which would, in the end, overwhelm them. All three emperors seemed to sense that their days were numbered. 'If the monarchy is doomed,' said Franz Joseph quietly to his chief of staff, 'let it at least go down honourably.'[3]

And Count Czernin, later Austria's foreign minister, had an even more trenchant comment to make on the downfall of the monarchic order of Central Europe. 'We were bound to die,' he afterwards said. 'We were at liberty to choose the manner of our death, and we chose the most terrible.'

Part Three

THE CROWNS
AND THE CANNON

11

Divided Houses

THE OUTBREAK of the First World War proved, once and for all, the irrelevance of the family ties between the various reigning houses of Europe. That the majority of Europe's leading sovereigns were closely related had made not the slightest difference to the course of events. Indeed, it was ironic that when the direct descendants of Queen Victoria sat on no less than seven European thrones, and her Coburg relations on two more, the Continent should have been ravaged by the greatest war that it had ever known.

Far from benefiting from this close relationship, they suffered because of it. For the royal cousinhood, these were to be heartbreaking days. Overnight, their world was split in two.

In the last hours before the outbreak of hostilities, there was a frantic scramble as holidaying royals hurried back to their countries. The Kaiser's brother, Prince Henry of Prussia, had to cut short his stay at Cowes; their sister, Queen Sophie of the Hellenes, had to quit Eastbourne, leaving two of her children in the care of her cousin, George V. Tsar Nicholas II's mother, the Dowager Tsaritsa Marie, who had been visiting her sister, Queen Alexandra, tried to cross hostile Germany by train, only to be turned back in Berlin, from where she had to make her way back to St Petersburg via Copenhagen. In every court in Europe, French governesses, English nannies and German maids packed their portmanteaux and headed for the railway station.

Once home, the majority of these royal relations did not see each other again for four years. Those mammoth pre-war gatherings – for christenings in Darmstadt, house parties in Copenhagen and weddings in Berlin – came to a sudden end. So, too, did any private visits. And not only could they no longer see each other but members of the same family were often completely alienated from one another. Cousins found themselves fighting cousins; brothers and sisters were on opposite sides. Few of them escaped the agony of divided loyalties.

The three Hesse sisters – the Tsaritsa Alexandra, the Grand Duchess Ella and Princess Louis of Battenberg – were cut off from their brother the Grand

Duke of Hesse, and from their fourth sister Irene, who was married to the Kaiser's brother Prince Henry. (Princess Louis and Princess Henry did have the foresight, though, to exchange maids on the outbreak of war; Princess Louis's German maid went to Kiel while Princess Henry's English maid went to the Isle of Wight.)

Princess Alexander of Teck, born Princess Alice of Albany, had a British-born brother, the Duke of Coburg, fighting with the German army on the Russian front, while her husband, who was Queen Mary's brother, was attached to the British Mission to King Albert of the Belgians. The war, claims Princess Alice, quite shattered her brother's life. The Duke of Coburg was denounced in Germany for being English and in England for being German. Also with King Albert's army were Prince Sixtus and Prince Xavier of Bourbon-Parma, French princes whose sister was married to the heir of their Austrian enemy, the Emperor Franz Joseph.

Queen Elisabeth of the Belgians, born a member of the Bavarian royal house, had a brother-in-law, Prince Rupprecht of Bavaria, in command of the German Sixth and Seventh armies, fighting Belgium's ally, France. When, before the war, the Kaiser had tried to break down King Albert's meticulous impartiality by appealing to Elisabeth's native loyalties, her answer had been discouragingly succinct. 'My husband and I are one,' she declared. 'I abide by his decisions.' It had proved to be the one occasion on which Wilhelm II had not given whole-hearted approval to wifely subservience. Now that Belgium and Germany were at war, Elisabeth identified herself unequivocally with her husband's country. 'It is finished between me and them,' she said of her German relations: 'henceforth an iron curtain has descended between us.'

King George V, although somewhat uneasy about his own ancestry, usually resisted the rabidly anti-German excesses of so many of his subjects. Yet he was compelled to deprive several of his German relations – among them the Kaiser, the German Crown Prince and Queen Alexandra's brother-in-law, the Duke of Cumberland – of their honorary British commands and to have their names dropped from the Army List. He also reluctantly agreed to the removal, from St George's Chapel at Windsor, of the banners of the various enemy Knights of the Garter and to the striking of their names off the roll of the Order. And – against his better judgement – he was obliged to accept the forced resignation of his close kinsman, Prince Louis of Battenberg, as First Sea Lord, for no better reason than that he had a German name. Queen Mary, too, had to play down her own interest in and affection for the members of her late father's family, the Württembergs.

The Kaiser made a point of returning to George V, by way of the departing British ambassador, his insignia of a British Field Marshal and Admiral of the Fleet. Wilhelm could hardly contain his disgust for what he regarded as

Britain's perfidy. This was the thanks, he said bitterly, for Prussia's help to the British at Waterloo.

But it would take more than gestures of this sort to still the widespread suspicions that royals with foreign blood secretly sympathised with the enemy. When the Kaiser, in his expansive fashion, was seen chatting in English to British prisoners-of-war, he was accused of being pro-British. In Russia, where the Tsaritsa Alexandra was German-born, rumours were rife about her supposed sympathy for her native land. The story would be told of a general who, one day in the Winter Palace, comes across the Tsarevich, weeping bitterly.

'What is wrong, my little man?' asks the general.

'When the Russians are beaten, Papa cries. When the Germans are beaten, Mama cries. When am I to cry?' answers the boy.

The story was nonsense but the fact that it was so widely repeated was significant.

Yet the Tsaritsa would have been less than human had she not worried about the fate of her brother, the Grand Duke of Hesse, who was in the German army. 'I have no news of my brother,' she once wrote to the Tsar. 'I shiver to think that the Emperor William may avenge himself against me by sending him to the Russian front. He is quite capable of such monstrous behaviour.'

And some sympathies were more robustly expressed than this. From her deathbed, the redoubtable old Grand Duchess of Mecklenburg-Strelitz, British-born Princess Augusta of Cambridge, was able to get a word through to George V.

'Tell the King,' came her message from Germany, 'it is a stout old English heart that is ceasing to beat.'

By the year 1914, kings no longer led their armies into battle. Along with their divine right had gone their right to command their country's armed forces. It was just as well. Kings were no more guaranteed to be good soldiers, or military strategists, than they were to be good rulers. In theory, sovereigns remained supreme commanders, but the actual waging of the war was entrusted to the generals. Not since the days of Napoleon had a leading monarch personally commanded a battle. By now sovereigns either remained firmly in their palaces, paying an occasional, morale-boosting visit to their troops, or else established themselves in some country house behind the front from where, surrounded by their equerries, secretaries, attachés, valets, footmen and cooks, they could follow day-to-day events. Either way, contemporary monarchs had very little say in the conduct of the war.

A shining exception to this rule was provided by Albert of the Belgians. Within days of the outbreak of the war, he proved that he was the

Commander-in-Chief of the Belgian army in practice as well as in rank. This was in accordance with the Belgian constitution. 'Soldiers,' ran his first rousing Order of the Day, 'I am leaving Brussels to place myself at your head.'

And in the course of the three months of August, September and October 1914, King Albert was transformed from an apparently colourless, if well-intentioned, sovereign into a bold and resolute leader of men, the symbol of little Belgium's stand against a powerful and ruthless invader. While his allies, Britain and France, floundered about in a swamp of indecision, his country was to bear the brunt of the German attack and he to earn for himself the title of Albert the Brave.

As soon as it was certain that the Germans had crossed the border, Albert felt free to abandon his country's strictly observed neutrality and to appeal to France and Britain for help. Confident that the Allies would hurry to his aid, the King prepared to hold up the enemy advance until the arrival of reinforcements. But, unsuspected by Albert, no such reinforcements were planned. France, obsessed with regaining the provinces of Alsace and Lorraine, lost to the Germans in 1870, was determined to make its thrust across the Franco-German frontier. Britain, after a period of uncertainty, sent four divisions to support, not the Belgians, but the French. And so, for over a fortnight, King Albert's forces faced the tremendous onslaught alone.

During the fortnight, the King was forced to make a series of momentous decisions. That they had to be made in the face of hostile criticism from his allies, his general staff, his troops and the civilian population, rendered them all the more significant. Two factors influenced his actions: he had to conserve his little army, and he had to keep it on Belgian soil as long as possible.

The first of these decisions was to prevent his army, which had early on repulsed the enemy before Liège, from launching an immediate counter-attack. The level-headed Albert realised that any such offensive would be suicidal. Another decision was to reject the Kaiser's suggestion that, as Belgium had 'upheld its honour' by this heroic resistance, she now allow the German army to pass through the country. His rejection of this tempting suggestion led to the bombardment of Liège into submission, and to a pouring of German troops across the River Meuse.

Again Albert made a sensible, if unpopular, move. He ordered his army to retreat to the fortified city of Antwerp, thus leaving central Belgium, including Brussels, to be overrun by the enemy.

'It isn't a question of shutting ourselves up in an entrenched camp,' explained Albert to the French, who had hoped that his army would fall back into France to join their left wing, 'but of taking breath before an eventual counterblow.'

So while he, with Queen Elisabeth and their three children, as well as his

17 Crown Princess, afterwards Queen, Marie of Romania in typically
   theatrical setting

18 Sandringham *circa* 1912. Second from left: Crown Princess, afterwards Queen, Sophie of Greece; fourth from left, Crown Princess, afterwards Queen, Marie of Romania; eighth from left, Dowager Empress Marie of Russia; ninth from

government, remained in Antwerp, the Germans occupied Brussels and, in accordance with the Schlieffen Plan, swung southwards in a massive curve towards France. All that the King could do as he waited – in vain, as it turned out – for Allied relief, was to harry the enemy's flank.

During these harrying attacks, Albert was always to be seen in the thick of the fighting. He moved openly among the men, encouraging them and sharing their dangers. Although never sparing himself, he was extremely sparing of his troops. His calm, his common sense and, above all, his unostentatious courage earned him the trust and then the whole-hearted devotion of his soldiers. 'The attitude of the King and Queen through these tense and tragic days was magnificent,' wrote Winston Churchill, who visited beleagured Antwerp at this time. 'The impression of the grave, calm Soldier-King presiding at Council, sustaining his troops and commanders, preserving an unconquerable majesty amidst the ruin of his Kingdom, will never pass from my mind.'

For that Albert's kingdom was being ruined, there was no doubt. The Germans, infuriated by the initial Belgian resistance, were carrying out a ruthless and systematic terrorisation of the country. Already the German advance had been delayed and the Schlieffen Plan disrupted; to prevent any further Belgian resistance, the civilian population would have to be intimidated. So while King Albert looked on in impotent horror, his country was subjected to a series of atrocities – looting, burning, mass executions, the destruction of the ancient city of Louvain – the like of which had never before been experienced in European warfare.

'My heart bleeds', protested the Kaiser in a telegram to the United States President, Woodrow Wilson, for the sufferings of Belgium, caused 'as a result of the criminal and barbarous action of the Belgians'. Their resistance, he claims, had been 'openly incited' and 'carefully organised'[1] by the Belgian government.

But the rest of the world knew better. If there had hitherto been any doubts as to why the war was being fought, the German rape of Belgium removed them. Not only had Belgian neutrality been violated but her stubborn stand against a powerful and merciless invader had won her widespread sympathy and adulation. A cartoon, published in *Punch*, captured this spirit of Belgian resistance. On the ruins of a devastated Belgium, the Kaiser and King Albert stand face to face.

'You see,' the Kaiser is saying, 'you've lost everything.'

'Not my soul,' replies Albert.

By this time, Wilhelm II was established in the German legation in Luxembourg. It had at first been assumed that, like his fellow monarchs George V, Nicholas II and Franz Joseph I, the Kaiser would remain in his capital; from there, acting as a national focal point, he would handle political and diplomatic affairs. But, for the Supreme War Lord, any such notion was out of the question: his place was with his army. In any case he – and almost every other sovereign in Europe – assumed that the war would last a matter of weeks only. Had he not assured his departing troops that they would be home before the leaves had fallen?

Wilhelm's intention was to remain on the western front until France had been defeated (the Schlieffen Plan reckoned on complete victory by 9 September) and then to travel to the eastern front for the last stages of the Russian campaign. 'Lunch in Paris, dinner in St Petersburg' was the Kaiser's neat summing-up of his plan.

And so, surrounded by a numerous suite, Wilhelm II set up his headquarters, first in Coblenz and then, with his troops swinging through Belgium, in Luxembourg.

If it had ever been assumed that Wilhelm II would become a supreme commander in the mould of Albert I, the assumption was short-lived. Living so close to the Kaiser, his entourage soon came to an appreciation of his military, and temperamental, inadequacies. Equally disillusioned about the Kaiser's qualities of leadership was his Chief of the General Staff, Field Marshal von Moltke. For all the belligerence of his peacetime attitudes, Wilhelm II was revealed as having no more understanding of military strategy than did the majority of his fellow sovereigns. 'Bloodthirsty details from the front he finds interesting,' noted Admiral von Muller, 'but he shows little comprehension of the gravity of the whole situation.'

Nor did he have any of the qualities essential in a military commander: he was too indecisive, too lacking in self-confidence, too unrealistic. He see-sawed between heady optimism and deep depression; between great generosity of spirit and savage vindictiveness. One moment he would be predicting imminent victory, the next humiliating defeat.

He was extraordinarily sensitive. Once, when he was strolling in the garden with two of his officers at a time when the news from the eastern front was bad, one of the men fetched a chair rather than sit beside him on a bench that was too short for the three of them. 'Am I already such a figure of contempt that no one wants to sit next to me?'[2] sighed Wilhelm.

But the news from the eastern front did not remain bad for long. To halt the unexpected Russian advance, Moltke appointed the retired General Paul von Hindenburg in overall command on the Russian front and, to serve under him, General Erich Ludendorff. Within a matter of days of their appointment, the two generals had won a resounding victory over the Russians at the Battle of Tannenberg. From that time on, Hindenburg and Ludendorff became progressively more powerful until, in the end, they would overshadow the irresolute Kaiser almost completely.

Victory in the east was counterbalanced by defeat in the west. By

9 September, the date which should have seen the final triumph of the Schlieffen Plan, the German army was in retreat. German muddling, combined with stiffening French resistance – typified by the celebrated shuttle service of the 'taxis of the Marne' – put paid to the Schlieffen Plan. Moltke, his spirit broken by the Allied victory on the Marne, delegated responsibility to a subordinate. It fell to the Kaiser to exercise his prerogative and appoint a new chief of staff. It was to be his last military decision of any significance. Wilhelm chose a court favourite, General von Falkenhayn. Under this new command, the German line steadied and the army dug in. The conflict on the western front now developed into what the Schlieffen Plan had been especially designed to avoid: a long war of attrition.

With the war bogged down in the trenches, the Kaiser moved again: this time to a rich industrialist's home in Charleville. But, for all the contact he had with military operations, he might just as well have been in Berlin. Occasionally, in his royal train, its blue, cream and gold glories disguised by a coat of khaki-green paint, or in his armoured motor car, Wilhelm would visit the front line. More often he remained at Charleville, all but ignored.

'If people in Germany think I am the Supreme Commander, they are grossly mistaken,' he once complained. 'The General Staff tells me nothing and never asks my advice. I drink tea, go for walks and saw wood . . .'[3]

While the war lord of the Second Reich was being kept well away from any fighting, the peace-loving Albert of the Belgians was covering himself in military glory.

The Allied victory on the Marne had brought no relief to King Albert, still holding out in fortified Antwerp. With the French and British forces remaining firmly in France, the Germans concentrated their attack on Antwerp; they could not risk leaving the entrenched Belgian army on their right flank. For three weeks, in the face of merciless German bombardment, Albert held out, but by 5 October he realised that if he did not soon evacuate his army, his line of retreat would be cut off and all hope of joining up with the Allied forces would be gone. Two days later his army quit Antwerp and fled southwards. It looked as if the two-month-long Belgian resistance, which had so impressed the world, had come to an end. Except that it had gained a little time for the Allies, the sacrifice had apparently been in vain.

In the midst of the confused and demoralised army, King Albert and Queen Elisabeth headed for France. It had become a *sauve qui peut*. The King, usually so unemotional, was deeply depressed; the Queen, always so vivacious, was at one stage discovered in a rose garden near Ostend, sobbing her heart out. Both realised that their kingdom would have to be abandoned and that the Belgian army, stripped of its independence, would become an anonymous part of that great host massed on the western front.

But by 13 October Albert's mood had changed. He had decided to retreat no further. He was resolved to remain, with his army, on Belgian soil.

A few miles south of Ostend, the river Yser flowed into the sea; some miles inland it was linked to the Ypres Canal. Together, these two waterways formed a natural barrier. Between them and the French frontier lay a few square miles of Belgian territory. On this last enclave of his country's soil, wedged in the far southwestern corner of Belgium, King Albert was determined to dig himself in.

Having made his decision, the King issued a resounding proclamation to his troops. They were to fall back no further. From this moment on, he seemed like a different man. 'This leader,' wrote one contemporary, 'who had always been ready to take advice, who preferred to persuade rather than to command, was transformed into a dominating personality, following his own counsel, acting with the utmost determination and speaking in such a stern voice that even those who were intimate with him wondered at the change.'[4]

Albert's new-found resolution was soon put to the test. On 18 October and for the following twelve days, the Germans launched a massive attack on the Belgian position along the Yser. The depleted and exhausted Belgian army fought magnificently. The Battle of the Yser, by which the Belgian army halted the German advance along the Channel coast, thus saving the French ports, was a superb achievement. It allowed the Belgian army, with its prestige restored and its independence guaranteed, to link up with, and form the extreme left wing of, the Allied front stretching all the way from Switzerland to the Channel. And it established King Albert's reputation as one of the wisest and most tenacious military leaders of the First World War.

When, after more than a week of almost superhuman effort, the Belgians were forced off the left bank of the Yser, Albert made yet another masterly decision. On the night of 29 October, he ordered the opening of the sluice gates at Nieuport, on the Channel, and the flooding of the valley of the Yser. From now on his army was to be separated from the enemy by an immense sheet of water.

With the battle of the Yser won, the Belgian army and the Belgian King were to remain, for the next four years, on twenty square miles of Belgian soil.

If the close family relationship between Europe's reigning houses had not been able to prevent the war, it might still, they imagined, prove useful in making the peace. The neutral monarchs – the three Scandinavian kings, King Alfonso XIII of Spain and Queen Wilhelmina of the Netherlands – were only too ready to act as mediators. The first one to do so was King Christian X of Denmark. First cousin to Britain's George V, Russia's Nicholas II and

Greece's Constantine I, the Danish King could, as a neutral sovereign, maintain direct contact with Germany's Wilhelm II and Austria's Franz Joseph I. He often acted as an intermediary for the exchange of letters between these opposing families.

In November 1914, he offered to initiate talks on a mediated peace between George V, Nicholas II and Wilhelm II. Although, at that stage, the Kaiser was not interested in coming to terms with Britain, he let Christian X know that he might consider an approach to Russia. He had always set a high value on his friendship with the Tsar, explained Wilhelm.

When the Danish King's emissary visited Nicholas II at Tsarskoe Selo he found the Tsar equally sympathetic, if characteristically hesitant. Taking things a stage further, Christian X then proposed that the Kaiser and the Tsar each send representatives to Copenhagen to open negotiations.

But the plan never materialised. By the spring of 1915, with Britain and Russia harbouring hopes of a victory at Gallipoli, Nicholas II had once again been mesmerised by that perennial Near-Eastern chimera – the taking of Constantinople. So he turned down the Danish King's offer.

But Wilhelm remained optimistic. He was convinced that, sooner or later, the Tsar would change his mind. He was also convinced – and this in spite of the fact that he was being cold-shouldered by the politicians and the generals – that peace was something to be made by kings and emperors. When an emissary of President Woodrow Wilson arrived at the Kaiser's headquarters with an offer of mediation, Wilhelm was dismissive. This really was not the business of republicans.

'I and my cousins George and Nicholas shall make peace when the proper time has come,' he declared.

By the time that Nicholas II finally turned down Christian X's offer of mediation, he had assumed personal command of the Russian army. Until then – August 1915 – the Tsar had remained at home to control affairs of state. The army had been under the command of one of Nicholas's relations, the efficient, popular and physically impressive Grand Duke Nicholas. The Tsar had confined his military involvement to prolonged stays at headquarters (always known as *Stavka*), where he was careful not to undermine the Grand Duke's authority. Nicholas, who was often accompanied by the eleven-year-old Tsarevich Alexis, enjoyed these visits immensely. After the claustrophobic, intensely feminine atmosphere of Tsarskoe Selo, there was something invigoratingly masculine about military headquarters. These visits also allowed him to forget, for a while, the pressures of political life in the capital.

General Sir John Hanbury-Williams, the British military attaché, meeting the Tsar for the first time at *Stavka*, was particularly impressed by his relaxed air. 'The Emperor received me alone,' he wrote. 'He was dressed in perfectly plain khaki uniform, the coat being more of a blouse than ours, with blue breeches and long black riding boots, and was standing at a high writing desk. As I saluted, he came forward at once and shook me warmly by the hand. I was at once struck by his extraordinary likeness to our own King, and the way he smiled, his face lighting up, as if it were a real pleasure for him to receive one. His first question was one of inquiry after our King and Queen and the Royal Family . . . I had always pictured him to myself as a somewhat sad and anxious-looking monarch, with cares of state and other things hanging heavily over him. Instead of that I found a bright, keen, happy face, plenty of humour and a fresh-air man.'

But Nicholas was not quite as satisfied with things as he appeared. In fact, he was very unhappy about his position. He would far rather have been in personal command of the army than a mere visitor to *Stavka*. He felt that his role should be that of warrior-tsar, not tame head of state.

In his dissatisfaction, Nicholas was being egged on by Alexandra. Even more than he, did this impassioned woman feel that the place for the Autocrat was at the head of his troops. It was surely quite wrong for the more masterful-looking Grand Duke Nicholas to be holding this all-powerful position. Might he not, in time, come to overshadow the small and mild-mannered Tsar? Already, by her unstinting work among the wounded, Alexandra felt that she had become the *Mutushka* – the mother – of the loyal and simple Russian soldiers; only by placing himself at the head of his men could Nicholas truly become their *Batiushka* – their father.

Encouraging the Tsaritsa in her thinking was Rasputin. In those tense days before the outbreak of war, the *starets* had tried to talk the Tsar out of committing Russia to the conflict. 'Let Papa not plan war,' he had telegraphed, 'for with the war will come the end of Russia and yourselves.' Nicholas had reacted angrily to what had seemed to him like unpatriotic sentiments and, since then, he had treated Rasputin's advice with a certain amount of scepticism. But Alexandra remained as besotted with the *starets* as ever. And as Rasputin shared her distrust of Grand Duke Nicholas (who had once threatened to hang him) he worked up the Empress's feelings against him.

While the Russian army was successful (if it was only just holding its own against the Germans, it was winning resounding victories against the Austro-Hungarians) there was very little that the Empress and Rasputin could do about getting rid of Grand Duke Nicholas. But when, in the spring of 1915, the Russian forces began to fall back in the face of a determined German onslaught, their position was strengthened. In letter after letter to her husband, Alexandra begged him to follow the advice of 'Our Friend' to dismiss Grand Duke Nicholas and assume supreme command himself. After the fall of Warsaw to the Germans in August 1915, Nicholas finally made up his mind to take their advice. Grand Duke Nicholas was dismissed and, against the pleas of his ministers and the example of most of his fellow sovereigns, the Tsar took personal command of the army.

The Tsaritsa was overjoyed. 'You have fought this great fight for your country and throne – alone and with bravery and decision,' ran her hectoring phrases. 'Never have they seen such firmness in you before . . . God anointed you at your coronation, he placed you where you stand and you have done your duty, be sure, quite sure of that and He forsaketh not His anointed. Our Friend's prayers arise day and night for you to Heaven and God will hear them . . . It is the beginning of the great glory of your reign. He said so and I absolutely believe it.'

But by no means everyone believed in this great glory lying just around the corner. With control of the army having passed from the resolute hands of Grand Duke Nicholas into the vacillating hands of Tsar Nicholas II, victory seemed less likely than ever. And with the disappearance of the autocratic head of state from the capital to the battlefield, a dangerous vacuum remained. It was a vacuum which the Tsaritsa felt increasingly confident of filling. While the Tsar managed the army, she would manage the government. Together, they would save Holy Russia and the Autocracy for their son.

And in case her weak-willed husband proved unequal to his great task, Alexandra chivvied him into being firmer, bolder, more autocratic. 'Be the master and lord, you are an autocrat,' she insisted. 'Never forget that you are and must remain autocratic Emperor.'

That she would prove equal to what she considered her divine mission, Alexandra never doubted. In this, she was being backed up by the wily Rasputin. Confidently, and with disastrous results, the Tsaritsa and the *starets* began to manage the affairs of the empire. And, in the unlikely event of her ever developing any reservations about him, Rasputin would remind her of his importance in her life.

'I need neither the Tsar nor yourself,' he would say. 'If you abandon me to my enemies, it will not worry me. I am quite able to cope with them. But neither the Tsar nor you can do without me. If I am not here to protect you, you will lose your son and your crown in six months.'[5]

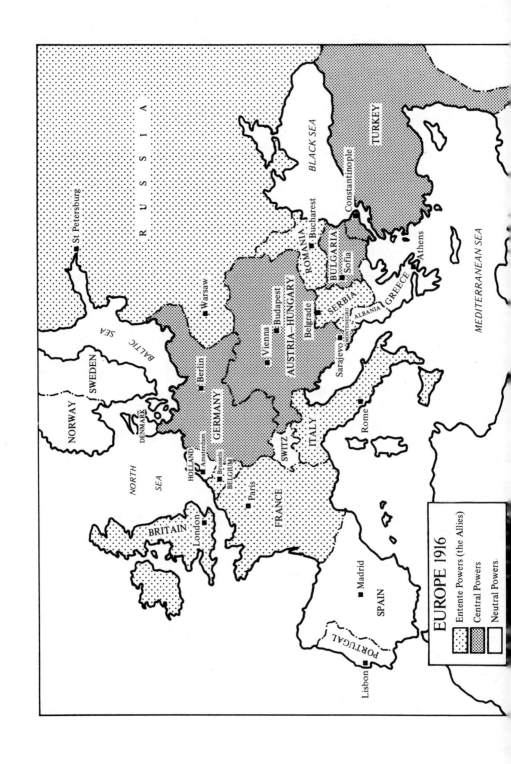

EUROPE 1916

Entente Powers (the Allies)

Central Powers

Neutral Powers

12

Taking Sides

ONLY GRADUALLY were the monarchs of southeastern Europe drawn into the conflict. Some were prepared to wait and see which of the rival contestants came up with the more attractive territorial offer; others faced agonising personal decisions. At the opening of hostilities, only those three venerable sovereigns – Franz Joseph of Austria–Hungary on the one side, and Peter of Serbia and Nicholas of Montenegro on the other – were involved. And of the three, King Peter alone was to be found in the field with his troops.

Just before the outbreak of war, the seventy-one-year-old King Peter, whose health had been steadily declining ('an old broken man on the edge of the grave' is how he described himself) had appointed his son, Crown Prince Alexander, as Regent. Yet this did not stop him from playing as active as possible a part in the fighting. In the opening weeks of the war, his army fought magnificently. Twice they repulsed the invading Austro-Hungarian forces, and by the end of September 1914, a combined Serbian and Montenegrin force had actually penetrated Austrian territory. But a third invasion by the Austrians forced the Serbs back and, at the end of October, Belgrade had to be evacuated.

It was now, with his armies on the defensive, that old King Peter came into his own. Almost overnight, he developed into the symbol of Serbian resistance. Rifle in hand, he would scramble into the trenches to fight beside his men. On one occasion, hobbling up to some troops who were wavering under sustained enemy artillery fire, he exhorted them, 'in the manner of a Homeric general', to hold firm.

'Heroes,' he shouted, 'you have taken two oaths: one to me, your King, and one to your country. From the first I release you, from the second no man can release you.'[1] Yet, always aware of the untameable temperament of his peasant subjects, the King went on to assure them that if they did decide to go back to their homes, they would not be punished.

They did not go back. Instead, by an almost superhuman effort, the fought their way back to Belgrade. In the midst of them, as they battled forward in the swirling dust, went their King. Seated in a ramshackle old car, he would urge on the driver with shouts of 'Faster! Faster!' By the middle of December 1914, the Serbs had retaken their capital. The Hungarian flag, which had been floating above the palace, was torn down and laid on the steps of the cathedral. Over it, as he went to celebrate a great victory mass, trod the triumphant King Peter.

And if, in his heart of hearts, the old monarch knew that his country's successes could only be temporary, he never publicly admitted it. Instead, he behaved with all the assurance of a victor. To his subjects, King Peter of Serbia was now wholly, says one chronicler, the Warrior King.

Also being hailed as a warrior king was the far more unlikely figure of little Victor Emmanuel III of Italy. On the outbreak of war, and in spite of a request from the Emperor Franz Joseph that the Italian King honour his treaty obligations, Victor Emmanuel and his government opted for neutrality. Although realising that, if Italy were to live up to her boast of being a great power, she would have to enter the war sooner or later, Victor Emmanuel decided to bide his time.

The King's main ambition remained the completion of the *Risorgimento*. So not only was he prepared to ally his country to whoever promised him the *terre irredente* – those Italian-speaking lands still held by Austria – but he had to be certain that the promise would be kept; that, to put it at its crudest, Italy would choose the winning side. 'The little thief', exclaimed Wilhelm II on hearing of Victor Emmanuel's decision of neutrality, 'always wants to swallow something more.'[2]

The Allied victory on the Marne helped make up his mind. Quite clearly the Kaiser's troops were not going to be marching home in triumph before the leaves had fallen. Victor Emmanuel would be wiser to opt for the Triple Entente rather than the Central Powers. So, by the Pact of London, signed on 26 April 1915, in which Italy was promised not only Trentino and Trieste but great tracts of Austrian-owned land on the Adriatic coast, the King allied his country to the Entente Powers. A month later Italy declared war on Austria; or, as Franz Joseph more grandiloquently put it, 'The King of Italy has declared war on Me.' Not until August did Victor Emmanuel pluck up the courage to declare war on Germany.

The Kaiser's reaction was predictable. When someone suggested that Victor Emmanuel's hand might have been forced by his politicians, Wilhelm refused to believe it. Kings' hands were never forced by politicians. When the Day of Judgement came, declared the Kaiser, the King of Italy would not be able to evade his responsibilities by blaming his government. God would say to him, 'No, no, my little man, that won't wash with me. Who made you a King? Your Ministers? Your Parliament? No, I placed you in that exalted position and you are responsible to me alone. Go to Hell, or at least to Purgatory.'3

By the year 1915, such robustly autocratic sentiments were sounding very strange indeed. And coming from Wilhelm II, who was by now little more than a puppet in the hands of others, they sounded stranger still.

Victor Emmanuel remained with his troops throughout the war. The government was presided over by his cousin, the Duke of Genoa, whom he had appointed as Regent. Although hailed as *Il Re Soldato*, Victor Emmanuel very wisely left the actual waging of the war to the generals. But, like his fellow sovereigns, Albert of the Belgians and Peter of Serbia, he became closely identified with the fighting men. Among the soldiers at the front – that mountainous terrain where Italy and Austria met – Victor Emmanuel earned the reputation of being a conscientious, courageous and deeply concerned monarch. From his quarters – most often the Villa Linussa in the Friuli valley – he emerged each day to make his rounds. The little figure, in his ankle-length greatcoat and tall peaked cap, was everywhere: inspecting installations, asking questions, handing out cigars, eating from a mess tin, murmuring words of encouragement, tending to the sick and comforting the dying. In all weathers and in all conditions, Victor Emmanuel carried out his self-imposed duties. *Il Fante dei Fanti* – the Foot Soldier of the Foot Soldiers – the men called him. Anecdotes about his bravery and his kindness were legion.

'It was a pleasure to see the King among his troops, encouraging them with a genial word and a friendly smile,' wrote the visiting British ambassador. 'One felt that when the war was over he would have friends in every village.' *Il Re Soldato* had not quite eclipsed the Liberal King.

'The King', declared the peasant recruits in wonderment at their monarch's daily appearance among them, 'is like the presence of God.'4

With the passing years, as the war on the Austrian front dragged inconclusively and murderously on, at the cost of Italian lives and morale, King Victor Emmanuel III developed into an almost legendary figure: a monarch who, no matter what his innermost feelings might be, appeared always calm, confident and defiant. His reputation had never stood higher. And it was never to stand so high again.

Another monarch who had been prepared to play a waiting game before committing himself to either side was that arch-intriguer, Tsar Ferdinand of Bulgaria. His position had been almost identical to that of Victor Emmanuel III. He was ready to link his country to whichever side promised better spoils, always provided that they were, or would one day be, in a position to deliver these spoils.

Ferdinand's overriding aim was to regain those areas of Macedonia lost to

Serbia after the Second Balkan War. 'The purpose of my life', he remarked with great bitterness, 'is the destruction of Serbia.' For the Entente Powers, this created a considerable problem. Serbia was their ally, and nothing, it seemed, would convince the Serbs of the advisability of ceding even an inch of their recently won territory to their enemy, Bulgaria. The Central Powers, on the other hand, were in the happy position of being able to offer Ferdinand as much of Macedonia as he liked, for the very good reason that it was not theirs to give away.

Yet Ferdinand was not really enamoured of either Germany or Austria-Hungary. His relations with Wilhelm II had always been strained, and the Habsburg Emperor he described, after a recent visit to Vienna, as 'that idiot, that old dotard of a Francis Joseph'.

Appreciating that the vain Bulgarian sovereign enjoyed being courted, both sides made a point of sending important emissaries to Sophia to try and win him round. (If the emissary happened to be accompanied by a good-looking young blond adjutant, his chances of a sympathetic hearing would be immeasurably improved.) To help entice the Bulgarian Tsar into the Entente camp, the French foreign ministry sent one of Ferdinand's relations, the Duc de Guise. As a prince of Bourbon–Orleans and future pretender to the French throne, the Duc de Guise was regarded as admirably equipped for his task. Who better to persuade Ferdinand, always so proud of his Bourbon blood, of his duty to France?

The mission raised the whole question of royal obligations and loyalties. Over a century before, when Louis XVI had lost his throne in the French Revolution, there was no doubt that he regarded himself – and was regarded – as a king first and a Frenchman second. But by now things had changed. The loyalty of all monarchs was to country before caste. The sympathy of the deposed French Bourbons, for instance, was with France, which happened to be a republic, rather than with Germany or Austria, which happened to be monarchies.

So it was with every justification that Tsar Ferdinand could protest that his first duty was to the country over which he reigned, Bulgaria, and not to the country of his maternal ancestry, France. To the accusation that it would be treasonable for a French Bourbon to join the enemies of France, he could rightly reply by asking if George V of Great Britain and the Tsaritsa Alexandra of Russia were to be blamed for 'betraying' their German blood. In any case, was he not as much his father's son as his mother's – as much German Coburg as French Bourbon? And were there not Coburgs fighting on both sides?

With his sharp sense of irony, Ferdinand would have appreciated the fact that the French republic had felt it necessary to send a prince to win him round; a prince, moreover, who like Ferdinand himself, was a descendant of the very King Louis Philippe whom France had overthrown in 1848.

Ferdinand, having heard the Duc de Guise out, refused to commit himself.

'And now that you have discharged your mission,' he said blandly, 'you must again become my nephew.'

Ferdinand's vacillation, or rather, his hesitation in joining the Central Powers, infuriated Wilhelm II. 'If he doesn't come to his senses,' threatened the Kaiser, 'I'll strike him off the rolls as Honorary Colonel of the Regiment.'

'That would, of course,' noted one member of the Kaiser's suite wryly, 'make him see reason.'[5]

Ferdinand's mind was made up for him by the successes of the Central Powers during the summer of 1915, in the same way that Victor Emmanuel's decision to join the Entente had been influenced by the earlier Allied victory on the Marne. A spectacular German breakthrough on the Russian front, coinciding with an Allied defeat at the hands of the Turks (who had joined the Central Powers in 1914) at Gallipoli, made a great impression on Ferdinand. On 6 September 1915 Bulgaria joined the Central Powers. He hoped, said Tsar Ferdinand to the astonished British minister, about to leave Sofia, that the war would not affect his good personal relations with King George V.

In October the Bulgarians launched their offensive against the Serbs in Macedonia. This time the campaign was glorious. With the combined German and Austrian armies attacking from the north, and the Bulgarians from the east, the Serbs were soundly beaten. By the end of December the whole of Serbian Macedonia was in the hands of Bulgaria. The humiliations of the Second Balkan War had been avenged. Tsar Ferdinand had been vindicated.

Ferdinand's finest hour was rendered finer still by his ceremonial meeting with Kaiser Wilhelm II in the Serbian town of Nish in January 1916. The Kaiser arrived in the new German Balkan Express, that luxurious symbol of the ascendancy of the Central Powers, that ran twice weekly from Berlin to Constantinople. Meeting on the station platform, the two sovereigns made an incongruous-looking pair: the German Kaiser much shorter and squatter than had been imagined, the Bulgarian Tsar tall and hawk-nosed but walking with 'a curious duck-like waddle'. Both were festooned with medals. Forgetting, in this moment of victory, their mutual antipathy, the two men walked arm-in-arm towards the waiting cars.

This new-found harmony pervaded that evening's banquet, when Wilhelm made Ferdinand a field marshal in the Prussian army. Only for a second was there a suspicion that the sly . ᷉dinand might be having a private joke at his fellow sovereign's expense.

'*Ave Imperator, Caesar et Rex, Victor et Gloriosus . . .*' intoned the Bulgarian Tsar to the serenely smiling Kaiser. Was Ferdinand's Latin really so uncertain that he did not know that the generally accepted meaning of the word *gloriosus* was braggart?[6]

★

While Ferdinand of Bulgaria was basking in the sunshine of victory, Peter of Serbia was suffering the darkest days of defeat. Faced by the combined force of the German, Austro-Hungarian and Bulgarian armies, the Serbs had been forced to abandon their recently recaptured capital. Although they fought as magnificently as ever, there was little that they could do to halt the enemy advance. The promised help from their French and British allies never materialised. After the battle of the 'Field of the Blackbirds' in November 1915, the Serbs were obliged to admit defeat. But determined to keep what remained of their army intact to fight another day, they decided to retreat westwards towards the Adriatic.

The retreat of the Serbian army formed one of the great heroic episodes of the First World War. This seemingly endless file of ragged men made, as they staggered along the rutted roads, an extraordinary spectacle: a spectacle rendered more extraordinary because of what they carried with them. To prevent the sacred bodies of their long-dead kings falling into the hands of the enemy, they had brought the royal coffins out of monasteries and had loaded them on to bullock-carts or, if the roads were too bad, on to the shoulders of the accompanying monks. Nor was it only the bodies of their dead kings that were being jolted along the tracks. King Peter, too old and rheumatic to walk, had to be borne, sometimes on an ox-cart, sometimes on a litter; and so did his son, the Regent Prince Alexander, who had been operated on for appendicitis in a wayside cottage.

'It is like some fantastic detail in a Byzantine fresco,' writes Rebecca West, 'improbable, nearly impossible, yet a valid symbol of a truth, that a country which was about to die should bear with it on its journey to death, its kings, living and dead, all prostrate, immobile.'

The most gruelling part of the retreat was across the mountain range that lay between Serbia and the Adriatic, on whose shores the Serbian army hoped to reorganise with French and British help. In appalling conditions, in mud, snow and piercing December winds, hungry, exhausted and dispirited, they battled across the jagged peaks. Almost half of them died on this epic journey.

Their desperate plight was worsened by the behaviour of King Peter's ally and father-in-law, the brigandly old Nicholas of Montenegro. At the beginning of the war, Nicholas had telegraphed Peter, promising him that he would stand by him until death. Serbian and Montenegrin troops had fought side by side during the first few weeks but then, inexplicably, Nicholas had withdrawn his army. It was assumed that, true to form, the old fox had made a secret deal with the Austrians.

When, late the following year, the Serbian army was battling across the mountains of Montenegro on their way to the sea, a royal order went out to the Montenegrin army and police, forbidding them to give or sell food to the starving Serbs. And although Nicholas's army did fight one more battle against the Austrians – at Mount Lovćen – the sudden Montenegrin capitulation merely strengthened Serbian suspicions that Nicholas had betrayed their cause. By January 1916, at the time when Wilhelm II and Tsar Ferdinand were meeting in triumph at Nish, King Nicholas had abandoned his army and fled the country.

Nicholas went to France where, in the fashionable Parisian suburb of Neuilly, he set up a court-in-exile. Living on handsome subsidies from the French, British and Russian governments and invariably sporting his country's colourful national dress, Nicholas was treated with all the deference due to an Allied sovereign. He was taken on an official tour of inspection of the western front; his views on the Balkan situation were listened to with flattering attention.

But as Nicholas had always been one to hedge his bets, he was careful not to sever all relations with the victorious Austrians. His second son, Prince Mirko, was in Vienna. Living on equally generous subsidies, Mirko was being hardly less assiduously courted. Nicholas's explanation – that his son was in the Austrian capital to receive treatment for tuberculosis – fooled very few. The old brigand was simply ensuring that, whatever the outcome of the war, the dynasty would be saved. Self-preservation, after all, was monarchy's first duty.

In the meantime, the tattered Serbian army, with old King Peter on his litter in its midst, reached the Adriatic. From here Prince Alexander appealed to Tsar Nicholas II of Russia for help. 'With feelings of anguish,' answered the Tsar, 'I have followed the retreat of the brave Serb troops across Albania and Montenegro. I would like to express to Your Royal Highness my sincere astonishment at the skill with which, under your leadership, and in face of such hardships and being greatly outnumbered by the enemy, attacks have been repelled and the army withdrawn.'[7]

The Tsar went on to promise that he would repeat his appeals to the French and British to ship the Serbian army to safety.

Help eventually came, and the Serbs were transported, in French and British ships, to the island of Corfu. While the men built up their strength for a counterblow, Prince Alexander, to whom old King Peter had by now delegated all effective power, took control of the situation. The Serbs could hardly have done better. With the look of an alert bantam cock and his air of quiet resolution, Prince Alexander made the ideal wartime leader. Travelling to Rome, Paris and London, he begged the Entente Powers to launch a determined reconquest of his country.

King Peter, meanwhile, moved on to the Greek mainland. He was to remain there for the rest of the war. Looking, in his long white beard, like an Orthodox priest, he survived to see the dream of a Greater Serbia – the creation of Yugoslavia – come true after the war, and to know that he had been proclaimed King of the Serbs, Croats and Slovenes. But by then he was living the life of a recluse.

King Ferdinand of Romania was the next monarch to join the conflict.

His uncle, the steely old King Carol of Romania, had died in October 1914. While this Hohenzollern-born monarch had been alive, there had not been much hope of Romania joining the Entente Powers. Nor would a council of ministers, specially convened by King Carol, permit him to honour his alliance with the Central Powers. Romania was to remain neutral.

But now that Carol had been succeeded by his weak-willed nephew Ferdinand, and, more importantly, by Ferdinand's strong-willed and pro-British wife Marie, the situation was more fluid. The Romanian prime minister, the astute Ion Bratianu, was certainly prepared to take advantage of the conflict for his country's benefit. The result was that both sides immediately began flooding Bucharest with emissaries (as Queen Marie had an eye for a handsome man, the Germans sent as many good-looking officers to the Romanian court as they had to the Bulgarian court of Tsar Ferdinand) and with promises of vast territorial rewards.

But King Ferdinand was not easily won round. He certainly did not share Queen Marie's whole-hearted enthusiasm for the Entente Powers. In truth, he did not even share his prime minister's less outspoken support for them. Like his late uncle, King Carol, Ferdinand was a Hohenzollern. Not only did he have brothers fighting on the German side but he had an unshakable belief in the invincibility of the German army. He realised, too, that his country was in a very bad strategic position for waging war against the Central Powers. Britain and France were far away, and with Austria–Hungary to the west and Bulgaria to the south, Romania would be almost completely surrounded by the enemy. As an ally, Russia, with whom Romania shared a northeastern border, would be too busily engaged elsewhere to give Romania much help.

On the other hand, most of Ferdinand's subjects shared his Queen's eagerness to join the Entente Powers. For one thing, the Romanians felt a close affinity with their fellow Latins in France (was Bucharest not known as 'the Paris of the East'?); for another, a victory over the hated Austro-Hungarian empire would give them Transylvania – that Romanian heartland now occupied by Hungary. Neutrality might have looked like the more sensible course, but only by taking up arms against the Central Powers could the Romanians hope to realise their dream of *Romania Mare* – the aggrandisement of their country and the unification of all their people.

But still, and very understandably, Ferdinand hesitated. In a letter to Wilhelm II, he outlined his dilemma. 'In spite of his personal feelings and

19 The Supreme War Lord: Wilhelm II at the front

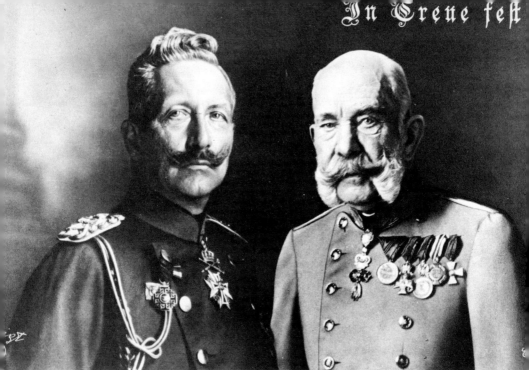

In Treue fest

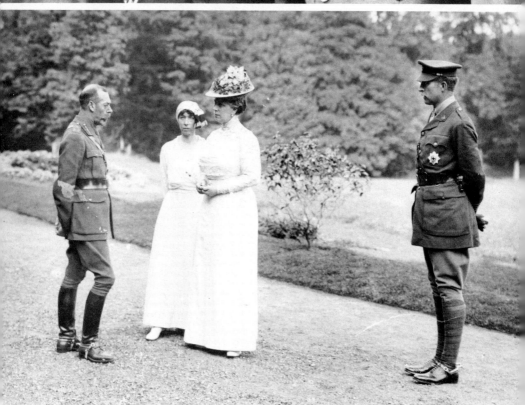

20 Propaganda postcard proclaiming the bond of loyalty between
Wilhelm II and Franz Joseph

21 George V and Queen Mary with King Albert and Queen Elisabeth of
the Belgians, behind the French front line

sympatheties', he explained to the Kaiser, 'he was before all else one with his people, who were clamouring for the liberation of the Romanians living beneath Hungarian sway . . . notwithstanding his old [German] loyalties, he was first and foremost King of his country, and bound by oath to serve it through every sacrifice.'[8]

Wilhelm remained unconvinced. His answer was to send telegrams, *en clair*, through Bucharest to his sister, Queen Sophie of the Hellenes (whose husband, King Constantine, was showing a similar disinclination to join the Central Powers) in which he threatened vengeance on any country who opposed his 'victorious armies and his *Deutscher Gott*'. To the astonishment of his entourage, the Kaiser even wondered whether Romania's hesitation in joining the Central Powers was due to the fact that he had not been pleasanter to Queen Marie during her pre-war visit to Berlin.

While Ferdinand was writing to the Kaiser, Marie – at the request of Bratianu, the prime minister – was writing much more impassioned letters to her cousins, George V and Nicholas II. At great length she described her own *impasse* ('my position is delicate and all my tact is needed, my own sympathies and feelings must be kept well in hand' reads one of her effusions to cousin Georgie) and, at even greater length, put forward Romania's territorial expectations.

Georgie's answers were characteristically terse. It was, thought Marie, more than likely that he simply did not understand the complexity of Romania's territorial ambitions: 'Geography had not been George's strong point,' she claims. But there was nothing wrong with Nicky's geography. 'I must frankly own that we are deeply amazed by your country's *enormous* demands,' he declared.

But, in the end, with the Entente Powers ready to pay almost any price, in the way of eventual territorial rewards, for his support (they were still sore at having let the Bulgarian Tsar slip through their fingers) and with his subjects itching to invade Hungary, Ferdinand made up his mind. On 27 August 1916, Romania declared war on the Central Powers. 'I always knew that it would end like this,' wrote Marie to George V, 'indeed I was confident that it would not be otherwise, but the struggles were hard and poor [Ferdinand] has made a tremendous sacrifice – the greatest that can be asked of a King and of a man . . .'

The decision finally made, the fifty-year-old King Ferdinand took nominal command of his country's armed forces. He did not cut much of a figure. His good qualities – his honesty, his unselfishness, his unswerving sense of duty – did not show to advantage in this particular situation. Nor were his interests suited to the times. Ferdinand enjoyed books, botany and a little quiet conversation. In war, as in peace, he remained diffident and self-effacing; ready to be guided by his government, by his general staff and, not least of all, by his wife.

For, with the outbreak of hostilities, Queen Marie of Romania came into her own. Until now, she had been known chiefly for her theatricality and her decorativeness. Only too aware of her considerable beauty, Marie had done everything to enhance it. Her manner was expansive (her beauty and vivacity were such, remembered Britain's Queen Mother, that even in the most illustrious company 'all eyes immediately turned when Queen Marie entered a room',[9]) her clothes were stagey, her famous gold rooms were furnished in a quasi-Byzantine, self-consciously Bohemian fashion. The courts of Europe seethed with rumours of her love affairs; the Kaiser referred to her as 'that meddlesome little flirt' or 'that English harlot'.[10] But all this she now put behind her. Self-dramatising Queen Marie might have remained, but to the changed situation she brought all her many great qualities: her courage, her compassion, her verve, her resilience and her conscientiousness.

All this, and more, she was to need in the years ahead. From the start, the war was disastrous for Romania. A resolute advance, to liberate their brothers in Transylvania, was checked almost immediately. With their Russian ally slow in coming to their aid (and this in spite of the Queen's hectoring letters to the Tsar) the Romanians faced two invading forces – the Germans and Austro-Hungarians from the north and west, and the Bulgarians from the south. Everywhere the army fell back in confusion. Abandoning hospitals, weapons and stores, the Romanians retreated helter-skelter towards the northeast. On 6 December 1916, just over three months after the Romanian declaration of war, the Kaiser's troops entered Bucharest in triumph.

By this time King Ferdinand had headquartered himself, with his family, his government and his ragged army, at Jassy, a provincial town not far from the Russian frontier. In a way, his position was similar to that of King Albert of the Belgians. For, once Russia had finally come to his aid (there was not really much love lost between the Russians and the Romanians) the German advance had been checked and the front line stabilised. This left the Romanian army in possession of only part of its country's soil.

With the war bogged down in the trenches, life behind the front line settled down to a grim and demoralising routine. Conditions were appalling. The winter of 1916–1917 was the coldest for fifty years. There was mismanagement and inefficiency everywhere. Typhus raged through the army. There was too little food, too few doctors and too few hospital beds. It was feared that the Romanians might be forced to give up what was left to them of their country and retreat into Russia.

The Queen remained the one bright flame in all the blackness of the Romanian situation. In her snowy nurse's uniform, with its vivid red cross on the armband, she was an inspiration to them all; the very symbol of fortitude. Never allowing herself to look anything other than optimistic, she was jolted along muddy roads to work in squalid hospitals and to bring solace to wounded men.

Yet there were times when even her indomitable spirit seemed about to give way. 'Everything seems too hard, too difficult, too completely dreadful, as though no human strength could stand such pressure and not give way to despair,' she once confided to her diary. 'But I *shall* stand it, I have sworn to stand it to the bitter end, it may even be a glorious end; at the deepest depths of my soul, I still believe it will be a glorious end, though I must admit that nothing at the present time justifies this optimism.'

There remained one uncommitted monarch in this turbulent corner of southeastern Europe: the bluff, realistic King Constantine of the Hellenes. And he had no intention of joining either side. Greece, Constantine believed, should remain neutral. Exhausted and depleted by the recent Balkan wars, Greece needed a period of peace to consolidate her gains. Conscious of a powerful bond between himself and his army, the King did not want to expose it to further dangers and privations. In any case, the conflict did not directly concern Greece; the country had no reason to side with any of the belligerents. It was true that Greece had agreed to come to the aid of Serbia, but only if Serbia were attacked by another Balkan state; the quarrel between Serbia and Austria–Hungary had nothing to do with Greece. Constantine's views were shared by his general staff and by many of the Greek people.

So when, just before the outbreak of war, the Kaiser sent Constantine a telegram appealing to him on grounds of 'family ties, friendship and as a field marshal in the German army' to join the Central Powers, the Greek King refused. One of the reasons he gave for remaining neutral was that Greece, if allied to the Central Power, would be at the mercy of the Entente fleets.

Dismissing Constantine's reasons as 'rubbish', the Kaiser sent him an altogether more forceful telegram. 'Things will go badly for anyone who opposes me,' threatened Wilhelm. But Constantine held firm.

The King's neutralist views were not shared by his prime minister, Eleftherios Venizelos. An astute, ambitious and patriotic man, who had held power since 1910, Venizelos had been largely responsible for forming the alliances which had resulted in Greece's spectacular gains during the Balkan wars. Anxious to achieve more spectacular gains still – to realise the 'Great Idea', the dream of an aggrandised Hellenic Empire – Venizelos was all for joining the Entente Powers. With Turkey now allied to Germany, there seemed no reason why Greece could not, by throwing in its lot with Britain and France, finally win Constantinople from the Turks.

This divergence of views between King and prime minister split the country into two irreconcilable camps. It was a situation of which the Entente Powers, anxious for Greek support, took immediate advantage. With

Venizelos's encouragement and despite the fact that Greece was neutral, a combined French and British force landed at Salonika, in northern Greece, in October 1915. From here they hoped to launch an attack on enemy-occupied Serbia. Their arrival led to yet another row between Constantine and Venizelos, and to the prime minister's resignation.

An extraordinary political situation now developed. In Athens, and the south, the King was in control; in Salonika, and the north, the Entente Powers behaved as though the country were theirs. From their entrenched position in Salonika they attacked both the enemy forces along the Serbian and Bulgarian borders, and Constantine's stubbornly neutralist stance in Athens.

Suspecting that Constantine was secretly in league with the Central Powers, Britain and France lost no opportunity of denouncing him. As the most obvious way of blackening his name was to accuse him of being pro-German, the Entente Powers raked up anything that might link the King to the Kaiser. His pre-war speech, for instance, delivered at the banquet at which Wilhelm II had made him a German field marshal, was now cited as 'irrefutable proof' of the King's pro-German leanings. The photograph of Constantine in his field marshal's uniform was used to back up the accusation.

It was in vain that Constantine could protest that George V had often worn the uniform of a German field marshal, and that Wilhelm II had worn a British one. Or that his professed admiration for the German army made him no more a German sympathiser than to admire the British navy made him pro-British. And had he not held firm in the face of the Kaiser's threats? And were not Germany's allies, Turkey and Bulgaria, Greece's bitterest enemies?

An undeniable link between the King and the Kaiser was, of course, Queen Sophie. As Wilhelm II's sister, she was in an invidious position. It was true that Sophie, forty-six years old in 1916, had what were generally considered to be 'Prussian' qualities: that she was efficient, thorough, unbending. With her erect carriage, high-piled hair and stern expression, she could look unapproachable. In lackadaisical Greece, Sophie was regarded as something of a martinet. 'I noticed', writes the celebrated hostess, Roma Lister, meeting Queen Sophie for the first time, 'a stronger personality than exists in most feminine royalties. She was friendly and gracious to all the party, but there was a latent power hidden in her, as in her brother [the Kaiser] – a reversion to the medieval type of sovereign that pierced through the banalties of life.'

But none of this meant that Sophie was in sympathy with Wilhelm II. On the contrary, there had never been much *rapport* between brother and sister; they had quarrelled incessantly. In earlier days, when Wilhelm had been treating their British-born mother, Queen Victoria's daughter the Empress Frederick, so cruelly, Sophie had always sided with the Empress. In fact, Sophie considered Wilhelm to be insufferably ostentatious and ludicrously conceited. Her feelings towards her cousin George V, on the other hand, and for his country generally, were warm. Time and again Sophie voiced her admiration for British institutions and British ways. Britain, not Germany, had always been her second home. Her 'beloved England', she would explain, was the place she loved to be in most.

All this, if it was ever known, was swept away in the flood of vituperation which now poured over Queen Sophie. In the eyes of her critics – the French and British press and those Greek newspapers sympathetic to Venizelos – she was presented as a fanatically pro-German, hard-hearted virago, determined to force her weak-willed husband into fighting for the Kaiser. No story against her was too bizarre to be believed. She would allow only those favourable to the German cause to see the King. She had a private cable installed at their country place, Tatoi, by which she would communicate with German submarines. Constantine's near-fatal illness in 1915 (it was pleurisy) was due to the fact that, during the course of a disagreement between them on the question of Greece joining Germany, Sophie had grabbed a dagger and stabbed him in the chest.

The unhappy Greek situation came to a head in the autumn of 1916 when Venizelos, working hand-in-glove with the Entente Powers, openly defied the King. Following a pro-Entente uprising in Salonika, he quit Athens and made a public announcement of his support for the Entente cause. Arriving in Salonika, he formed a revolutionary Provisional Government in opposition to Constantine's government in Athens.

At this insult to a fellow monarch, Constantine's cousins, George V and Nicholas II, became seriously alarmed. They suddenly found themselves torn between monarchial solidarity and national interests. 'It seems to me', wrote the worried Tsar to the British King, in customary English, 'the protecting powers [Britain and France] in trying to safeguard our interests concerning Greece's neutrality, are gradually immersing themselves too much in her internal home affairs to the detriment of the King.'[11]

After two of Constantine's brothers, Prince George and Prince Andrew of Greece, had visited George V, the British King took the unusual step of approaching his prime minister on the subject. 'Are we justified in interfering to this extent in the internal government of a neutral and friendly country?' he asked. He could not help feeling that 'we have allowed France too much to dictate a policy, and that as a Republic she may be somewhat intolerant of, if not anxious to abolish, the monarchy in Greece.'[12]

George V's apprehensions were justified. On 24 November 1916 Venizelos formally declared war on the Central Powers. With Constantine still stubbornly refusing to abandon his neutrality, the French attitude became more menacing. The French fleet had been anchored off Athens for some months; now a contingent of troops landed at Piraeus and marched on the capital. Much to their astonishment, they were resisted by Greek troops loyal to the King. This was not what Entente propaganda had led them to expect. After a short skirmish, they were forced back.

Constantine's telegram to George V, justifying the action of his troops, received a coldly formal answer. Whatever the British King's personal feelings might have been, as a constitutional monarch he was bound to echo his government's defence of the French action.

The French land attack having floundered, they resorted to bombarding Athens from their ships. When even these bullying tactics failed to coerce those Greeks loyal to the King into joining them, the Entente Powers applied another method. They imposed a strict blockade. For the following eight months, the Greeks all but starved.

'Can Belgium have suffered more at German hands?' demanded the embittered Queen Sophie.

By this stage, Constantine was little better than a prisoner of the Entente. His every move was watched; he almost never left the palace. Convalescence from his attack of pleurisy the year before was slow. For three years after his illness he wore a tube in his back through which a poisonous discharge passed from an incision in his lung. Gradually, this suppurating wound weakened his once powerful physique. According to his brother, Prince Christopher, he 'lost much of his vigour and the capacity for crisp decision that had carried him through so many difficulties in the past. He was no longer master of the situation.' Once so dynamic and impatient, Constantine became dispirited and lethargic.

To see all his work for Greece ruined and his people hounded and hungry depressed him deeply. 'How weary I am of these dirty politics!' wrote Constantine to a friend at the time. 'I have periods of disgust and lassitude which almost bring tears to my eyes . . .'

The quiet centre of all these Balkan upheavals was Schönbrunn Palace outside Vienna where the long life of the eighty-six-year-old Emperor Franz Joseph was coming to an end. The old monarch, whose ultimatum to Serbia had unleashed the whole terrible struggle, had ceased to be in control of either military or civilian affairs. Everything was now being run by the generals and the politicians. His last days coincided with a curious calm in his empire: Serbia and Montenegro had been conquered, the Russian and Italian fronts were static, Romania had been overrun. With the Reichsrat – the Austrian parliament – having been prorogued in 1914, there was a political silence as well. News of the unrest being fomented among the various racial groups hardly penetrated the walls of the palace. In Vienna the populace was apathetic and war-weary.

But, to the end, the old Emperor kept himself busy. On the last day of his life, 21 November 1916, he rose before dawn as always, was rubbed down in cold water and dressed in his uniform. All day long, and in spite of not feeling well, he sat at his desk, reading, writing and signing. When his heir, his great-nephew the young Archduke Karl, came with his wife, Archduchess Zita, to see him, the Emperor told them that he *had* to get well, this was no time for being ill. Soon after six that evening his daughter, Archduchess Marie Valerie, finding him looking flushed, made him go to bed. When his valet asked for instructions, Franz Joseph asked to be wakened, as usual, at half past three the following morning.

Franz Joseph died just after nine that evening. The new Emperor, Karl, brought the old Emperor's long-standing companion, Katherina Schratt, in to see his body. She laid two white roses on his breast.

The funeral was conducted with all the baroque pomp and pageantry of the Habsburg court. Everything – the slowly-pacing troops, the black-plumed horses, the elaborately draped hearse, the massive coffin under its embroidered pall – was in accordance with long-established tradition. But where, in pre-war days, every monarch in Europe would have followed the remains through the streets of Vienna, the Tsar of Bulgaria and the King of Bavaria were the only rulers of any importance – other, of course, than the new Emperor and Empress – to take part in the procession. Not even Kaiser Wilhelm II, who had spoken of Franz Joseph as 'my sole surviving friend in the world', attended. Although in Vienna, it was decided for 'security reasons' that he should not take part in any public ceremonial. It was just as well. Jubilant about the recent victory in Romania, Wilhelm could hardly have matched his mood to the occasion.

For the funeral of the old Emperor was a particularly poignant occasion. Among the tens of thousands of spectators who lined the hushed and wintry streets, few would have remembered the time when Franz Joseph had not reigned over them. And how many of them would have imagined that, in two years time, they would be witnessing the death of his six-hundred-year-old empire?

13

Uneasy Heads

BY THE END OF 1916 Europe's leading monarchs were coming to a fuller realisation of the nature of the conflict in which they had become embroiled. The war had not been the swift, glorious campaign of their early imaginings. Instead of being home by Christmas 1914, their troops were about to face a third winter in the trenches. Any dreams they might have had of spectacular advances, lightning strikes and swashbuckling victory parades had long since faded: the embattled monarchs now found themselves all but powerless witnesses of the most horrific struggle the world had ever experienced.

The days when war had simply been an extension of diplomacy, a sure means of redressing the balance between conflicting claims and interests, had gone forever. Kings would no longer be able to offer up their swords to a fellow monarch after one major defeat, nor wars end with some minor territorial adjustment. The concept of total war, of unconditional surrender, of a fight to the finish, had taken hold. It had become a war of annihilation.

With the conflict deadlocked on all fronts, tens of thousands of lives were being lost in titanic battles, usually for the gain, or loss, of a couple of hundred yards. The casualty lists at such murderous encounters as Verdun, the Somme and on the Russian front were appalling; equally desperate were the lesser-known battles being fought on the Balkan hillsides or the Italian mountains or the plains of Galicia. Millions upon millions of men were being slaughtered. By the end of 1916 the outcome of the war was as uncertain as it had been two years before. 'This war', admitted the Kaiser privately, 'will not end in a great victory.'

The sovereigns were deeply conscious of the mounting death-toll. Misguided and unimaginative they might sometimes have been, but these kings and emperors were none of them heartless men. George V was often on the verge of tears as he read the casualty lists or visited the wounded. 'When I think', wrote the Tsaritsa Alexandra to the Tsar, 'what the losses of lives mean to your heart.' Wilhelm II could sometimes not sleep, it was said, for worrying about the dead and the wounded. 'I never wanted this, I never wanted this,' he was heard to mutter on one occasion.

★

A royal awareness that things had got out of hand, that monarchy must reassert itself, that kings must resume control before it was too late, led to several royal peace feelers being put out during this period.

The first such move, in the spring of 1916, was shrouded in mystery. In conditions of the utmost secrecy, the Grand Duke of Hesse, brother of the Tsaritsa Alexandra of Russia, travelled to Tsarskoe Selo to see Tsar Nicholas II. The step seems to have been taken with the knowledge of the Kaiser but in defiance of the German High Command. This would explain why the Grand Duke never afterwards admitted to it. To this day, the visit is denied by the Hessian archives. But both the Kaiser's daughter, the Duchess of Brunswick-Lüneburg, and his daughter-in-law, Crown Princess Cecilie, referred to it in later years.

'My nephew Prince Friedrich Ernst of Saxony-Altenburg . . .' writes the Duchess of Brunswick-Lüneburg, 'maintained that the Grand Duke of Hesse, with my father's consent, had personally sought out the Tsar in order to get a separate peace, and had gone to Russia under the pseudonym of Thurn-und-Taxis. The Tsar had given his brother-in-law an escort who had been sworn to absolute secrecy. At the transit point which the Grand Duke had to pass through the lines, he was recognised by one of his escort's acquaintances and he, too, was sworn to complete silence.'

But nothing came of this meeting. Today, the chief interest lies in the fact that, years later, Anna Anderson, in her claim to be the Tsar's daughter, Grand Duchess Anastasia, mentioned having seen her 'Uncle Ernest', Grand Duke of Hesse, at Tsarskoe Selo in 1916. As the visit was such a closely guarded secret, known only to a few members of the German and Russian imperial families, Anna Anderson's claim caused a considerable stir.

In later years the Kaiser's family was always to maintain that both Wilhelm II and Nicholas II had been anxious to negotiate a separate peace but that their efforts had been repeatedly foiled by the French and British authorities.

Wilhelm II's next peace feeler, put out in December 1916, was a more overt gesture. He agreed to a proposal by his chancellor, Bethmann-Hollweg, that Germany make a peace offer. With the Romanian capital having fallen to the Germans earlier that month, the Kaiser considered the situation of the Central Powers just good enough for the offer to be made from a position of strength.

But there was more to it than this. The German civilian population, feeling the strain of the British blockade, was becoming increasingly hungry and discontented. Only by allowing unrestricted submarine warfare – which Wilhelm II was anxious to avoid – could the blockade be broken. Peace would avoid the need for this. In addition, President Wilson was about to come up with a peace initiative of his own, and Germany was anxious to beat him to it.

The German Peace Note, issued on 12 December 1916, was purposely vague in tone. Because of this George V, anxious for peace, was afraid that his new prime minister, the impulsive Lloyd George, might reject it out of hand, 'so putting ourselves in the wrong' and 'alienating the sympathy of the moderate party in America'. He begged him to give it most careful consideration.

While the German Peace Note was being considered, President Wilson issued an invitation to the opposing powers to state their peace terms. Neither move achieved anything. The Allies – as the Entente Powers and their co-belligerents were by now being called – saw the German initiative as little more than an empty gesture and rejected it. Yet their own peace terms, drawn up in response to Wilson's request, were so unrealistic that the President found himself unable to discuss them. In any case, the Germans had by then turned down Wilson's invitation. 'I go to no conference,' declared the Kaiser. 'Certainly not to one presided over by him.'

Wilhelm's reaction to the Allies' rejection of the German peace offer was equally high-handed. Switching, with characteristic abruptness, from peacemaker to war lord, the Kaiser announced that Germany's war aims would now have to be extended. 'No concessions to France, King Albert not to be allowed to stay in Belgium, the Flemish coast must be ours,'[1] he thundered.

All this bold talk might have been more impressive had the Kaiser not, by now, been completely subservient to that duo-dictatorship of Hindenburg and Ludendorff. Not only did Wilhelm II have very little say in military matters but the control of civilian affairs was also passing into their hands. In the long run, their brand of authoritarianism was to be disastrous for the monarchy.

The next in the series of peace moves came from Europe's newest monarch – the Emperor Karl of Austria–Hungary.

Twenty-nine in the year that he succeeded his great-uncle the Emperor Franz Joseph, Karl was in many ways an admirable man: honest, goodnatured and well-intentioned. A spell at the Vienna Schotten-gymnasium and two years in various garrison towns and on the Italian and Russian fronts had given him some understanding of the aspirations of ordinary men. They, in turn, had been attracted by his approachability and his simplicity. It was as much for this as for his subsequent efforts at democratising his court and regime, that Karl became known as 'the People's Emperor'.

If some cynics considered the young ruler to be a little naïve and a little too trusting, he was undoubtedly capable of inspiring great loyalty and affection. With his good looks, his boyish smile and his charming manners, the

Emperor Karl brought a humanity to the Austro-Hungarian throne; a humanity notably lacking during the last arid years of Franz Joseph's long reign. He also, despite his almost knightly idealism (and the medievalism of his coronation in Budapest) brought an air of modernity to the hidebound Habsburg court. Unlike Franz Joseph, Karl had a taste for such modern inventions as fast cars and telephones.

The new Emperor's aura of youth and decency was greatly enhanced by the presence of his wife, the twenty-five-year-old Empress Zita. One of the no less than twenty-four children (by two wives) of Duke Robert of Bourbon-Parma – head of Europe's most illustrious non-reigning royal family – the Empress Zita was a beautiful, intelligent and accomplished figure. The couple had been married in 1911 and were to have eight children. Although the Empress in some ways resembled those other strong-minded consorts, Alexandra of Russia, Sophie of Greece and Marie of Romania, she by no means ruled her husband to the extent suggested by Entente propagandists. Being more vivacious, more assertive and more outspoken than Karl, Zita gave the impression of being the dominant partner but, in truth, she was quite ready to follow her husband's lead. Her political interests had a strongly dynastic bias: her Bourbon blood, of which she was inordinately proud, ensured that she favoured France above Prussia.

Together, this young couple exemplified all the cosmopolitanism, courtliness and self-discipline of Europe's royal brotherhood at its best.

If the new Habsburg Emperor was neither iron-willed nor intellectual, he did have a strong sense of vocation. Karl's dedication to the dynasty and the empire was unquestioned. He was also intelligent enough to appreciate that his realm was in need of radical reform; that some sort of federal remedy would be necessary to save the empire. Indeed, his ideas for reform were considerably in advance of his time. Not only was he anxious to reject the latent absolutism of the old Habsburg order and rule as a true constitutional monarch but he was quite prepared to countenance the existence of republics within a federated state.

But as any such scheme would be impossible to implement in wartime and as, in any case, the empire was in grave danger of being torn apart by the war, Karl began to think in terms of ending hostilities. A pious and peace-loving man he wanted, as he made clear in his first public pronouncement, 'to banish, in the shortest possible time, the horrors and sacrifices of war'.

It would not be easy. Karl appreciated that any open peace move would be scotched by his German allies. And so he, the most open of men, was obliged to resort to conspiratorial methods. Within days of his accession, Karl set in train the famous peace move for which he was later to become known, not only as the 'People's Emperor', but as the 'Peace Emperor'.

In a way, the Emperor Karl's peace plot was a reversion to Old World diplomacy. It was a quintessentially royal gesture: the last attempt of twentieth-century monarchy to influence international events to any significant degree. To the horror and hopelessness of war-weary Europe, Karl's peace plot brought a whiff of the *ancien régime*.

The dramatis personae were all royal: the Emperor Karl, the Empress Zita, Zita's mother the Duchess of Bourbon-Parma and two of Zita's many brothers, Prince Sixtus and Prince Xavier. In pre-war Paris these two Bourbon-Parma princes, who considered themselves French, had been well-known figures in social and diplomatic circles. Prince Sixtus, whose name was to be particularly associated with the Peace Plan, was a politically conscious young man. Alive to the obligations of his Bourbon ancestry ('a Bourbon is always a Frenchman', he would say) Sixtus had always favoured an Austro-French alliance; in common with his sister Zita, he had very little love for a Prussian-dominated Germany. As the law of the Third Republic debarred any members of a French royal family from serving in the country's army, the Bourbon-Parma princes had joined the army of the King of the Belgians, where they were serving as lieutenants in the artillery.

But early in 1917 their brother-in-law, the new Habsburg Emperor, entrusted them with a far more important job. They were to sound out the French authorities on the possibility of a negotiated peace. Although Karl did not really favour a separate peace, he would consider one if forced to do so. In the meantime, he planned to keep all knowledge of the negotiations from the Kaiser until a later date. As, technically, they were his enemies, Karl was obliged to make use of a complicated network of royal connections in order to contact his brothers-in-law. His mother-in-law, the Duchess of Bourbon-Parma, acting through the Grand Duchess of Luxembourg, made contact with Queen Elisabeth of the Belgians who, in turn, arranged for King Albert to ask the two Bourbon-Parma princes to go and meet their mother, incognito, in Switzerland.

There now followed several weeks of highly secret diplomacy. Trailing an aura of romantic conspiracy – false papers, confidential letters, clandestine meetings, journeys in and out of neutral Switzerland – the Bourbon-Parma princes acted as negotiators between the Emperor Karl and his foreign minister on the one hand, and the French president and his prime minister on the other. At one stage President Poincaré even suggested that they go and see Tsar Nicholas II: as princes they would have immediate access to and considerable influence on the Tsar.

Climax to all this frenzied activity came with a secret meeting between the Habsburg Emperor and the Bourbon-Parma princes. The meeting took place, on a snowy day in March 1917, in the old Habsburg castle of Laxenburg, just south of Vienna. The princes found their brother-in-law looking pale and worried: his hair was already touched with grey. 'It is absolutely essential to make peace, I want it at any price,' announced Karl. If his German allies proved unco-operative, then Austria could not 'continue to fight for the King of Prussia'.[2]

The family greetings over, Karl, Zita and the two princes were joined by Count Czernin, the Austrian foreign minister. While agreeing that all knowledge of the negotiations should be kept from their German allies, Czernin, unlike Karl, would not even consider the possibility of a separate Austro-Hungarian peace. At the end of their talks, the following day, Karl handed the princes a letter written in his own hand. In it he agreed, among other things, to the restoration of the sovereignty of enemy-occupied Belgium and Serbia and, more important, to what he called the 'just claims' of France to Alsace-Lorraine. This *Kaiserbrief*, which Czernin was afterwards to claim he had not seen or sanctioned, was to cause poor Karl considerable distress in due course.

The reaction of both the French and British authorities to the Emperor Karl's overtures was reassuring. Lloyd-George, who was particularly taken with Karl's proposals, suggested a meeting between the three Allied heads of state – George V, Victor Emmanuel III and President Poincaré – and their prime ministers, to discuss the matter. He also arranged for Prince Sixtus to see George V. The meeting went very well. 'It would be a great thing if [the peace negotiations] could be brought about,' noted the King in his diary.

There was less progress in the opposition camp. In fact, there was no progress at all. On 3 April 1917, Karl and Zita travelled to the Kaiser's headquarters at Homburg on the pretext of introducing the two empresses. Karl had already referred, obliquely, to his peace proposal during the Kaiser's visit to Vienna a few weeks before; now he hoped to discuss it more fully. He never did. Somehow the opportune moment never presented itself; Wilhelm seemed reluctant to enter into any serious discussion. Perhaps he had been warned not to. 'If we had a friend in Germany it was the Emperor William,' the Empress Zita afterwards said, 'but he was completely under the thumb of his generals.'[3]

King Victor Emmanuel, too, was at the mercy of others. Although he was in favour of talks, his prime minister, Baron Sonnino, was not. The Italian government was simply not prepared to negotiate with Austria, other than after an Italian victory. Having been enticed away from the Central Powers by Entente promises of vast spoils from the Habsburg Empire, Italy was not prepared to settle for anything less. And whereas the Emperor Karl was quite happy to hand over German-occupied territory to France, he was not quite so ready to give up any of his own inheritance to Italy. Italy, after all, was Austria–Hungary's chief enemy; the Italian campaign was the only 'popular' campaign of the war.

None the less, appreciating that some sacrifice would have to be made, Karl agreed to meet certain Italian demands. He wrote a second letter, in which he offered to give up Trentino. But, for Italy, this was not enough. She wanted all her *terre irredente*. And so, whatever King Victor Emmanuel's thoughts on the Emperor Karl's offer might have been, he was obliged, as a constitutional monarch, to accede to the wishes of his prime minister.

Once again, then, the hopes of a negotiated peace, presided over by the various crowned heads, faded away. It had been, perhaps, the last chance for the monarchs of central Europe to save their thrones. Other feelers were to be put out: through the mediation of the Pope, and of the neutral sovereigns King Alfonso XIII of Spain, Queen Wilhelmina of the Netherlands and King Christian X of Denmark, but they, too, were destined for failure. For by that time there would have been a dramatic transformation in the progress of the war.

The collapse of the Kaiser's peace moves, early in 1917, had given his High Command – Hindenburg and Ludendorff – exactly the excuse they needed for the introduction of unrestricted submarine warfare. They felt certain that this would bring Britain to its knees in six months. But what it did was to bring the United States into the war. On 6 April 1917, after the sinking of several American merchant vessels by German submarines, the United States declared war on Germany.

And there was another reason for the United States' entry into the war. President Wilson's not quite valid claim – that this was a struggle between democracy and autocracy, between liberal parliamentarianism and monarchic militarism – had been given credence by the removal of one major obstacle: on 15 March 1917, three weeks before the American declaration of war, the autocratic Tsar Nicholas II of Russia had been forced to abdicate.

'There are rumours of serious trouble at the Russian court,' wrote Queen Marie of Romania in her diary on 8 January 1917, two months before the Tsar's abdication. 'It is said that the much-hated Rasputin has been killed . . . and that the Imperial Family is in revolt against the Empress, clamouring that she should be sent to a convent. She is extraordinarily hated and some event unknown to me must have brought this hatred to a climax. Anyhow, something uncanny and dreadful is going on there . . .'

Queen Marie was right. Something uncanny and dreadful was indeed going on at the Russian court. On the first day of January 1917 Rasputin's corpse had been found under the ice of one of the tributaries of the frozen River Neva in the capital. He had been murdered three days before by a party of conspirators headed by young Prince Felix Yussoupov.

The Kaiser, in his convoluted fashion, saw the murder of Rasputin as a deliberate move against his plans for a separate peace with the Tsar. The *starets*, claimed Wilhelm, had always favoured such a peace. 'Against him was the party of Princes, the nationalistic bourgeoisie organised by parliament and the English will for war incorporated in Ambassador Sir George

Buchanan and the military commander, Colonel Knox. As these adversaries recognised Rasputin's influence, they went to work. Rasputin was just murdered and the Tsar's kingdom wiped out by the democratic revolution supported by England.'[4]

This was nonsense. Rasputin's murder had been, from first to last, a monarchist act: a desperate attempt by the monarchists to save the monarchy. Both the effete Prince Yussoupov and the other leading conspirator, Grand Duke Dmitry Pavlovich, were members of the imperial family; and if Rasputin's murder did not actually have the sanction of other family members, they were certainly not sorry to see the end of the *starets*. They hoped that his murder would weaken, and indeed destroy, the Tsaritsa's power, leaving the Tsar free to follow a less authoritarian and less disastrous course.

That some sort of drastic action needed to be taken in Russia had been apparent for some time. Between them, the Tsaritsa and Rasputin had reduced the government to a mockery. Determined that the principle of autocracy should be upheld and that ministers were there simply to carry out the Tsar's will, they had dismissed – or had insisted that the Tsar dismiss – anyone who disagreed with them. One by one competent ministers had been replaced by nonentities. And even ministers of unquestioned loyalty to the autocratic ideal had fallen from power because of Rasputin's antipathy towards them. In the end, the government consisted mainly of Rasputin's nominees.

Nor did their combined meddling stop with the appointing and dismissing of ministers. There was no aspect of national life to which the pair did not turn their attention. The *starets* advised the Tsaritsa on economic and military matters as well. His instructions, coming from God and passed on by Alexandra, reached the harassed Tsar in a steady stream. And if ever Nicholas hesitated to put these instructions into effect, Alexandra would back them up with her hectoring letters.

'Be firm,' she wrote on one occasion, 'one wants to feel your hand – how long, years, people told me the same – "Russia loves to feel the whip" – it's their nature – tender love and then the iron hand to punish and guide. How I wish I could pour my will into your veins . . . Be Peter the Great, Ivan the Terrible, Emperor Paul – crush them all under you . . .'

By the end of 1916 it was the Tsaritsa's famous mauve boudoir at Tsarskoe Selo, and not the Tsar's wooden pavilion at *Stavka*, that had become the nerve centre of the Russian empire. Serenely unaware of her limitations, obsessed by her inaccurate picture of Holy Russia, convinced that everything she was doing was for the good of the country, Alexandra battled on. Not an evil, nor a heartless, nor even an entirely foolish woman, the Tsaritsa was an extremely misguided one.

22 Nicholas of Montenegro, in customary national dress, with
General Allenby

23 Peter of Serbia being helped onto his horse during the disastrous campaign of 1915

24 Victory in Serbia: Wilhelm II drives in triumph beside Ferdinand of Bulgaria

Inevitably, she was accused of being Rasputin's mistress. For what other reason, it was argued, would she be so intimate with this coarse-mannered and lecherous *moujik*? And, just as inevitably, she was accused – this German-born Tsaritsa – of working together with Rasputin for a German victory. No less than other sovereigns was Alexandra paying the price for belonging to Europe's inter-related family of kings. Was not her brother, the Grand Duke of Hesse, fighting with the German army, and one of her sisters married to the Kaiser's brother? Indeed, was the Kaiser not her cousin?

It was conveniently forgotten that the Tsaritsa was also Queen Victoria's grand-daughter; that, because of the early death of her mother – Queen Victoria's daughter Alice – Alexandra had spent a great deal of her youth at Victoria's court. And surely George V was as much her cousin as Wilhelm II?

Just as yet another of her cousins, Queen Sophie of Greece, was being accused of being in direct touch with the Kaiser, so was Alexandra. The palace at Tsarskoe Selo was said to have been fitted with secret wireless sets by which the Tsaritsa and Rasputin communicated with the enemy. She even had a direct telephone line to the German Emperor. Military information, nagged out of her husband, was either passed direct to the Kaiser or else sold by Rasputin to the German authorities. How else could Russia's military disasters be explained away? And for what other reason was the populace suffering such serious food shortages than to facilitate the handing over of the country to the Germans?

As hunger and dissatisfaction spread, so did the cry against the 'traitress' become louder. On the streets they were openly calling the Tsaritsa *Nemka* – 'the German woman' or, more graphically, 'the German whore'.

Rasputin's murder, early in January 1917, did little to temper the widespread hatred of Alexandra. Those who had imagined that the death of the *starets* would put an end to her political influence were soon proved wrong: she played a more active part than ever. To any suggestion that she withdraw from the political scene, the Tsar turned a deaf ear. Nor would he listen to any talk of choosing a government more acceptable to the Duma. Time and again he was warned – by members of the imperial family, by ambassadors, by politicians – that the Tsaritsa's attitude was leading, not only the dynasty, but all Russia, to disaster.

'Your Majesty,' begged Rodzianko, chairman of the Duma and one of the last to warn the Tsar of the dangers of the Tsaritsa's insistence on autocratic rule, 'do not compel the people to choose between you and the good of the country.'

For a moment the Tsar seemed to waver. 'Is it possible', he asked, 'that for twenty-two years I tried to act for the best and that for twenty-two years it was all a mistake?'

'Yes, Your Majesty,' was Rodzianko's frank answer, 'for twenty-two years you have followed the wrong course.'

But Nicholas's spasm of self-doubt – or rather, of doubt in the autocratic principle – was short-lived. Completely in tune with Alexandra's thinking, he was determined that the autocracy should be passed on, untainted by democracy, to their son.

With the Tsar refusing to listen to reason, there were mutterings about more drastic methods of getting rid of Alexandra. Once more the imperial family felt that it was up to them to save the monarchy. The Tsar's grand-ducal relations decided to stage a palace revolution: the Tsaritsa would be arrested, the Tsar forced to abdicate in favour of his son, and Grand Duke Nicholas proclaimed Regent. For several weeks, the plot was the talk of the capital.

'Yesterday evening,' noted the French ambassador, 'Prince Gabriel Constantinovich gave a supper for his mistress, formerly an actress. The guests included the Grand Duke Boris . . . a few officers and a squad of elegant courtesans. During the evening the only topic was the conspiracy – the regiments of the Guard which can be relied on, the most favourable moment for the outbreak, etc. All this with the servants moving about, harlots looking on and listening, gypsies singing and the whole company bathed in the aroma of Moët and Chandon *brut impérial* which flowed in streams.'[5]

But nothing came of it. In the spring of 1917 the Tsar returned to the front and the Tsaritsa continued to rule through the utterly incompetent ministers.

The storm broke on 8 March 1917. The immediate cause was a drastic lack of food and fuel in the capital. A mob, cold and hungry, broke into several bakeries. During the following days the rioting became more serious and workers came out on strike. On 12 March the soldiers – many of them new, undisciplined, disaffected recruits – began joining the mob, with regiment after regiment rising against its officers. By the following day almost the entire capital was in the hands of the revolutionaries. The imperial government collapsed and power passed to the Duma. A rival assembly – a 'Soviet of Soldiers' and Workers' Deputies', created by the fiery Kerensky – took its place beside the more moderate Duma. On 14 March the Tsar's last bastion, the Imperial Guard, pledged allegiance to the Duma. Leading the Marine Guard on its way to support the Duma was the first member of the imperial family to break with the Tsar: his cousin, Grand Duke Cyril. The revolution had triumphed.

Yet, in triumphing, the revolution had taken not only the monarchy, but the revolutionary leaders themselves, by surprise. The revolution of March 1917 might have been prepared for by the men of the Left, but it was not they who had started it.

Nicholas had just arrived back at headquarters when the trouble erupted. At first, he refused to take it seriously. The disturbances in the capital, five hundred miles away, were described to him as 'street disorders'; and street disorders were nothing new to the Tsar. His response, on finally appreciating that the situation was more serious than he had imagined, was to send military reinforcements and to suspend the Duma. Only after receiving a telegram from the Tsaritsa and a telephone call from his brother, Grand Duke Michael, did he decide to return to Tsarskoe Selo. He left the front on 13 March, the day after the Duma assumed power.

His train never reached Tsarskoe Selo. It was obliged to halt, some hundred miles south of the capital, at Pskov. While he waited there, the situation steadily deteriorated. By the morning of 15 March, Nicholas had heard that the Provisional Government had decided that he must abdicate in favour of his son, with his brother Michael acting as Regent. This decision was backed up by a series of telegrams from the generals commanding the various fronts, all urging him to give up the throne.

Without the support of either the politicians or the generals, Nicholas had no choice. Displaying, in this moment of supreme crisis, his customary blend of dignity, courtesy and fatalism, the Tsar agreed to abdicate. In the hushed drawing-room of the imperial train he renounced not only his own rights but those of his invalid son. He dare not expose the haemophilic boy to the rigours of ruling a country such as Russia.

'For the sake of Russia and to keep the armies in the field,' he wrote in his diary that evening, 'I decided to take this step.'[6]

The imperial crown now passed to Grand Duke Michael. His reign was all too brief. Within hours the ineffectual Tsar Michael had been talked into abdicating.

In the course of one week, to the astonishment of the world and the consternation of Europe's monarchs, the proud, powerful, three-hundred-year-old Romanov dynasty had collapsed.

14

'Thrones at a Discount'

THE OVERTHROW of Tsar Nicholas II sounded like a death knell through the courts of Europe. No matter how much the monarchs might tell themselves, and each other, that Russia was a special case, that the circumstances of the Tsar's fall had been exceptional, that it was really the Tsaritsa and Rasputin who were to blame, they could not help feeling apprehensive about their own thrones. Might not the overthrow of autocratic rulers – or, indeed, of any rulers – prove infectious?

The young Emperor Karl certainly thought so. It gave his search for a negotiated peace an added urgency. 'We are fighting against a new enemy which is more dangerous than the Entente,' he warned Wilhelm II, 'against international revolution which finds its strongest ally in general starvation. I beseech you not to overlook this portentous aspect of the matter and to reflect that a quick finish to the war – even at the cost of heavy sacrifice – gives us a chance of confronting the oncoming upheaval with success.'

If the monarchs of the Central Powers were not able to conclude peace during the next few months, he added, 'the peoples will go over their heads and the waves of the revolutionary flood will sweep away everything for which our brothers and sons are fighting and dying.'[1]

Whether all their 'brothers and sons' were fighting to preserve the monarchical system was debatable, but more enlightened monarchists were coming to the realisation that the days of even semi-autocracy were numbered. President Wilson's peace aims, ringingly announced on the entry of the United States into the war, strengthened this realisation. Eyes gleaming with idealistic fervour, Wilson claimed that Americans were fighting 'for democracy, for the right of those who submit to authority to have a voice in their own government, for the rights and liberties of small nations . . .'

His pronouncement was not lost on the Kaiser's chancellor, Bethmann-Hollweg. Three days after Wilson's speech, Bethmann, who was also prime minister of Prussia, proposed an immediate introduction of universal suffrage to replace the present élitist suffrage in the Prussian parliament. His proposal was backed up by an Easter Message from the Kaiser to the effect that 'after the massive contributions of the entire nation in this terrible war, I am sure that there is no room left for Prussia's class suffrage.'

But Hindenburg and Ludendoff were having none of it. First they engineered Bethmann's dismissal and then, having assured the appointment of a more amenable chancellor, saw to it that the 'class suffrage' remained unchanged. Nor would they have any truck with the Reichstag's proposal for a compromise peace; not, at least, until it had been couched in the most innocuous terms.

The Emperor Karl was finding it equally difficult to introduce constitutional changes. If his first reaction to the Tsar's overthrow had been to urge the Kaiser to make peace, his second was to give his regime some semblance of democracy. The Austrian parliament, which had been suspended at the beginning of the war, was hastily recalled. Nor did Karl intend to leave it at that. Already this humane and sensible monarch had amnestied many political prisoners; now he planned to take an even bolder step. He would grant national autonomy to all the peoples of his empire. But his conservative politicians would not hear of it. And lacking both the strength to push through these sweeping changes himself and a sympathetic prime minister to do it for him, Karl was obliged to give way. His constitutional project was shelved.

Like the failure of his peace plan, Karl's inability to reform his empire meant that a splendid opportunity had been missed. Seldom has a road to hell been paved with better intentions.

Other monarchs, such as Ferdinand of Romania, acted, or were encouraged to act, more resolutely. To forestall any revolutionary uprising by the Romanian peasantry, the King made a 'historic' promise to his troops. Standing in the chill spring wind on the plains beyond Jassy, he assured the assembled soldiers that after the war there would be a more equitable distribution of land. The great estates would be broken up and divided out among the peasants. They would also be allowed to take 'a larger part' in public affairs.

It was a bold move, especially for a Balkan monarch. By risking the wrath of the wealthy, landowning classes, the monarchy was loosening its close ties with its natural supporters. Yet it was a step that had to be taken. And it had to be taken, not only by the King of Romania, but by all monarchs. Only by distancing itself from the conservative aristocracy and by developing into a supra-national institution, could monarchy hope to ride out the storms already breaking about its head. Where a sovereign, such as the Kaiser, relied too heavily on the support of the military and civilian élite, he was doomed. For it was usually the monarchists themselves who undermined the monarchy by refusing to allow it to broaden its base.

'Most of the monarchies of Europe', claimed Prince Philip, Duke of Edinburgh, in later years, 'were really destroyed by their greatest and most ardent supporters. It was the most reactionary people who tried to hold on to something without letting it develop and change.'[2]

Even that apparently unassailable sovereign, George V, was experiencing a distinct feeling of apprehension. As early as 1915, Lord Esher, the *eminence grise* of Edward VII's reign, had warned Queen Mary 'that after the war thrones might be at a discount'. Now, with the Russian throne having been well and truly discounted, Esher's warning took on an added significance. A mass meeting, held in the Albert Hall to celebrate the fall of Tsardom, seemed, to some, to herald the birth of revolutionary republicanism in Britain. It was followed by a letter to *The Times* in which the celebrated H.G. Wells claimed that the moment had come to 'rid ourselves of the ancient trappings of throne and sceptre' and for the setting up of republican societies.

Within the palace itself there was an awareness that something must be done to counteract this anti-monarchist chill in the air. 'We must endeavour', wrote the King's private secretary, Lord Stamfordham, 'to induce the thinking working classes, socialist and others, to regard the Crown, not as a mere figurehead and as an institution which, as they put it, "don't count", but as a living power for good . . .'[3] And George V's assistant private secretary, Clive Wigram, suddenly woke up to the fact that more use should be made of the hitherto ignored press to advertise the tireless wartime activities of the King and Queen.

For there was no doubt that the royal couple had fully identified themselves with their country's struggle. Although George V was not actively involved in the military conduct of the war, he followed its progress with great interest. On five occasions he crossed to France to spend a few days with the army; on one of these he was thrown from his horse and severely injured. At home he dedicated himself to an apparently ceaseless round of gruelling duties: reviewing troops, inspecting naval bases, conferring decorations, touring munitions factories and visiting hospitals.

But not even these conscientiously undertaken tasks could counteract the rumours that the King's support for the Allied cause was less than whole-hearted. As much as any other sovereign, George V suffered for his mixed ancestry. By the year 1917, with victory over Germany seeming as remote as ever, his German blood – and alleged German sympathies – had become the subject of malicious slander. H.G. Wells spoke out against the 'alien and uninspiring court'; to which jibe the King answered, 'I may be uninspiring, but I'll be damned if I'm alien.'

Yet George V took the criticism of his German ancestry seriously enough to come to a momentous decision: he would change the name of his House. He had ascended the throne as a member of the House of Saxe-Coburg and Gotha (although, on being consulted, the College of Heralds thought that the name might more properly be 'Wettin' or even 'Wipper'). In any case, it was agreed that the King should adopt the uncompromisingly British name of

'Windsor'. This was done and the new name was proclaimed on 17 July 1917.

All in all, this royal name-change was a supremely nationalistic and patriotic gesture. No less than someone like Tsar Ferdinand, who had felt that his duty to Bulgaria overrode his duty to his Bourbon ancestry, was George V putting his country before his dynasty.

Nor was the change confined to the King's immediate family. Various Teck and Battenberg princes re-emerged with such mellifluously Anglicised surnames and titles as Mountbatten, Cambridge, Athlone, Milford Haven and Carisbrooke; while those two grand-daughters of Queen Victoria, the princesses of Schleswig-Holstein, became, as the King robustly put it, 'Helena Victoria and Marie Louise of *Nothing*'.

The change did not please everyone. Some regarded it as a betrayal of monarchical clanship; it has even been described as 'a loss of nerve'[4] on the part of George V. Prince Alexander of Teck, who had been metamorphosised into the Earl of Athlone, announced himself 'furious' at the change. 'He thought that kind of camouflage stupid and petty,' said his wife, Princess Alice. And another dynastically conscious observer, the Bavarian nobleman, Count Albrecht von Montgelas, considered that 'the true royal tradition died on that day in 1917 when, for a mere war, King George V changed his name.'[5]

But perhaps the wittiest reaction came from the Kaiser. The title of that well-known Shakespearean play, he scoffed, was to be changed to 'The Merry Wives of Saxe-Coburg and Gotha'.

The King whose kingdom had been reduced to a mere twenty square miles of his country's soil – Albert of the Belgians – had little reason for fearing a revolutionary upheaval. It was true that, in occupied Belgium, the Germans were doing their utmost to divide the country along racial lines by encouraging Flemish nationalism but, in the main, the Belgians remained loyal to their absent King. To the members of all political parties, Albert had become the symbol of Belgian resistance, their hope for a better future.

Among the soldiers, crowded on to that strip of featureless Flemish landscape behind the sandbags and barbed-wire entanglements of the front line, the King was immensely popular. The royal family – Albert, Elisabeth and their three children – had established themselves in a doleful little villa in the seaside resort of La Panne, eight miles from the front line and a stone's throw from the French frontier. The house was spartan in the extreme. When the visiting Princess Alice, Countess of Athlone, once asked Queen Elisabeth how she could bear to go on living, for year after year, in such discomfort, the Queen explained that to make the house more comfortable would be to accept it as home. She would not allow herself to believe that they would go on living there much longer.

From this villa, the royal couple would emerge each day to carry out their self-imposed duties. Although the war had become largely one of attrition, not a day passed without some action along the Belgian front, often slight, occasionally massive. Danger was as prevalent as boredom, frustration and despair. The King and Queen faced all these trials with equanimity. Like Marie of Romania, similarly established in a corner of her country on the far side of the Continent, Elisabeth devoted herself to nursing the wounded. It was she who had encouraged the doctors in the setting up of field hospitals and who, faced with the lack of even the most elementary medical facilities, had simply telephoned Harrods in London to order whatever was needed. Harrods had fulfilled the order in a matter of days.

The Queen visited the hospitals every day. Sometimes she assisted the doctors, at other times she comforted the wounded. Her calm in the face of danger always astonished the men. Whether in the wards or in the trenches, she would continue her rounds, seemingly impervious to bursting shells. Once, when a hospital was struck and set ablaze, she refused to be whisked away to safety. She worked tirelessly, helping the nurses get the patients out of the burning building. When the raid was over and the wounded accommodated elsewhere, the doctor in charge complimented her on her courage. In what way, answered the Queen with a wry smile, had her courage differed from that of the nurses?

Dressed in white, Elisabeth would spend hour upon hour with the wounded. She would move from one bed to the next, smiling, questioning, comforting. Dying soldiers would call to her as to a mother; many died in her arms. The face of their little Queen was the last thing to be seen by many a Belgian soldier.

As the years went by, so more and more did Queen Elisabeth become an object of veneration. She was the sun, it has been said, of that grey winter. So small, so frail, she seemed to epitomise the spirit of her country's struggle. She became 'The Heroine of the Yser', 'The Mother of the Army', 'The Soul of Belgium'. To the men, bogged down for year after year in the hell of the trenches, it seemed in no way excessive when it was predicted that their Queen would one day be known as Saint Elisabeth of Belgium.

Yet not even the gloom and danger of her surroundings could repress the Queen's startling individuality: the romantic, theatrical, bohemian side of her nature. She was, after all, a member of the artistic and eccentric Wittelsbach family. In the grounds of that bleak villa, she had had a movable wooden pavilion erected. Here she would entertain those poets, musicians and artists in whose company she always took such delight. The interior of the bungalow, says one visitor, the French writer Pierre Loti, was entirely hung with pale blue Persian silk, relieved with a touch of rose-pink and decorated with a large design representing the portico of a mosque. Its furniture consisted solely of divans, piled high with brightly patterned cushions. Here, in her animated, sharp-witted fashion, Elisabeth talked to him about the religions of the East. And there were not many courts in Europe in which the religions of the East could be discussed with any degree of intelligence.

In a rather different way, King Albert was also winning the devotion of the troops. By now this shy, gauche and diffident sovereign had emerged as a man of immense stature: brave, resolute, realistic. Yet for all his worldwide reputation, Albert remained self-depreciating, with a solemn, preoccupied air and a painfully slow way of expressing himself. To read through the war diary he kept during these dismal years on the Yser is to come to some appreciation of his strength of character. He emerges from the scrawled pages as simple, as modest, as prudent, as sensible and as brave as legend has always claimed him to be. There are no histrionics, no delusions, nor is there any vindictiveness; the tone throughout is practical, highlighted by that vein of cynicism which ran so strongly through his nature.

In spite of all temptation he remained level-headed, refusing to indulge in what he called the 'exaggerated patriotism' of some of his fellow monarchs, or in the defeatist attitudes of some of his colleagues. So honest himself, he found the rhetoric of some of the Allied politicians highly distasteful. 'What does the *struggle for right* mean?' he asked himself; or 'a fight for civilisation', or 'to go on to the end'?

Albert's war aims, from first to last, remained constant. He was dedicated to defending Belgian independence and Belgian neutrality. He was seeking neither glory nor revenge nor gain. He was simply fighting for the right of his country to live in peace, free of any international entanglements. With those members of his government, by now established at Le Havre in France, who cried out in terms of vengeance, of eventual territorial aggrandisement at the expense of Germany, he would have no truck. He was too good a European, and too much of a monarch, to join in the clamour for a war of annihilation.

When the Allies compiled their joint answer to President Wilson's note on their war aims, Albert resisted his government's pressure to include Belgium in the answer. Belgium's war aims were not the same as France's or Britain's, he explained to his ministers; they were not fighting to destroy Germany. As a result of his stand, Belgium sent a separate answer to Wilson.

These same, very human qualities were evident in the King's dealings with his soldiers. 'In the name of so-called liberty,' he afterwards wrote, 'we asked of free men, in the twentieth century, much more than what was ever extorted from the serfs in the Dark Ages – and they gave it.'[6] Conscious of this, he did what little he could to lighten their load. No aspect of their daily lives was too trivial for his notice. Were they warm enough? Did they get enough vegetables? Were they bothered by rats?

Stories of his unheralded appearances amongst them, so different from the carefully orchestrated visits of sovereigns like Wilhelm II or George V, were legion. 'Close the bloody door!' shouted a private as his monarch, with characteristic awkwardness, came shuffling into a wooden hut. 'Careful with the sandbags!' barked another when the King looked in to see what he was doing. On asking a soldier the time and finding out that the embarrassed man had no watch, Albert saw to it that one was delivered to him the following morning.

One day, on walking past the villa in which one of his officers was billeted, Albert noticed the young officer sitting in the garden with his wife. As this was contrary to regulations and as it was too late for the young woman to escape into the house, the officer hurried forward to make his excuses.

'Your Majesty has caught me out,' he stammered. 'I am here with my wife.'

'And I also am here with mine,' answered the King quietly.

On another occasion, when two soldiers were wandering about the dunes in search of rabbits, they spotted an officer trudging towards them.

'A general!' exclaimed one, preparing to bolt.

'No,' answered the other, greatly relieved, 'only the King.'

Albert returned their salutes gravely and strode on across the sands.

Perhaps the most telling tribute to King Albert's fortitude comes from his biographer, Emile Cammaerts. 'Those who saw La Panne during the years of waiting', he afterwards wrote, 'will never forget that tall and austere figure on that last strip of Belgian shore confronted with stormy clouds and foaming sea, watching with calm courage during that long vigil, with all the regal splendour stripped from his Court, and almost all his land torn from his friendly grasp, alone against the blind elements and blinder injustice of man, with no comfort but his Queen, brought as low as any Sovereign could be brought by the forces of destiny, and as high as any man can be raised by the conviction of his right and the faith in his cause . . .'

One afternoon, when the King was visiting the trenches to ask the men if there was anything they needed, one soldier, bolder than the rest, asked in return, 'And you, Sire, don't you want anything?'

For a moment the King was silent. Then, in his halting way, he gave his answer. 'I should like to go back to Brussels,' he said.

As one, the men moved forward and crowded around him.

'Let us take you there!' they cried.

Seldom has the royal instinct for self-preservation, already brought into play on the fall of the Russian throne, been more graphically illustrated than in George V's handling of the matter of the Tsar's future.

On first hearing of Nicholas II's abdication, the King was all sympathy. 'Events of last week have deeply distressed me,' he wired to the Tsar on 19 March 1917. 'My thoughts are constantly with you and I shall always remain your true and devoted friend, as you know I have been in the past.'

Wilhelm II was hardly less distressed. Regarding the Tsar as a fellow monarch rather than as an enemy, he gave secret orders that the Russian imperial family should be allowed to pass freely through the German lines and that a special train and guard of honour should be placed at the Tsar's disposal. Through the offices of Christian X of Denmark, he offered the Russian Provisional Government safe passage for any warship carrying the imperial family through the Baltic. Wilhelm's brother Henry, as Commander-in-Chief of naval forces in the Baltic, was told to make sure that any ship flying the Tsar's personal standard was to pass unmolested. 'I have done everything humanly possible for the unhappy Tsar and his family,'[7] claimed the Kaiser.

For it was generally assumed that the Tsar would be allowed to share the fate of most other fallen monarchs by being sent into exile; and that – again like many another fallen monarch – this exile would be spent in Britain.

But it was not going to be quite so simple. Although the Russian Provisional Government was ready enough to get the imperial family away to safety, the Soviet – that more militant assembly of soldiers' and workers' deputies – was determined that the Tsar should be kept imprisoned. So while the imperial family and a band of loyal attendants remained under guard in the echoing rooms of the Alexander Palace at Tsarskoe Selo, the Provisional Government considered how best to spirit them out of the country.

George V's telegram to Nicholas had strengthened the conviction of Russia's new foreign minister that it must be to Britain that the imperial family should go. He asked the British ambassador, Sir George Buchanan, to approach his government on the matter. In a series of increasingly urgent telegrams, the ambassador begged the British government to agree to the Russian request. Finally, after a meeting attended by George V's private secretary, Lord Stamfordham, on 22 March 1917, Lloyd George decided to grant asylum to the imperial family. His decision had not been taken lightly: the Liberal prime minister had very little sympathy for the fallen Tsar. But as he had the highest regard for the new revolutionary government in Russia, and as the request had come from them and not from the Tsar himself, Lloyd George agreed to it.

The King's reservations, expressed through Lord Stamfordham, seem to have been confined – at this stage – to the practicalities of the business. George V did not want to be saddled with the expense of accommodating and keeping the Tsar and his court. None the less, he concurred with his government's formal offer of asylum.

Within a matter of days the King had changed his mind. On 30 March, in a letter to the government, he mentioned his reservations. In spite of 'a strong personal friendship for the Emperor' and a willingness 'to do anything to help him in this crisis', George V now doubted the wisdom of offering him sanctuary. Politely, the government waved the sovereign's objections aside. The invitation had already been extended; it was too late to withdraw it. But George V refused to be fobbed off. In letter after letter, each more adamant than the last, he begged the government to reconsider the invitation.

In the end he was successful. The government was persuaded to withdraw its offer.

Why was George V so determined to deny asylum to Nicholas II? After all, the Tsar and Tsaritsa were not only his fellow sovereigns and allies, but his first cousins. There were several reasons. The King realised that, whatever the truth of the matter, it would generally be assumed that he had been the one to initiate the offer of sanctuary. And no matter what he might think of them, there was no denying the fact that, in the eyes of many of George V's subjects, the imperial couple were far from blameless victims of the revolution. In left-wing circles, Nicholas II was regarded as a bloodstained tyrant whose fall from power had been richly deserved. Why, they wanted to know, should this reactionary autocrat be given a home in freedom-loving Britain? No sooner had the offer of asylum been made public than the King was inundated with letters from people 'in all classes of life' objecting to the proposal.

Already, a few months before, the King had been subjected to considerable abuse because of his sympathetic attitude towards his other first cousins, Constantine and Sophie of the Hellenes. Strong exception had been taken to the fact that George V had recently entertained two of Constantine's brothers. According to Allied propaganda, the entire Greek royal family were vehemently pro-German. And so, it was widely believed, was the Russian Tsaritsa. When the British government, egged on by the King, suggested that the imperial family be granted asylum in France instead, the British ambassador in Paris replied in no uncertain terms.

'I do not think that the ex-Emperor and his family would be welcome in France,' he wrote. 'The Empress is not only a Boche by birth but in sentiment. She did all she could to bring about an understanding with Germany. She is regarded as a criminal or a criminal lunatic and the ex-Emperor as a criminal from his weakness and submission to her promptings.'[8]

It was throughout this period, too, that George V was having to contend, not only with that whispering campaign against his own German ancestry and rumoured pro-German sympathies, but with a revival of republicanism. This was really not the time for a constitutional monarch, feeling apprehensive about his own throne, to be seen extending the hand of friendship to an autocratic Tsar and his allegedly pro-German Empress who had just been overthrown by their own subjects. George V's first duty was to survive. Set against this, all other considerations – compassion, personal loyalty, blood relations, monarchical solidarity – counted for almost nothing.

Yet, allowing for all this, could George V not have done *something* to save his relations? Two years later a British warship was to rescue his aunt – the Tsar's mother, the Dowager Tsaritsa Marie – from the Crimea; could the King, in the days immediately after the Tsar's fall, not have urged his government to take advantage of the Kaiser's offer of safe passage through the Baltic to send a similar warship to rescue the imperial family? Could the family not then have found sanctuary in some neutral country, such as Denmark or Switzerland?

But the Russian Provisional Government, loath to antagonise the more extreme elements in the Soviet, might not have been able to carry out their plan. And the longer they left it, the less chance they had of carrying it out. With each passing week the government's grip on affairs was becoming shakier (Lenin had by now arrived back from exile); once that grip was lost, the imperial family were to be in grave danger.

If, in the early days of the revolution, the Tsar had enjoyed the protection of the Provisional Government because they had considered vengeance unworthy of the new Russian regime, many of its members had by now come to respect him as a man. Alexander Kerensky, the new minister of justice, was especially impressed by him. It had not taken Kerensky long to appreciate that the accusations of treason made against Nicholas – which he, as minister of justice, had been delegated to investigate – were absurd. Nicholas was an unequivocal nationalist and patriot. Moreover the Tsar's behaviour, in captivity, was exemplary. In spite of the humiliating conditions of his imprisonment at Tsarskoe Selo, Nicholas remained uncomplaining and courteous. Those – Kerensky among them – who had expected to find either a hard-hearted autocrat or a simple-minded weakling, were astonished to find an unassuming and sensible gentleman.

Even the Tsaritsa had surprised them by her simplicity and her resignation. She was far from being the virago of popular legend. 'Did you know, Alexandra Fedorovna,' admitted a common soldier after speaking to her in the garden one day, 'I had a quite different idea of you. I was mistaken about you.'

By August 1917, having failed to get the family out of Russia, Kerensky decided that they must be moved away from the capital as soon as possible. He no longer felt able to guarantee their safety. He chose the provincial town of Tobolsk, in western Siberia, as their place of refuge. Perhaps from here, by way of the trans-Siberian railway, they could eventually be moved eastwards, to Japan. On 14 August, with considerable relief, Kerensky got the family safely aboard a train bound for Tobolsk.

His relief was not shared by everyone. 'News has reached us that the Tsar and his family have been transported to Tobolsk, no one knows why,' wrote Queen Marie of Romania. 'What are they going to do with my poor Nicky? I am so anxious . . .'

15

The Gathering Storm

THE NEXT MONARCH to lose his throne was King Constantine of the Hellenes.

Ever since the autumn of 1916, when Venizelos, with Entente encouragement, had set up a rival government in Salonika, the Allies had been unremitting in their efforts to force the Greek King to abandon his neutrality. They had systematically slandered both King Constantine and Queen Sophie. They had first marched on and then bombarded Athens. When what Constantine's cousin, George V, called these 'bullying' tactics had failed, the Entente powers had enforced a rigid blockade of the country. They were determined to starve the Greeks into submission.

On Constantine, the effect of all this was disastrous. The masterful sovereign, the Victor of the Balkan Wars, the 'Son of the Eagle' had disappeared; Constantine was now an unhappy, disheartened, thoroughly disillusioned man. For a monarch whose chief characteristic was his honesty, the Greek King was sickened by the atmosphere of intrigue and duplicity in which he was being forced to live.

Sophie was equally disillusioned. But being by nature more spirited than her husband, she was not nearly so resigned. If, at the outbreak of the war, there had been no substance in the rumours of her German sympathies, the same was not quite true by the summer of 1917. By this time Sophie had become, if not exactly pro-German, certainly anti-Entente. She was ready to forget past disagreements with her brother, the Kaiser, and to call on him for help.

The only thing to sustain the royal couple during this time of trial was the affection and loyalty of the majority of their subjects. In spite of all the Allied propaganda, Constantine remained a hero in the eyes of most of his people. When, during his illness the year before, the King was thought to be dying, the crowds stood for days in anguished silence outside the palace. As a last hope, the miraculous ikon of the Madonna from the island of Tinos was brought to Athens. As it was borne through the streets, the people fell to their knees to pray for the King's life. Many believed that his recovery dated from the moment that the Madonna was placed in his sickroom.

But, quite clearly, the division of the country between Constantine and Venizelos could not continue indefinitely. Already the Entente governments had recognised Venizelos and appointed diplomatic representatives to his Provisional Government. It would not take much more, they reckoned, for Constantine's hungry and dispirited supporters to give in. 'The Greeks', as the Russian minister informed his government in April 1917, 'are ready for any capitulation, provided that the King is left untouched.'

But the Entente Powers had no intention of leaving Constantine untouched. They were determined that both the King and his allegedly pro-German eldest son, Crown Prince George, must go. In June 1917 a French warship, carrying Senator Charles Jonnart, the fancifully titled High Commissioner of the Protecting Powers of Greece, arrived off Athens. Summoning the Greek prime minister aboard, Jonnart presented him with an ultimatum. Either King Constantine abdicated or Athens would be bombarded and Greece subjected to a full-scale military occupation. But, as the Allies planned to retain the monarchy, the King would be allowed to choose a successor from among his younger sons.

Looking, according to Constantine's brother Christopher, 'white-faced and haggard', the prime minister came to the palace to deliver the ultimatum. The King had no choice. He was afraid that any Allied attempt to land their troops would again be resisted by the Greeks. Constantine was determined that no more blood should be spilt for his sake. To one of his daughters, who begged him not to give way, the King answered quietly, 'It is out of the question that I should cause more bloodshed. Don't you understand the meaning of sacrifice?'

So ingrained, though, was Constantine's belief in the sanctity of monarchy that he was determined to find a way whereby he could give up his throne without actually abdicating. He finally decided that neither he nor his eldest son would sign any act of abdication: they would merely leave the country, with royal power passing pro tem to the King's second son, the twenty-three-year-old Prince Alexander. Constantine knew his countrymen well enough to appreciate that, at some future date, they might well want to recall him.

That same afternoon, at a sad little ceremony attended by only four people – Constantine, Alexander, the prime minister and the Archbishop of Athens, who had been smuggled in by the back door of the palace – the new King took the oath of allegiance. Just over four years had passed since Constantine, at the height of his popularity and surrounded by gorgeously robed clergy and beaming ministers, had taken his oath. Where, Prince Christopher asked himself, 'were those crowds who had cheered the King so frenziedly' on that occasion?

They were nearer than he imagined. And they were no less frenzied. Although the news of the King's imminent departure was meant to have been

25 Tsar Nicholas II and the Tsarevich
    Alexis in 1916

26 Queen Marie of Romaniá in her
    famous Red Cross uniform

27 King Constantine and his officers. Behind him stands his second son, the future King Alexander

28 George V, Queen Mary and the Prince of Wales at Château Tramecourt, France

secret, it had spread rapidly through the city. Already a small crowd had gathered outside the palace. Their keening, 'that age-old lament in a minor key with which Greeks proclaim death and disaster', brought yet more people hurrying through the streets. By nightfall a vast multitude had collected outside the building, all shouting, 'He shall not go! He shall not go!' Nothing would disperse them. Any attempt to get the royal family away was thwarted by the vociferous mob. People simply flung themselves to the road to prevent the cars from moving forward. In desperation Constantine issued a proclamation. 'Bowing to necessity, and fulfilling my duty towards Greece, I am leaving my beloved country . . .' he explained. 'I appeal to you, if you love God, your country and myself, to submit without disturbance.'

He could have saved himself the trouble. The crowd refused to move. All night they surged about the palace. In the morning they were still there, their lamentations louder than ever. But by now, in the blazing sunshine, their grief was turning to hysteria: there were cries that it would be better to kill the King than to let him leave Greece.

In the end, the family decided on a ruse to get away. A rumour was spread among the crowd that the King was to slip out of a little-used back gate. While several cars were being drawn up outside the gate, others were driven into the wooded grounds of the Old Palace, which stood alongside. With the mob surging to the back of the palace, the royal family dashed out of the front entrance, crossed a road, pushed through a gate in the railings surrounding the Old Palace and flung themselves into the waiting cars. They were just able to drive off before the crowd, realising what had happened, came streaming back.

The family were driven to Tatoi, their country place. Here, if the atmosphere was less menacing, it was hardly less emotional. A stream of people – 'smart cars bearing ministers and society people, lorries laden with workmen, peasants in their rough country carts, farmers on horseback, city workers on bicycles' – made their way to Tatoi. Many brought gifts of fruit or flowers; all begged the King not to leave.

But he had to go. On the following day, 12 June 1917, the royal family left Greece. Jonnart's suggestion, that the King, the Queen and the Crown Prince be granted asylum on the Isle of Wight, had aroused George V's 'strong disapproval'. Having just weathered the storm about the Tsar's projected place of refuge, King George was not prepared to face another for the sake of King Constantine. So Switzerland was chosen as the place of exile. Despite the fact that the royal family set sail from a small fishing port, the scenes were hardly less frenzied than they had been in Athens. Again the royal party had to fight their way through a lamenting crowd to the boat that was to ferry them to their yacht, *Sphakteria*. Some of them, in their eagerness to catch a last glimpse of the King, waded shoulder-deep into the water. 'The whole bank', says Prince Christopher, 'was lined with men and women waving frantically to that solitary figure standing alone in the stern of the boat with his eyes fixed on the shores of his beloved Greece.'

'You will come back!' cried the crowd.

'Yes,' shouted the King in return, 'be sure I shall come.'

While King Constantine of the Hellenes was tasting the bitterness of dethronement and exile, King Victor Emmanuel III of Italy was basking in a sudden sunburst of glory.

For year after year the King had remained with his army. It had proved a dispiriting experience. In common with their Entente allies, the Italians were bogged down in a war of attrition. Conditions in the Dolomites – the South Tyrolese Alps dividing Italy from Austria – were appalling. Murderous battles were being fought in sub-zero temperatures, in ice and snow, in clinging mud, and in damp, impenetrable mists. The line was held at the cost of tens of thousands of lives; such trifling advances as were made were never worth the loss of men and material. The King could only look helplessly on while disillusion and defeatism spread through the ranks. Shouts of 'Down with the war!' and, even more chillingly, 'Long live the Revolution!' were heard more and more frequently.

The King's lot was not made any easier by his realisation that the Commander-in-Chief, General Cadorna, was a tyrannical and unimaginative man, apparently oblivious to the sufferings of his men. 'Cadorna', wrote one observer, 'was a seventeenth-century general, who understood war as nothing more than a gigantic siege operation – those sieges where the soldier was kept at his post by the whip.'[1] *Il Re Soldato* did what he could to counteract this harshness by his obvious concern for the men's welfare. Quite often, though, his activities were reduced to the taking of photographs. By his recording of the scenes at the battlefront on his bulky, plate-back camera, Victor Emmanuel became known as 'the Photographer King'.

It took a humiliating defeat to reveal Victor Emmanuel III at his most heroic. Towards the end of October 1917 the Italians were soundly beaten by a combined German and Austro-Hungarian force at Caporetto. Nearly 600,000 men were lost and, as the enemy came pouring down from the mountains, Venice and Milan were in danger of being overrun. Everywhere the Italians fell back in confusion; there were wholesale desertions. The rout was stopped only by the re-establishment of the line along the River Piave, less than twenty miles from Venice, and by the arrival of French and British reinforcements. Caporetto was the worst single military disaster in Italian history; the Italian army was never to recover from the accusations of cowardice and incompetence.

Victor Emmanuel was mortified. 'What caused it all?' he asked in an

English-language entry in his diary. So profound was his sense of shame that he thought of abdicating.

Yet out of the blackness of his despair was born the King's most glorious hour. The British and French, no less appalled by the magnitude of the defeat of their Italian allies held a conference at Peschiera on Lake Garda to establish the causes. The conference was attended by, among others, the French, British and Italian prime ministers, and General Foch. To state Italy's case came King Victor Emmanuel.

The King received the delegates in a gloomy building beside that symbol of the days of the Austrian occupation, the fortress of the Quadrilateral. 'Physically,' wrote Lloyd George, 'he is not a commanding figure, but I was impressed by the calm fortitude he showed on an occasion when his country and his throne were in jeopardy.' As the conference progressed, so did Lloyd George find himself struck by the Italian King's exceptional qualities: his courage, his cheerfulness, his determination to defend the honour of his soldiers. 'His sole anxiety seemed to be to remove any impression that his Army had run away. He was full of excuses but not of apologies for this retreat.'

With great plausibility the King explained the reasons for the defeat; he was able to convince his sceptical listeners that his country would continue to fight on beside its French and British allies until final victory. He undercut their insistence that General Cadorna be replaced by assuring them that this had already been decided upon. Indeed, throughout the conference, Victor Emmanuel proved himself to be articulate, adroit, well-informed and, above all, a supreme patriot. When the reputation of the Italian army was at its lowest, the King was able, almost single-handed, to save it.

If, to his allies, Victor Emmanuel had emerged from the Peschiera conference as an exceptionally impressive figure, to his countrymen he had emerged as a hero. 'It is well', wrote the Italian prime minister, 'that the Italian people know that the humble and anonymous Italian fighting man . . . had in his King a stirring and tenacious defender, at a time when it was fashionable to blame [the fighting man] for the causes of the military upset.'[2]

In time, the King's stand at Peschiera was to become legendary, played up for considerably more than it was worth. Victor Emmanuel, who was a modest man, appreciated this. 'Peschiera?' he would say. 'What I did? Much exaggerated . . . It was nothing.'

But if Victor Emmanuel was a modest man, he was also an astute one. He had consciously made full use of his kingly office, both to plead his country's cause and to enhance his own reputation. By presenting himself as the champion of the Italian fighting man, Victor Emmanuel had saved, not only the honour of his army, but his own throne.

★

The Austro-German victory over the Italians at Caporetto enabled the Kaiser to pay one of his triumphant visits to a theatre of war. He travelled to the Austrian seaport of Trieste, from where he went on to inspect various military and naval installations. His journey also allowed him to see the Emperor Karl and the Empress Zita of Austria–Hungary. This coming together of the sovereigns was hardly a success. 'The atmosphere', says a member of the Kaiser's suite, 'was very unpleasant throughout the meeting.' The young couple found the Kaiser insufferably bombastic and patronising ('Who', Wilhelm II had once asked of Karl, 'does this young man think he is?'); nor could they share the Kaiser's exhilaration over the recent victory. To the Austrian Emperor, Caporetto had merely set back any chances of a speedy negotiated peace. But, not wishing to appear defeatist in the eyes of their exultant guest, the imperial couple limited their conversation to polite generalities.

From Austria the Kaiser's green-painted train continued on its round of apparently endless journeys through Central Europe. Hindenburg and Ludendorff, anxious to keep Wilhelm out of the way, encouraged him to undertake extensive tours. Once again, Wilhelm II had become *der Reise Kaiser*, travelling from Flanders in the southwest to Riga in the northeast, from Heligoland in the icy North Sea to the sun-baked frontiers of Greece. He laid a wreath on the tomb of King Carol of Romania in German-occupied Bucharest; he had a meeting, against a fiery sunset sky, with Tsar Ferdinand of Bulgaria beside the Czernavoda Bridge over the Danube; he drove in state to the Yildiz Palace in Constantinople. Sometimes he was to be found in the castle of Pless in Upper Silesia, at others he was at Homburg in the Taunus Mountains, occasionally he spent a few weeks at Potsdam.

To the members of his entourage, the Kaiser seemed to be living in a fantasy world. More and more did he see-saw between spells of black depression and heady optimism. At one moment he would be obsessed with trivialities; at another he would be expounding grandiose theories for the future of Europe. He had aged considerably. His face, wrote one observer at this time, 'is that of a tired and broken man. His hair is white, though his moustache is still suspiciously dark. There was an absence of the old activity of gesture, a quick, nervous wheeling about and unstable manner of the man . . . He held in his hand a handkerchief which he was perpetually using, and I noticed later he seemed to require it to assuage his continual coughing . . .'[3]

By now the Kaiser was existing in an almost complete political vacuum. In Russia the October Revolution – Lenin's overthrow of the Provisional Government and the assumption of power by the Bolsheviks – led directly to the fulfilment of Wilhelm's long-standing ambition: a separate peace with Russia. Lenin, to consolidate his still precarious hold on the country, needed peace at almost any price. But Wilhelm was not involved in the complex details of the negotiations. Any attempt on his part to intervene was invariably slapped down by the High Command. Even his family seemed to be deserting him. More often than not, the Empress and the Crown Prince supported Hindenburg and Ludendorff against him. Indeed, throughout much of this negotiating period, the Kaiser remained at Homburg, far away from any centre of activity.

He was still there when the Treaty of Brest-Litovsk, ending the war between Germany and Russia, was signed on 3 March 1918. By its terms, Germany gained considerably in territory, population and resources. The Kaiser hailed the treaty as 'one of the greatest victories in history, the significance of which will only properly be appreciated by our grandchildren'. What German grandchildren probably appreciated more was being given a day off school by their delighted Kaiser.

How much understanding did Wilhelm II have of the true significance of the Russian Revolution? He certainly did not regard it as the dawn of a new age, as the start of a new order of society. At one stage he even thought that once peace had been signed between them, Germany might be able to form some sort of alliance with Russia. Neither the overthrow of Tsardom, nor the publication of Woodrow Wilson's famous 'Fourteen Points' by which the United States President made clear that he would like to see the overthrow of Kaiserdom as well, could convince Wilhelm II that the days of monarchy in Central Europe were numbered. He was still capable of declaring that if a British emissary came to ask for peace, he would have to kneel down before the German imperial standards, since what would be happening would be a victory of monarchy over democracy.

The Kaiser was not alone in his blindness. Although by now the various monarchs appreciated that democracy would have to be spread more widely if they hoped to safeguard their thrones, they could not really envisage a Europe in which the monarchical system was not the natural order of things. On the contrary, and even at this eleventh hour, some of them were thinking in terms of extending the system.

The Kaiser, in positively Napoleonic fashion, was giving a great deal of thought to the creation of new kingdoms out of recently conquered territories. He would pontificate on the setting up of kings in Courland, Finland, Poland and Lithuania; or on replacing the kings of Belgium and Romania. Wilhelm was particularly interested in getting rid of Ferdinand of Romania, whom he denounced as 'the traitor Hohenzollern'. After what one of Wilhelm's entourage calls 'some discussion with the ladies of the court', the Kaiser proposed that his youngest son, Prince Joachim, ascend the Romanian throne. When it was tentatively suggested that Joachim might not have quite the right qualities, Wilhelm gave a brusque answer.

'Qualities', he announced grandly, 'are not really necessary.'

It needed the Austrian foreign minister, Count Czernin, to bring a little realism to these imperial daydreams. With the fall of the Tsar and with the flight of the kings of Greece, Serbia and Montenegro from their countries, this was not the time for further dethronements. 'At this time', he says, 'there was a certain decline in the value of kings on the European market, and I was afraid that it might develop into a panic, if we put more kings off their thrones.' So Ferdinand was allowed to keep his.

However, this argument did not affect the creation of new thrones or the resurrection of old ones. With Poland now freed of Russian domination, both the Kaiser and the Emperor Karl were anxious to revive the old Polish kingdom. The most promising of the rival candidates was thought to be the fifty-six-year-old Archduke Charles Stephen of Austria. Central Europe was flooded with Austrian propaganda in an effort to secure the Archduke's nomination. 'Sheaves of printed matter have been circulated,' runs one report, 'declaring that he has the blood of sixteen Polish kings in his veins, is a Catholic, speaks Polish perfectly, and has given his elder children a Polish education . . .'[4]

But perhaps the most bizarre suggestion concerning the restoration of thrones came from George V. The British King's belief in the efficacy of monarchy had already been illustrated by his conviction that India's problems would best be solved by a strengthening of the rule of the hereditary princes. When the war was over, he now ventured, the German empire should be dismantled and the various kings, princes, grand dukes and dukes restored to the positions of prestigious independence which they had enjoyed before Bismarck's wars had united Germany under Prussia half a century before.

It was a splendidly impractical notion. At the very time that Woodrow Wilson was advocating republicanism as the New World's cure for the Old World's ills, the Old World – in the person of King George V – was recommending the renaissance of no less than twenty-five monarchs.

16

The Beginning of the End

THE PEACE of Brest-Litovsk, signed between Russia and Germany on 3 March 1918, finally extinguished any hopes of victory for King Ferdinand and Queen Marie of Romania.

Ever since the fall of the Tsar, a year before, Russian support, on which the embattled Romanian army depended utterly, had been increasingly unreliable. With the collapse of the Russian Provisional Government and the triumph of Lenin's Bolsheviks, it had ceased almost entirely. In their hundreds of thousands, Russian troops had deserted the Romanian front; by the middle of December 1917, an armistice had been signed between Russia and Germany. With the Germans occupying most of the country, the Romanian army could not possibly hang on to their remaining territory much longer.

The turn of events depressed King Ferdinand greatly. Only reluctantly had he joined the Entente Powers; he had no taste for war; he was too much of a realist to imagine that his troops were any match for the Germans. There was little point, he reckoned, in carrying on. 'I understand the King's despair,' wrote Queen Marie; 'the strain has been too awful, never any good news, all hopes crushed again and again and again. The situation is getting more and more impossible and nowhere to turn.'

The impossibility of the situation was emphasised by a telegram from Marie's cousin, George V, offering asylum in Britain for the Romanian royal family (the Romanian sovereigns, unlike the Russian or Greek, were very popular in Britain). It was emphasised more vividly still by the official visit of the Queen's other cousin, Wilhelm II, to German-occupied Romania. How ironic, thought Ferdinand, after the Kaiser had laid a wreath on the grave of King Carol, that the late King, who had always longed for a visit from the illustrious German Kaiser, should receive one only after he was dead and his country occupied.

If Ferdinand's spirit was broken, Marie's was characteristically defiant. She simply could not bring herself to believe in the inevitability of a German victory. Although it would be too much to claim that she was actually enjoying the war, there is no doubt that it had given her a tremendous sense of achievement. Time and again, as she carried out her many duties, as she visited the hospital wards, the soup kitchens, the parade grounds, even the trenches and battlefields, the Queen felt that she was fulfilling a great destiny, that she was making a significant contribution to the life of the nation.

The soldiers idolised her. 'Looking into the eyes of their Queen', she wrote in her self-congratulatory but strangely moving fashion, 'they had sworn to stand up like a wall to defend the last scrap of Romanian territory which was still ours. Many a dying soldier whispered to me with his last breath that it was for me that he was fighting, for was I not his home, his mother, his belief and his hope?'

This was why she refused to listen to any talk of giving up. 'I do not know how to accept defeat, not this kind of defeat!' she cried. Anyone mentioning the hopelessness of continued resistance would be treated to a flood of frenzied counter-argument. While King Ferdinand sat silently by, his beautiful Queen would hold forth on the necessity for *la grande aventure, le grand geste*, some heroic last effort. With part of the army, the sovereigns must cut their way through the Russian 'traitors' to link up with the 'still faithful Cossacks' in the south of Russia. 'To sit still and die,' she exclaimed, 'suffocated between Russian traitors and German haters, is really too poor a death!' Or what about *la guerre à outrance*, with the King and Queen, encircled by their loyal troops, fighting to the very last. Alone, if necessary, like some ancient or medieval heroine, she would face the oncoming hordes: 'fantastic, I know, hardly belonging to our days, but honourable, brave and free!'

'Oh God, if only I were a man, with a man's rights and the spirit I have in a woman's body!' she exclaimed. 'I would fire them to desperate, glorious resistance, *coûte que coûte!*'

This was all very well in its way but it was having no real effect on the course of events. Queen Marie was like some great tragedienne playing to an empty house. The fate of Romania was being decided elsewhere. In January 1918 the Germans sent King Ferdinand an ultimatum. He was to send a deputation to treat with them. The King was given four days in which to reply. His government promptly resigned and a new government, headed by one of the generals, decided to sue for peace. There was little else that they could do. The German peace terms, thrashed out during the following weeks, were harsh. Yet if Ferdinand did not accept them, warned Czernin, the Austrian foreign minister, the Central Powers would carry out their threat to replace him on the throne with another German prince. This was 'the dynasty's last chance'. Ferdinand took the hint.

Facing the German demands was one thing; facing Queen Marie quite another. The war might have brought husband and wife together in some ways ('we have become the firmest possible friends,' claimed Marie at one stage) but in others it had emphasised the differences between them. The

King realised that, in the Queen's eyes, he was far too phlegmatic, too resigned, too defeatist. So who can blame poor Ferdinand if, during these agonising days of decision, he avoided his wife as much as possible? He simply could not stomach another of her impassioned harangues. 'I feel that I can terrify him because of my passionate attitude,' she admitted. 'I can never be luke-warm.'

Yet he could hardly avoid her altogether. Things came to a head between husband and wife on the morning that the King was due to accept or reject the final peace terms. On his way to the fateful crown council, she tackled him. 'Woman-like,' says Marie, 'I had my say.' She certainly did. Yet even she was too embarrassed by her tirade to repeat it word for word. Her paraphrasing of it strikes a suitably heroic note. 'If we are to die, let us die with our heads high, without soiling our souls, by putting our names to our death warrant. Let us die protesting, crying out to the whole world our indignation against the infamy which is expected of us.'

She even sent Crown Prince Carol into the crown council to deliver one last, hectoring protest 'in my name and in the name of all the women of Romania against the horror of peace in such a form'. Perhaps it would be uncharitable to suggest that, as much as anything, Queen Marie was ensuring her place in history.

She could have saved her breath. Influenced, no doubt, by the fact that the Peace of Brest-Litovsk was being signed on the very day that he was holding his crown council, Ferdinand agreed to the peace terms. ('He whimpered', as the Kaiser put it, 'like a lap dog' during the negotiations.) To Marie, the capitulation marked one of the bitterest, most tragic hours of her life: 'dark', she wails, 'as death'.

'The King and I could hardly face each other,' she afterwards admits, 'he was a completely broken man. I did not try to argue any more: I knew that all was over; I knew that I was defeated.'

But not quite so defeated as to cause her to neglect to write a letter to her cousin, George V. In it Marie was careful to draw his attention to the hopelessness of the Romanian situation, to the sacrifices of the Romanian army, to Romania's unshakable fidelity to the Allied cause and, not least of all, to her own willingness to have fought on. 'Rather would I have died with our army to the last man, than confess myself beaten, for have I not English blood in my veins?'

She ended with the earnest hope – and here lay the heart of her letter – that her cousin George would not forget Romania in the final hour of victory.

Cousin Georgie's answer was laconic. 'You may be confident', ended his telegram, 'that we and our Allies will do our utmost to redress the grievous wrongs Romania has suffered in the great cause for which we went to war.'

What the Queen histrionically described as 'a fate almost too dark to be conceived' turned out to be not quite as dark as she had imagined. A new government, sympathetic to Germany, managed the country's affairs and the royal family remained at Jassy.

As that dedicated monarchist Count Czernin had said, this was not the time 'for putting kings off thrones', even if they were one's enemies.

There were times, though, when kings proved to be their own worst enemies. In the spring of 1918 the image of monarchy was seriously debased by that hitherto irreproachable sovereign, the Emperor Karl of Austria–Hungary.

Things, at that stage, were looking more promising for the Habsburg empire. Both Serbia and Montenegro had been conquered, Italy had been dealt a severe blow at Caporetto, peace had been made with Russia and Romania, and a great new German offensive on the western front – the so-called 'Kaiser's Battle' – was going well. To improve this shining hour, Count Czernin made a speech in Vienna designed to show that a battered France was anxious to end the war. He had recently rejected a French peace offer, boasted Czernin, because their proposals had included the return of Alsace-Lorraine to France.

Georges Clemenceau, the new and dynamic prime minister of France, promptly denied this. France, he declared, had received no such rebuff from Austria. But Czernin, refusing to be silenced, blustered on. He met each French claim with a counter-claim. When Clemenceau, playing his trump card, mentioned the hitherto secret *Kaiserbrief*, in which the Emperor Karl had alluded to France's 'just claims' to Alsace-Lorraine, Czernin denied that the Emperor had written any such thing.

It was at this stage that Karl himself plunged into the increasingly murky and dangerous waters. Not only did he send the Kaiser a telegram denying that he had ever recognised France's claims to Alsace-Lorraine (Wilhelm's answer was that he had never doubted his ally's loyalty) but, pressed by the almost hysterical Czernin, foolishly signed what he assumed to be a confidential document to that effect. One can only suppose that the guileless Karl, having been assured by both the French authorities and Czernin that his secret peace negotiations would remain so, believed them. He should have known better. Czernin promptly published the Emperor's signed denial, and Clemenceau, just as promptly, published a photographic copy of the *Kaiserbrief*.

The whole affair, although more complex than many supposed, revealed an indisputable fact: the Emperor Karl of Austria–Hungary had lied.

Equally indisputable, to Karl's indignant German allies, was the fact that, behind their backs, he had pledged himself to the return of Alsace-Lorraine. In an effort to patch things up, Karl hurried to German headquarters, now in the Belgian town of Spa. The price of Karl's pardon was the loss of almost all independence of action. From now on the Habsburg empire was to be firmly shackled to the Hohenzollern empire. Politically, economically and militarily, Austria–Hungary was to be subservient to Germany: she was to become little more than a German satellite.

This, in turn, destroyed any possibility, not only of a separate Austrian peace with the Allies, but of the Allies preserving the Habsburg empire after the war. The champions of the sort of nationalism advocated in President Wilson's famous Fourteen Points – of self-government for the various national minorities – were able to out-argue those who wished to maintain the multi-national Habsburg empire. From now on the determination to dismember the empire was all but universal in the Allied camp.

For the Emperor Karl, the affair of the *Kaiserbrief* had a deeply personal significance as well. It showed that he was simply not equipped to play a Machiavellian role. So honourable, so trusting, he should never have become involved in this sort of diplomatic double-dealing. It was both foolish and unworthy. Monarchs should not lie – or, at least, should not be caught lying – to each other. 'In those days Europe, even in its death throes,' writes Edmond Taylor, 'was not hardened to such violations of the gentleman's code.'

Indeed, everything that poor Karl touched seemed to be turning to ashes. Having ascended the throne with the best of intentions, he had inherited an extraordinarily difficult situation. An accumulation of problems, built up during the long reign of the Emperor Franz Joseph, had had to be tackled in the worst possible circumstances. A man of peace, he had been obliged to wage war; a democrat, he was allied to one of the most authoritarian states in Europe; a reformer, he was surrounded by some of the most hidebound, bureaucratic and conservative politicians on the Continent; a straightforward and deeply moral man, he ruled over one of the most complex and corrupt empires in the world. 'Everything failed', as his biographer Gordon Brook-Shepherd has put it, 'because everything was interlocked.'[1]

And it was the affair of the *Kaiserbrief* that dealt the *coup de grâce*. Not only was it a fatal blow to Karl's personal prestige; it somehow 'tarnished the fading magic that still surrounded the Habsburg throne itself, the only remaining link between the peoples of the empire'.[2]

The Romanian sovereigns were not the only ones to feel the effects of the Treaty of Brest-Litovsk. For the Russian imperial family the coming of peace was equally disturbing and, in the end, infinitely more tragic.

Since late August the year before, the Tsar, the Tsaritsa, their five children and their little household had been living in comparative comfort in the house of the provincial governor of Tobolsk in Siberia. But not long after the signing of the peace, a new commissioner arrived at Tobolsk. His name was Yakovlev and he appears to have had orders to take the imperial prisoners to

Moscow. The family could only speculate on the reason. Perhaps the Tsar was going to be forced to sign the peace treaty; Nicholas imagined that the Kaiser would much rather have dealings with a brother monarch than with a revolutionary government.

The prospect appalled the Tsaritsa. Like her cousin Marie of Romania, Alexandra could not bear the thought of her husband debasing himself before the victorious enemy. She feared that without her to support him, he might agree to some shameful course of action. Yet there was a strong likelihood that she might not be in a position to support him. The thirteen-year-old Alexis, who had suffered a fall that spring, was still in bed. The boy was certainly in no condition to be moved. The Tsar, decided Yakovlev, would have to go to Moscow without his family. After an agonising period of indecision, Alexandra decided that she would accompany her husband. After all, Alexis was getting better and would be left in the devoted care of three of his sisters and his tutor Gilliard. The Empress and her daughter Marie would go with the Tsar.

On 25 April 1918, the little party set out for Moscow. They never reached it. Near Omsk their train was stopped and diverted to the town of Ekaterinburg. Here Nicholas was delivered into the hands of the Ural Regional Soviet, a group of ruthless and hostile men with an almost pathological hatred of him. Whether it had all been part of a plan by the Bolshevik government to rid themselves of their embarrassing prisoner is uncertain. What is certain is that everyone, other than the Ural Regional Soviet, now washed their hands of any responsibility for the imperial family.

Within a month the entire family had been reunited in a two-storied house in the centre of Ekaterinburg. Gilliard and some of the others were set free. Where the family's detention at Tobolsk had been relatively relaxed and conditions not uncomfortable, their imprisonment at Ekaterinburg was both severe and humiliating. The accommodation was cramped; the family was closely guarded; only short periods of exercise were allowed in the walled-in yard; they were subjected to petty cruelties and lewd indignities. Not even in the single lavatory were the young grand duchesses safe from the crudities of their captors: the door had to be left open and on the walls were scrawled obscene drawings of the Empress and Rasputin.

Yet the behaviour of the family was never anything less than exemplary. It is a curious fact that adversity often brings out the best in crowned heads. Sovereigns, known for their cruelty, stupidity or authoritarianism when on the throne, quite often conduct themselves with extraordinary humility, dignity and resignation when they have lost them. There is very little harking back to past glories, or complaining about reduced circumstances, or railing against an unjust fate. On the contrary, these fallen sovereigns often reveal a real nobility of spirit. Rejected monarchs such as Louis XVI and Marie Antoinette, or Napoleon III, behaved with a stoicism not far removed from saintliness in their time of darkness.

'Kings in exile', Tsar Ferdinand of Bulgaria was to explain after he, too, had lost his throne, 'are more philosophic under reverses than ordinary individuals; but our philosophy is primarily the result of tradition and breeding, and do not forget that pride is an important item in the making of a monarch. We are disciplined from the day of our birth and taught the avoidance of all outward signs of emotion. The skeleton sits forever with us at the feast. It may mean murder, it may mean abdication, but it serves always to remind us of the unexpected. Therefore we are prepared and nothing comes in the nature of a catastrophe. The main thing in life is to support any condition of bodily and spiritual exile with dignity. If one sups with sorrow, one need not invite the world to see you eat.'[3]

This was certainly true of Nicholas and Alexandra. Sustained by their unquestioning faith in God and by their deep love for each other and for their children, they endured their long martyrdom uncomplainingly. They were greatly helped, of course, by the fact that neither of them had ever had much taste for the pomp and glitter of their position; their preference had always been for a tranquil, domesticated, bourgeois way of life. Nicholas remained the polite, simple, fatalistic man he had always been; even in his shabby clothes, expertly patched by the Tsaritsa, he managed to look neat and somehow dapper. Alexandra, with her piety, integrity and sincerity un-altered, achieved an almost sublime serenity.

Quite naturally, they hoped that they might be released or rescued (and with the breaking out of civil war in Russia and with a strong anti-Bolshevik force already sweeping westwards towards Ekaterinburg, there was a strong likelihood of this) but their chief characteristic seems to have been their resignation. If, in their years of power, Nicholas and Alexandra had some-times given the institution of monarchy a bad name, they were now adding considerably to its lustre.

In recent years there have been conflicting theories about the date and manner in which the members of the Russian imperial family met their end. What is certain is that the rapid approach of the White forces convinced the Bolsheviks that the family must be got rid of before they could be rescued and so become a rallying point for the counter-revolutionary movement. Perhaps they *were* all shot in the cellar of the Ekaterinburg house on the night of 16 July 1918; perhaps the Empress and her daughters *were* moved elsewhere to be killed later; perhaps the Grand Duchess Anastasia *did* escape the slaughter. What is indisputable is that when, on 21 July 1918, Ekaterinburg fell to the Whites, there was no trace of the imperial family whom they had come to rescue.

The crowned heads of Europe were horrified by the murder of Nicholas II. For a monarch to lose his throne was not so unusual; for him to fall to an assassin's bullet or an anarchist's bomb was one of the hazards of his vocation;

even for him to be murdered in some political coup or torn apart by some frenzied mob was understandable; but for a sovereign to be killed in cold blood by his subjects in civilised, twentieth-century Europe struck Nicholas's fellow monarchs as the most dastardly of crimes. It had not been equalled since the guillotining of Louis XVI. The murder brought home to them, as nothing had done before, the dangers which they now faced from the forces of revolution. It would also help them to make up their minds about abdicating and getting out when their particular day of decision dawned.

And the sovereigns mourned Nicholas to a man. The Kaiser could not sleep, claimed his daughter-in-law, Crown Princess Cecilie, for thinking of the slaughter of the Tsar and his family. 'It was a foul murder,' noted George V, conveniently forgetting that it was he who had denied the Tsar refuge. 'I was devoted to Nicky, who was the kindest of men and a thorough gentleman; loved his country and people.'[4]

'Poor Nicky!' wrote Marie of Romania in her diary. 'I shudder to think of your end, you, who knew all of power and glory; and such a death! . . . Surely God recognises in you the good man you were. He alone will be the fair judge of the mistakes you made whilst on the throne, for all men are mistaken, and probably you had to die for sins not your own.'

Only very rarely did Albert of the Belgians leave his patch of Belgian soil. Except for short visits to the French and Italian fronts, he remained among his troops. His decision was a wise one. Although some thought that he should have made more use of his royal status by paying formal visits to his brother monarchs or other heads of state, there is little doubt that, by remaining at La Panne, Albert kept intact that enormous prestige won during the early months of the war. 'The whole world felt his debtor', wrote on observer, 'because he behaved as if no debt were due to him.'[5]

The only wartime royal visit paid by King Albert and Queen Elisabeth was in July 1918 when they went to London to attend the Silver Wedding celebrations of King George and Queen Mary. They were given a tumultuous welcome; the royal couple were amazed by the warmth of their reception. 'In the King and Queen of the Belgians', enthused *The Times*, 'Great Britain salutes the very soul of loyalty to a word pledged, high minds not cast down by long misfortune, hope and confidence indomitable.' The couple stayed at Buckingham Palace; they attended a family luncheon where all available members of the British royal family were gathered to greet them; they went, with King George and Queen Mary, to a concert in the Albert Hall. As they entered the royal box, they were given an almost overwhelming ovation. Tactfully, the British sovereigns stood back so that their guests remained the centre of attention.

'So very small she looked,' wrote the watching Lady Diana Cooper of Queen Elisabeth, 'and dressed in gleaming white from head to toe.' Beside her King Albert, his face ruddy and his hair bleached from long exposure to sun and wind, stood in bemused and embarrassed silence while the great hall echoed and re-echoed with applause. They cheered, claimed Lady Diana, 'as I have not heard cheering before'.

The loudest cheers came when, in his speech, Lord Curzon revealed the hitherto carefully guarded secret that the Belgian sovereigns had arrived in England by seaplane.

From the triumphs of London, the royal couple returned to the dreariness of life in the red-brick villa at La Panne. 'It is impossible', noted the Belgian writer Louis Dumont-Wilden, when he visited the villa, 'to imagine a sadder place of exile.' Its windows, he said, 'opened on a grey seascape veiled in thick mist: the sky seemed melting into water. The rain, which had already lasted several days, was still falling.'6 At that stage there was not even the excitement of battle to relieve the monotony of the days; nothing seemed able to break the murderous deadlock of trench warfare. It must have seemed to Albert, at times, as if the war would go on forever.

But he never complained. His concern was for his army and his country, not for himself. Whatever his innermost feelings might have been, the King, like most of his brother sovereigns, never allowed himself to appear anything other than confident and steadfast.

By this stage the Kaiser was also permanently headquartered in Belgium, in the little watering resort of Spa. His accommodation was infinitely superior to King Albert's. A mock-medieval chateau – all turrets and gables and arches – set in a hundred-acre park, had been requisitioned from a Belgian textile magnate. Much of its furnishings came from Albert's palace at Laeken; the highly polished floors resounded to the click of heels as the Kaiser's dashingly uniformed equerries and adjutants hurried about their sovereign's business. The exact nature of this business was becoming increasingly unclear. Photographs showing the Supreme War Lord, in *Pickelhaube* and greatcoat, inspecting the troops, were invariably taken in the park where a sandbagged trench had been especially constructed for the purpose. Military and political decisions were taken, just as invariably, at the headquarters of the High Command at the Hotel Brittanique.

The 'Kaiser's Battle' – that great German offensive on the western front – which had started so gloriously in the spring of 1918, had petered out by the summer. Wilhelm II had never approved of his name being given to the offensive. In its early, successful phase, the title 'Kaiser's Battle' had somehow implied that Wilhelm had had nothing to do with any previous battles; now that it had failed, he tended to be too closely associated with this failure.

The Kaiser took this latest check to his armies very badly. 'I am a defeated War Lord to whom you must show consideration,' he once said to his entourage. That same night he had a terrifying vision. Not only all the ministers and generals of his reign, but all his royal relations had filed before him, holding him up to scorn. Only Queen Maud of Norway, George V's youngest sister, had shown him any pity. This waking nightmare suggested to him that he was 'an outcast among the kings, a crowned reprobate spurned with revulsion by those whose friendship he had once enjoyed'.[7] To a man of Wilhelm's sensitivity and conflicting loyalties, such a vision was a deeply disturbing experience. His companions could only sit in silence as, in the unlikely setting of the dining saloon of his train drawn up in a Belgian railway station, he recounted his night of horror.

Things became worse when, on 8 August 1918, the Allied counter-offensive was successful and the British broke through the German lines. What Ludendorff called 'the Black Day of the German Army' was an even blacker one for the Kaiser. Although he behaved with commendable calm and dignity, he began to talk again in terms of ending the war. Less than two months before, when the new state secretary for foreign affairs, Richard von Kühlmann, had bravely hinted at the possibility of an approach to the Allies on the question of a negotiated peace, the Kaiser had been pressured by Hindenburg and Ludendorff into dismissing him. Now, to the dejected Ludendorff, Wilhelm admitted that 'things can't go on like this indefinitely and we must find a way to end it all.'

But not quite yet. To get away from the tension of headquarters at Spa, Wilhelm went to Wilhelmshöhe, one of the imperial seats, near Cassel. Here, almost half a century before, the defeated Napoleon III had been held captive by Wilhelm's grandfather, Kaiser Wilhelm I, during the Franco-Prussian War. An added reason for this move to Cassel was to enable Wilhelm to be with his ailing Empress: Dona's heart was giving cause for concern. Yet, as always and in spite of her own condition, it was she who had to bolster him. When Wilhelm took to his bed in a state of collapse, she forced him up. When his old friend, the Jewish shipping magnate Albert Ballin, came to see him, the Empress begged Ballin to treat the Kaiser gently. To ensure that he did, Dona saw to it that the two men were never left alone. She had never liked Ballin: she was afraid, not only that he might depress Wilhelm further, but that he might encourage his growing defeatism.

Yet to Ballin, the Kaiser seemed curiously out of touch with reality. Wilhelm told his friend that he expected the front to be stabilised soon. He had received an offer of mediation from Queen Wilhelmina of the Nether-lands but the time was not quite right for an acceptance of the offer. As always, he wanted the German approach to be made from a position of strength.

That Germany would ever again be in a position of strength was becoming

29 The Emperor Karl and the Empress Zita visiting Innsbruck

30 Victor Emmanuel III, Queen Elena and Crown Prince Umberto at the front

31 Kaiser Wilhelm II and the Emperor Karl after the victory over the Italians at Caporetto

increasingly unlikely. And, in his heart of hearts, Wilhelm realised this. One evening, as the company was sitting on the terrace at Wilhelmshohe, someone brought out a picture and asked the Kaiser if he had painted it. No, he admitted, and went on to tell them whose work it was.

'You know,' he added quietly, 'if I had that man's talent, I should have been a seascape painter and not an Emperor, and I shouldn't be in such a horrifying position today.'[8]

The Fall of Kings

THE YEAR 1917 had marked the thirtieth anniversary of the reign of the flamboyant Tsar Ferdinand of Bulgaria. Yet for all his delight in ceremonial, Ferdinand had decided against any public celebrations. His second wife, the Tsaritsa Eleonore, had been seriously ill. For years this capable and kind-hearted woman, whom Ferdinand had always neglected so shamefully, had devoted herself to the welfare of the Bulgarian people. Her wartime work in the Clementine hospital in Sofia had been unstinting; she had, says one witness, 'a special gift for relieving suffering'. Eleonore had died in September 1917 and had been buried, at her own request, in the little twelfth-century church at Boynara near Sofia.

But there had been another reason for dispensing with any anniversary celebrations. Ferdinand, and his people, were suffering from extreme war-weariness. Indeed, there seemed to be no good reason why they should still be fighting at all. Their war aim – the conquest of Macedonia – had been realised by the end of 1916. And President Wilson's Fourteen Points (later augmented by his Four Principles) which had been widely distributed throughout the country, had convinced the Bulgarians of the justness of their cause. As Macedonia was peopled largely by Bulgarians, its annexation confirmed Bulgaria's status as – in Wilson's phrase – a 'well-defined national element'.

To wish to end the war was one thing, to achieve it another. Although Ferdinand, in his Byzantine fashion, had been involved in various secret negotiations with the Allies, he had never dared to defy the Kaiser openly. Any such move would have meant a German occupation of his country and even more suffering for his nearly starving people. In fact, as late as August 1918, much to the gratification of the Kaiser, Ferdinand knelt beside Wilhelm before the high altar of the church in Homburg and swore undying loyalty to his ally 'whatever the outcome may be'.

On the other hand, Germany was not giving Bulgaria anything like the military support she had once promised. By June 1918 it was apparent that the Allied forces, who had been building up their strength in Salonika in northern Greece, were preparing to launch an attack along the Bulgarian front. Yet repeated Bulgarian requests for German reinforcements were ignored.

In spite of this threat, Ferdinand remained his usual, pleasure-loving self. Daily life within his palaces was still conducted with strict punctiliousness and lavish ceremonial. The gardens and conservatories of his country places were still tended with great care and affection. When he travelled by train, it was still in conditions of the utmost luxury. Not until after the war would monarchs begin to feel guilty about their vast wealth and sumptuous lifestyles.

Nor, in his mid-fifties, had Ferdinand lost his sexual appetites. His *penchant* for blond, blue-eyed young men was as strong as ever; indeed, the war presented endless opportunities for spotting new ones. A young courier of the German military attaché was appointed – much to the consternation of Ferdinand's entourage – 'official reader of German newspapers'. To the even greater consternation of the commander-in-chief of the army, Ferdinand insisted that a certain cadet be promoted to full officer rank so that he might serve as the sovereign's orderly. On one occasion the Bulgarian war minister, anxious to discuss some urgent military matter with the Tsar, was astonished to hear that he had gone off with his chauffeur, in a car loaded with delicacies, in order to visit the young man's parents in their humble village home.

And while Ferdinand fiddled, Rome was about to burst into flames. On 14 September 1918, the Allied forces – among them the Serbs under old King Peter's son, Prince Alexander – launched their offensive along the southern Macedonian frontier. Within days they had broken through the Bulgarian front. As the Bulgarians retreated helter-skelter through the mountains, and mutinous troops marched on Sofia, Ferdinand concurred with his ministers' request to seek an armistice. The Bulgarian peace delegates travelled to Salonika and on 29 September agreed to the cessation of all hostilities between Bulgaria and the Allies.

'Was anything said about me?' asked an apprehensive Tsar Ferdinand of the head of the returning armistice delegation.

'I do not wish to discuss that subject,' came the diplomatic answer. 'But the Allies spoke in terms of admiration about the Crown Prince.'

Ferdinand understood. For the following three days he shut himself up in his rooms, seeing no one. Then, on 3 October, he called together his two sons, Boris and Cyril, and his secretaries. He informed them that he had decided to abdicate in favour of the twenty-four-year-old Prince Boris. The secretaries drew up a document and he signed it. Summoning his prime minister, the Tsar handed him the document.

'My abdication!' he announced baldly. 'Accept it!'

And then, turning from the prime minister to Prince Boris, he said, 'Let us two be the first to swear allegiance to the new Tsar.'

'From now on,' he declared to his son, 'I am your subject but I am also Your Majesty's father.'[1] Not even in this desperate moment had Ferdinand's sense of theatre failed him.

The following evening, accompanied by a small suite, Ferdinand left his kingdom.

For over thirty years, by a combination of guile, tenacity, ability and audacity, Ferdinand had managed to hold on to his crown. And even though he had finally lost it, he had been able to save the monarchy. It would be left to Hitler and Stalin, between them, to destroy that.

'The sensational news today', wrote an exultant Queen Marie of Romania on 4 October 1918, 'is that Ferdinand of Bulgaria has abdicated in favour of his son Boris, who was immediately crowned in Sofia.'

Suddenly, the long deadlock had been broken; everything was becoming fluid again. The abdication of Tsar Ferdinand marked the beginning of a complete transformation in southeastern Europe. 'For the first time', wrote Marie, 'we really see light ahead.' She, who since the German conquest of Romania, had been regarded as something of an embarrassment, now suddenly found herself acclaimed. Her flicker of resistance was developing into a great blaze of triumph.

'There are fearful battles being raged on all fronts,' she noted a few days later. 'French troops have entered Sofia, the Allies are advancing into Serbia and Albania. Turkey is going to pieces, in Palestine her armies are almost completely destroyed. The German front is at last crumbling everywhere.'

One afternoon a French aeroplane, flying up from Salonika, dropped a message for the excited Queen. It was from her cousin, George V. Written on a tiny scrap of paper, it promised Marie that 'Romania would not be forgotten'. 'All this is tremendous news for us, makes us tremble with excitement and expectation,' she gushed. For, by his message, the British King meant that the territorial promises, made to Romania when she joined the Entente Powers two years before, would be remembered on the day of victory.

But, in truth, the Great National Dream was already coming true. Earlier that year, the previously Russian-controlled territory of Bessarabia, on Romania's northeastern frontier, had been annexed. Now, with the gradual crumbling of the Habsburg empire, Romanians living in Transylvania and Bukovina were clamouring to join their mother country. 'The dream of *Romania Mare* seems to be becoming a reality,' wrote the gratified Marie. 'It is all so incredible that I hardly dare believe it.'

In his less demonstrative fashion the Serbian Regent, Prince Alexander, was also rejoicing in this sudden turning of the tide. No less were his years of defeat and waiting being rewarded. With his father, the old and increasingly eccentric King Peter I, living the life of a recluse in Greece, it had been left to Alexander to reclaim the kingdom. And, as much as Queen Marie, could the small, austere, highly disciplined Serbian Regent look forward to the aggrandisement of this kingdom.

Already, the year before, the exiled royal Serbian government had met a delegation of South Slavs from the Austro–Hungarian empire and had together issued a manifesto proclaiming a 'Kingdom of Serbs, Croats and Slovenes, a democratic and parliamentary monarchy under the Karageorgevic dynasty'. It had been, in effect, a declaration that from out of the ruins of the Habsburg empire, a new South Slav state, eventually to be known as the Kingdom of Yugoslavia, would be born. Now, in the early days of October 1918, as the Serbs, led by Prince Alexander, came marching triumphantly back towards Belgrade, the age-old dream of Greater Serbia was indeed coming true.

Victor Emmanuel III of Italy was also tasting the fruits of victory achieved and ambitions fulfilled. On 24 October 1918, he had the satisfaction of seeing his troops, together with their French and British allies, finally moving forward from the River Piave. After two days of determined resistance, their Austro-Hungarian enemy began to flag. First the Hungarian divisions, declaring that they would defend only Hungarian soil, headed for home. Their defection seriously undermined the morale of the remaining troops. They fought on, but their hearts were not in it.

On 29 October the Emperor Karl, pressed by his desperate general staff, asked for an armistice. On 4 November the Austrians surrendered. By then the victorious Italians were in control of their longed-for *terre irredente*: the army was in Trento and the navy in Trieste. Yet another national dream was being realised. Victor Emmanuel III had finally achieved the ideal of the *Risorgimento*.

For the Emperor Karl of Austria–Hungary, there was no dream to be realised; only a nightmare to be lived through. It was at his expense that his fellow sovereigns – the kings of Romania, Serbia and Italy – were seeing their territorial ambitions fulfilled. From the great white and gold rooms of Schönbrunn Palace outside Vienna, Karl looked out on an empire that was fast disintegrating. The remorseless Allied advances, through the Balkans in the south and from Italy in the west, considerably worsened the troubles already raging throughout his realm. To widespread hunger and war-weariness was now added defeatism. This, in turn, encouraged the empire's endemic separatist movements: movements that had been given a tremendous boost by Wilson's Fourteen Points. By now self-determination for all minorities had become not only respectable; it had become almost imperative.

In a desperate effort to ride out this storm, Karl issued a manifesto. With the exception of the always intractable Hungary, the Habsburg empire would be converted into a federal state with complete self-government for the various nationalities. The well-meant gesture came too late. The Emperor's manifesto was coolly received throughout the empire. Backed up by President Wilson's insistence that it was up to them – and not to him or the Emperor Karl – to decide their fates, the various minorities promptly cut loose. Czechoslovakia declared itself a republic. The South Slavs declared for union with Serbia in what would become Yugoslavia. The Polish minority joined the newly independent Poland. Transylvania and Bukovina asked Romania to annex them. Trieste and Trentino went to Italy. Hungary, deciding that it was also a national minority, seceded.

Within weeks the vast Habsburg empire had been reduced to German-speaking Austria alone. The Emperor Karl now reigned over an empire that had shrunk to less than one-fifth of its original size. But he did not reign over it for long. The Austrians, no less impressed by Wilsonian theories of freedom and democracy, wanted as much self-determination as any of the other peoples in the rapidly dissolving realm. Karl could only sit helplessly by while the political parties wrangled about the form this new state should take. Some favoured a constitutional monarchy, others a republic. One Socialist deputy even went so far as to suggest that a republic, with Karl as president, would satisfy both the republicans and the monarchists.

'My only wish', sighed Karl, 'is that everything shall be liquidated peacefully.' In the end a republic was decided upon. Yet even now the politicians could not decide on whether they should recommend immediate abdication or wait for the Emperor to be formally deposed.

Their minds were made up for them by the threat of violence. It was feared that the increasingly unruly workers and soldiers might stage a march on Schönbrunn. The country could not possibly afford a civil war. On Monday 11 November 1918, a deputation of desperately worried ministers arrived at Schönbrunn. They brought with them a document for the Emperor's signature. By signing it, he would be relinquishing 'all participation in affairs of state'.

Regarding it as an act of abdication, Karl refused to sign. 'This crown is a responsibility given to me by God and I cannot renounce it,' he claimed. Zita was equally adamant and, as always, more vehement. 'A sovereign can never abdicate!' she cried. 'He can be deposed and his sovereign rights declared forfeit. All right. That is force. But abdicate – never, never, never! I would rather fall here at your side . . .'[2]

Zita's passionate outburst was to give rise to the rumour that, whereas Karl had been prepared to abdicate, she would not allow him to. This she always denied. Karl was just as determined to resist abdication. And indeed, no more than those other high-spirited and brave-talking consorts – the Tsaritsa

Alexandra, Queen Marie of Romania, Queen Sophie of Greece or even the Empress Dona – could the Empress Zita really influence events.

In mounting agitation the delegation explained to Karl that the document was not exactly an act of abdication: it was simply a renunciation of his political powers. And, in any case, there was really no alternative. Reluctantly, Karl signed. But he made it clear that he was neither abdicating nor renouncing his dynastic rights. Just before leaving that evening, he issued a proclamation.

'Filled, as ever, with unwavering devotion to all my peoples, I do not wish to oppose their free growth with my person. I recognise in advance whatever decision that German–Austria may take about its future political form. The people, through its representatives, has taken over the government. I renounce all participation in the affairs of state.'[3]

There was not much more to be done. Before leaving the palace, the Emperor, the Empress and their five children went to the chapel to pray. Those members of the household who would not be following the imperial family into retirement assembled in the sumptuously gilded and tapestried Hall of Ceremonies. Slowly, in his charming, unassuming way, the young Emperor made the *cercle*, shaking hands and saying a few words to each of them. Then, having been warned that it would be unsafe to travel in the royal cars, Karl reluctantly agreed that the family should leave in private vehicles. It was to be a singularly undramatic exit for the last monarch of this once-mighty, six-hundred-year-old empire.

At dusk, on 11 November 1918, the heavily laden cars were driven out of the gates of Schönbrunn, headed for the temporary refuge of Eckartsau Castle, fifteen miles away.

Two days later a delegation from the new Hungarian government arrived at Eckartsau. As Karl's Hungarian crown had always been separate from his Austrian crown, he was being asked to give that up as well. On the same conditions – that he was renouncing only his share in the government and not his dynastic rights – Karl acquiesced.

The brotherhood of kings, which had been such a feature of pre-war Europe, was to come into play once more for the Emperor Karl. A few months after his fall, with the imperial family still living at Eckartsau, there were rumours of a Bolshevik-inspired plot against them. The Empress's brother, Prince Sixtus, with the fate of the Russian imperial family very much in mind, begged the President of France to grant them some protection. Poincaré was sympathetic but unhelpful. So Sixtus went to see George V. Both King George and Queen Mary were very disturbed by the Prince's news.

'What Sixtus has told us is very serious,' said the Queen.

The King agreed. 'We will immediately do what is necessary,'[4] he assured the Prince.

So George V arranged for a British officer to be assigned to the Emperor and Empress for their protection. He was still with them when, a few weeks later, they left Austria for exile in Switzerland.

'No ruler has experienced a fate so ill as that which befell the Emperor Karl,' wrote the socialist chancellor, Kurt von Schuschnigg, in later years. 'Whether he was a great monarch, was wisely advised at all times, did the right thing always, is not the question here. To recognise that he was thoroughly good, brave and honest, and a true Austrian who wanted the best, and in misfortune bore himself more worthily than many other men would have done, is to assert the truth – and this truth has been suppressed far too long.'[5]

The last drama of the reign of the Austro-Hungarian Emperor had been acted out amidst the splendours of Schönbrunn; the German Emperor played his final scene in the altogether less palatial setting of the Château de la Fraineuse at Spa.

The Kaiser had returned to Spa, after a short spell at Potsdam, on 29 October 1918. He had been urged to do so by the Empress and Hindenburg. Both of them imagined that the Kaiser would be better able to save his crown among his generals at headquarters than among his ministers in Berlin. For with crowns, as the leader of the Independent Socialists in the Reichstag so graphically put it, 'rolling about the floor', the possibility of the Kaiser being able to hang on to his was becoming increasingly remote.

The crisis had begun exactly a month before. On 29 September, Hindenburg and Ludendorff had admitted to Wilhelm that the German army could not hold out much longer. Everywhere the Allies were breaking through. An armistice, on the basis of Wilson's Fourteen Points, would have to be asked for. But, in the meantime, the system of government would have to be reorganised so as to make it more acceptable in the eyes of the American President. This was done. The Kaiser's kinsman, the generally respected and relatively liberal Prince Max of Baden was appointed chancellor; long-promised democratic reforms were introduced; the Kaiser was transformed into something more like a true constitutional monarch.

But it had all come too late. President Wilson was unimpressed. While Wilhelm II remained, he argued, there was no guarantee that these hastily instituted changes would be permanent or effective. The Kaiser had spent too many years boasting about his personal power for anyone to believe that he was prepared to give it up now. What Wilson wanted was the Kaiser's abdication.

On finally appreciating this, both Wilhelm and Dona were incensed. 'The hypocritical Wilson has at last thrown off the mask,' thundered the Kaiser. 'The object of this is to bring down my House, to set the Monarchy aside.'

The Empress lashed out at 'the audacity of the parvenu across the sea who thus dares to humiliate a princely House which can look back on centuries of service to people and country'.

Yet, had they realised it, it was probably still within their power to save, if not their own crowns, at least that 'princely House' of which they were so proud. Wilhelm could have sacrificed himself for the sake of the monarchy. This is what the adroit Tsar Ferdinand of Bulgaria had just managed to do. Nor, by this stage, was it only President Wilson who was so anxious to get rid of the Kaiser. There was a growing conviction, among the German government and people, that the abdication of the Kaiser would ensure a better peace. The only hope of saving the monarchy would be for both the Kaiser and his feckless heir to abdicate their rights in favour of the Crown Prince's twelve-year-old son, Wilhelm. Even the Majority Socialists in the Reichstag were prepared to support such a move.

But Wilhelm would not hear of abdicating. He had previously assured his new chancellor, Prince Max, that 'a successor of Frederick the Great does not abdicate.' Now, to prevent Prince Max from pressing the point, the Empress urged her husband to get away from Berlin. Already the chancellor had prevailed upon the Kaiser to dismiss Ludendorff: Dona was determined that Wilhelm should agree to no more such demands from Prince Max or his government.

This was why, on the night of 29 October, the Kaiser set out for Spa. Among Hindenburg and the other generals, in the bosom of his adored army, Wilhelm would be safe.

It was a grave error of judgement. Although there was no certainty that by remaining in the capital the Kaiser would have been persuaded to abdicate in time to save the monarchy (or even that the monarchy could have been saved by such a move) any chance of this happening disappeared once Wilhelm fled to Spa. When, three days later, an emissary from the chancellor arrived at his château with a plea for the Kaiser to abdicate, Wilhelm was dismissive.

'I have no intention of quitting the throne because of a few hundred Jews and a thousand workmen,' he declared loftily.

In the course of the following ten days – from 1 to 10 November – the old ordered world of Kaiser Wilhelm II fell apart. The fleet mutinied at Kiel; revolution broke out in the industrial cities; the troops at the front were no longer prepared to fight; soldiers' and workers' councils were being formed. Turkey had already capitulated on 30 October; on 4 November Germany's other ally, Austria, signed an armistice. One after another the reigning kings, grand dukes and dukes of the empire were overthrown by revolutions and their kingdoms and duchies converted into republics. 'The Wittelsbachs ruled over Bavaria for seven hundred years,' boasted Kurt Eisner on the dethronement of Ludwig III. 'I got rid of them in seven hours with seven men.'

In the face of this revolutionary disorder and in spite of the fact that armistice talks were already under way at Compiègne, the Kaiser and his advisers thrashed about for some way the monarchy could be saved without his abdication. He should go to the front and die a glorious death at the head of his troops; he should abdicate as German Emperor but remain as King of Prussia; he should lead the army back into Germany to put down the 'Bolshevik revolution'. This particular scheme was quashed when the astonished Wilhelm was assured that the army was no longer prepared to march behind its Supreme War Lord.

Wilhelm even, at one stage, came up with the extraordinary suggestion that the Germans should combine with the monarchical British and Japanese to 'fling' the republican Americans out of Europe.

Saturday 9 November was the day of decision. The weather was cold and damp; a thick mist shrouded the Château de la Fraineuse. All morning, sometimes in the sodden garden, sometimes in the almost equally cold rooms of the house, the Kaiser deliberated. While Prince Max kept telephoning from Berlin, urging him to abdicate in order to avoid civil war, Wilhelm conferred with the newly arrived Crown Prince and with his various generals.

Not long after luncheon his mind was made up for him. He was told, via that ceaselessly ringing telephone, that Prince Max, on his own initiative, had already announced the abdication of both the Kaiser and the Crown Prince. Soon after, a republic was proclaimed from the steps of the Reichstag.

Wilhelm was furious. 'Treason, gentlemen! Barefaced, outrageous treason!' he exclaimed. 'I am King of Prussia and I will remain King. As such I will stay with my troops!' He then fired off a salvo of telegrams to Berlin, each more explosive than the last. It was all to no purpose. A visit from Admiral von Scheer convinced him that he could no longer rely on the navy, and by now even that dedicated monarchist, Hindenburg, had advised him to go. Afraid that the Kaiser might suffer the same fate as the Tsar, Hindenburg begged his master to take refuge in Holland. A body of mutinous troops was said to be marching on Spa. Finally, after several more hours of indecision, Wilhelm agreed to go. He would leave for Holland at five the following morning. Not until two weeks later, though, did he sign a formal act of abdication.

It has been claimed that George V had earlier asked Queen Wilhelmina of the Netherlands to grant the Kaiser asylum. If this is true, the request would have had to have been made in the greatest secrecy. With feeling against the Kaiser running so high in Britain, the King would never have risked an overt gesture towards his brother monarch and cousin; the question of the Tsar's future had given him quite enough trouble. But it is not improbable that George V had approached Queen Wilhelmina.

After a six-hour wait at the frontier, Wilhelm was given permission to enter Holland. He was told that he was to be the guest of Count Bentinck at his castle of Amerongen.

On the afternoon of 11 November 1918, the day that was from now on to be known as Armistice Day, Wilhelm arrived at Amerongen. The first words of this monarch who was regarded – in Britain particularly – as a blood-thirsty, bloodstained monster who deserved to be hanged, were richly typical, both of his contradictory nature and of his royal internationalism.

'Now', he said briskly to his host as they drove through the castle gates, 'for a cup of real good English tea.'[6]

While the monarchs who had lost their crowns were everywhere scuttling to safety, those who had managed to keep theirs were basking in the sunshine of victory. Overshadowed for so many years by the generals and the politicians, humiliated by the defeat of their armies or the occupation of their countries, they had again come, gloriously and triumphantly, into their own. Sovereigns were being hailed as the hierophants of victory; they were once more the focal points for national loyalties. Just as support for the vanquished monarchs had evaporated almost overnight, so did support and adulation burgeon for those kings whose countries had been victorious.

When an American division attached to a force commanded by King Albert of the Belgians broke through the German lines in October 1918 and freed a group of Flemish civilians, the deliverers were astonished by their first question. 'The King!' shouted the excited civilians. 'How is the King?'

Paradoxically, the only monarch to remain impervious to this sudden surge of public acclaim was the King whose countrymen had sparked off the great conflict: old Peter I of Serbia. In spite of the fact that he had been proclaimed King of the Serbs, Croats and Slovenes on 4 December 1918, he played no part in the state entry into Belgrade. Indeed, he did not return to his aggrandised kingdom until late in 1919. Nor, bent over a stick and wearing a long white beard, was he recognised by his subjects. When his son, the Regent, begged him to take up residence in his former palace, he refused. Instead, he went to live with his other son, the deranged and dispossessed Prince George, in a modest villa at Topchider. King Peter was to die, at the age of seventy-seven, in 1921.

For George V and Queen Mary, the end of the war brought tremendous public acclaim. All those wartime carpings about the King's German ancestry and his alleged German sympathies were forgotten. Cheering crowds surged to Buckingham Palace on Armistice night; time after time, and deep into the night, the sovereigns were obliged to show themselves on the palace balcony. On five successive days the royal couple drove in an open carriage through the streets of the capital. 'Nine miles through masses of cheering crowds,' noted the King in his diary. 'The demonstrations of the people are indeed touching.'

Rome, too, echoed to vociferous cheering as, on that same Armistice day, Victor Emmanuel III returned to his capital. 'As I watched his triumphant progress from the station to the palace down the Via Nazionale in a blaze of flags through a rain of flowers,' wrote the British ambassador, 'I felt a sense of happy exultation because the King, for whom as a man I had such a profound regard, whose judgements had been right and sound throughout, who had never lost faith or courage in the grimmest hours of those dark years, might now feel proudly conscious that under his guidance the unity of his kingdom and the old Italian dream had been fulfilled.'[7]

But possibly no crowned head felt so profound a sense of elation as did Marie of Romania. Not until the end of November did King Ferdinand and Queen Marie return from Jassy. Their state entry into Bucharest was set for 1 December 1918. For the diffident Ferdinand it was a particularly triumphant homecoming. With Romania about to be more than doubled in size, he was bringing more than mere victory in his train. 'Kaiser Wilhelm, when drunk with success,' wrote Marie, 'had cried out in a loud voice that King Ferdinand would be the last of the Hohenzollerns to sit on a Romanian throne. King Ferdinand had said nothing but he had quietly, humbly, pursued his thorny way. Today, the Kaiser and his son were without a country, and King Ferdinand, loyal and modest, was hailed as a deliverer, was the King of *all* the Romanians! How not to bow my head in the wonder of what had come to pass.'

But bow her head was the very last thing that Queen Marie intended to do on the day of the state entry into Bucharest. It was an unforgettable occasion: a day of 'wild, delirious enthusiasm'. As the bands played and the troops marched and the flags fluttered and the crowds cheered, the King and Queen rode their horses through the streets of the capital. Both were in uniform. On her head Marie wore a grey astrakan busby and, over her tunic, a long military cloak with a fur collar. At one point they halted to kiss a great cross held up by a group of chanting, lavishly vestmented priests; at another, they were presented with the traditional gifts of bread and salt by the mayor of the city.

The parade was followed by a *Te Deum* in the Cathedral. For over two years this showiest of queens had seldom been seen in anything other than her Red Cross uniform or Romanian national costume. Now for the *Te Deum* she changed into one of her floating, glittering garments and, kneeling beside Ferdinand in 'the dusky church lighted by a thousand candles', gave thanks for their great victory.

But the most poignant homecoming of all was that of King Albert and Queen

Elisabeth of the Belgians. Their return had been gradual, for the King, commanding a combined force of Belgian, British, French and American troops, had had to battle his way towards Brussels. For a month, while the fighting continued, the royal family had lived in the Château de Lophem, just south of Bruges. Not until the armistice had been signed, on 11 November, could Albert think in terms of a formal entry into his capital.

At least though he had the satisfaction of knowing that the tide had turned; that those four long years on the Yser had not been in vain. Even before taking up residence at Lophem, Albert had heard that the Bulgarian resistance had collapsed and that his Coburg uncle, Tsar Ferdinand, had lost his throne. This turn of events gave him some wry satisfaction. He remembered that, at the beginning of the war, Ferdinand had called him a fool for not allowing German troops to pass freely through Belgium. 'Today', mused Albert, 'he must have altered his opinion; he must understand that it is always in a man's best interests to remain honest.'

It was while he was at Lophem that King Albert, in consultation with his ministers, inaugurated several radical political changes. During the last weeks of the war a certain section of the Belgian population was anxious for the King to take advantage of his enormous prestige to assume dictatorial powers. For four years he had governed by decree: why, it was asked, should he not continue to do so? Even if he were not to go so far as to stage a *coup d'état* he should at least take advantage of this opportunity to strengthen the executive. The monumental task of reconstruction, they argued, would be simplified were the King able to work unhampered by party political squabblings.

To these urgings Albert did not even deign to reply. He was bound to the constitution by his oath. That, as much as his distaste for autocratic rule, ensured his rejection of any such scheme. In common with kings like Ferdinand of Romania, Albert realised that the day of the power-wielding monarch was over. In fact, far from assuming more power for himself, he was determined to grant more to his subjects. While at Lophem Albert agreed to the immediate introduction of universal suffrage and to the gradual granting of various reforms to the Flemings. These moves were to be accompanied by sweeping social legislation.

It was rumoured, at the time, that the King had been frightened into these reforms. A riot, instigated by dissatisfied German soldiers and supported by some Belgian revolutionaries, had erupted in the streets of Brussels during the last days of the war. Tricolour cockades, red flags and the strains of the *Marsellaise* had scared some of the populace into believing that a revolution was imminent. The disturbances had been quelled but news of the revolutionary threat was said to have been purposely exaggerated in order to frighten an unwilling King Albert into conceding reform.

The rumour was nonsense. Few things were guaranteed to make the King more annoyed than the mention that he had granted these concessions under pressure. 'I want you to know that what I did at Lophem, I did of my own accord, actuated by no one but myself,' he afterwards declared.

By this broadening of the base of political life, Albert was to place himself, once and for all, above party politics. No longer would the socialists, growing yearly more powerful, be able to identify him with the privileged classes. The introduction of universal suffrage was to increase his prestige enormously; he was to become less of a political figure and more of a national symbol – the respected and impartial arbiter between the Catholic, Liberal and Socialist parties.

King Albert, claimed Emile Vandervelde, the great Belgian socialist leader, in later years, 'was the ideal incarnation of the "Republican Monarchy" which the authors of our Constitution wished deliberately to create in 1831'.

It was on 22 November 1918 that King Albert finally re-entered his capital. Dressed in khaki, with a steel helmet topping his lined and weather-beaten face, he rode slowly through the gaily decorated streets. Beside him, mounted on a huge white charger and wearing a faded grey riding habit, rode the Queen. Behind rode their sons, Prince Leopold and Prince Charles, and among the horsemen who followed after were Britain's Prince Albert – the future George VI – and Queen Mary's brother, the Earl of Athlone.

They say that no one who was in Brussels that day could ever forget this homecoming. For years afterwards it was spoken about with something like awe; it came to constitute one of the great royal set-pieces of the First World War. Every rooftop, every window, every inch of pavement was packed with people. Flags fluttered, handkerchiefs waved, cheer upon tumultuous cheer rose up as the procession passed by. Throats were hoarse, arms were limp, faces were wet with tears. Even the King, usually so serious, smiled with happiness at this heartfelt welcome.

It was the Queen, though, who was the most moving sight of all. 'Plainly overwhelmed by their reception,' remembered one eyewitness, 'she sat erect and motionless on her white horse, her face piteously grave in the midst of so much rejoicing and her eyes stonily fixed on the road ahead, as though she dare not glance to right or left for fear of breaking down.'[8]

No amount of public acclamation could blind Europe's triumphantly returning monarchs to the fact that their world had ended. With the coming of peace, the old Europe – the Europe of the Kings – disappeared. The fall of the three great dynasties – the Hohenzollerns, the Habsburgs and the Romanovs – meant that the only major European throne still standing was the British. Victor Emmanuel III was soon to be completely overshadowed as head of state by Mussolini; Greece would become a republic in 1924; the Spanish throne would fall a few years later. The remaining monarchies would be confined to the opposite corners of the Continent: to the Balkans (and they would be swept away by the Second World War) and to the countries bordering the North Sea.

The days when sovereigns could bestride the Continent like gods had gone forever. Although there would still be exchanges of royal visits among Europe's dwindling band of monarchs, their scale and significance would be altered. Their political importance would be minimal; their power to influence international affairs negligible; their function purely ceremonial. Never again would the myth that the destinies of the world were being controlled by a family of kings have the slightest substance. Monarchs would become little more than figureheads.

The reasons for the fall of these long-established European thrones at the end of the First World War varied from country to country. Military defeat, an inability to adapt to the democratic spirit of the times, President Wilson's anti-monarchist attitudes and his encouragement of nationalism – all these contributed to the overthrow of the old monarchical order. In the main, it was the sovereigns without personal power who kept their thrones and those wielding too much power who lost them. By behaving like autocrats, these monarchs had become identified with the shortcomings of their regimes. Tsar Nicholas II was regarded as the symbol of the tyranny and inefficiency of his empire; the Emperor Franz Joseph was held responsible for the subjugation of the minority races in his realm; Kaiser Wilhelm II was seen as the very personification of the militarism, élitism and aggressiveness of the Second Reich.

These lessons were not lost on the kings who survived. More than ever did they ensure that the crown was kept well above politics and faction; that it was identified with all the people and not the aristocracy alone. Those kings like Ferdinand of Romania and Albert of the Belgians, who were still in a position to shape and influence affairs, used their remaining powers to urge political and social reform. Victor Emmanuel III handed over several of his palaces and much of his wealth to the state. Even the politically powerless George V felt the need to safeguard his throne. 'The Crown and its cost', warned Lord Esher, 'will have to be justified in the future in the eyes of a war-torn and hungry proletariat, endowed with a huge preponderance of voting power.'

Once the dust, raised by the revolutionary and nationalistic upheavals that followed the fall of the three empires, had settled, and the peacemakers of Versailles had gone home, the Continent embarked on what was optimistically called a 'new order'. The old order – the dynastic, monarchical order – was held responsible for all the disasters that had fallen upon Europe. The war had been the result of the despotism, ambition and aggression of the kings. The old world of deference and discipline, of oppression and exploitation, of

32 Tsar Ferdinand of Bulgaria and the Emperor Karl of Austria–Hungary
during the last months of the war

33 Victory in sight:
George V and Albert
the Belgians lunching
off a railway goods
truck near Zeebrugge
November 1918

34 Ferdinand of Romani
and George V drive i
triumph through the
streets of London afte
the war

militarism and autocracy, was to be replaced by the Wilsonian dream of democracy and nationalism.

In its stead would rise that other Wilsonian conception – the League of Nations. 'Europe', announced the United States President, 'is being liquidated and the League of Nations must be the heir to that great estate.' The League, wrote his fellow visionary, General J.C. Smuts, 'will have to occupy the great position which has been rendered vacant by the dissolution of many of the old European empires and the passing away of the old European order'.

It was true, of course, that the old monarchical order had a great deal to answer for; that it was guilty of many of the things of which it stood accused. The monarchs – particularly the monarchs of Central Europe – with their monumental palaces, their glittering courts and their rigid ceremonial, had formed the apex of a pyramid; in this way, they had perpetuated a hierarchical and inequitable system. Their political positions had been too powerful; their governments too unrepresentative.

But if the monarchical system had not been perfect, it was certainly preferable to what followed. For the fall of the kings ushered in, not the utopian world of the League of Nations, but the altogether more draconian world of the dictators. In the place of the hereditary kings came the totalitarian men of the people: men 'risen up from the masses and established by the masses'.

'The day of the Kings was over, not because despotism was out of date,' writes Edmond Taylor, 'but because harsher and more efficient patterns of despotism were beginning to emerge. Above all, the old dynasties were discredited in the eyes of their former subjects because they had been so international, even when they were not, like the Habsburgs, explicitly supranational. As a democratic credo, Wilsonism might be ebbing, but the tide of nationalism that the Fourteen Points had helped to set in motion was running stronger than ever in Europe . . .'

Gradually, as this nationalism gathered strength, a new autocracy replaced the old. Dictatorships of one sort or another were established in almost every country over which the monarchs had once reigned; in very few cases were the personal liberties of these former royal subjects enhanced. In place of men like Nicholas II, Franz Joseph I and Wilhelm II, there now stood the infinitely more menacing figures of Stalin, Hitler, Mussolini and others. It was almost as though, in a nostalgia for their monarchical past, the peoples of Europe had raised up a new race of still more powerful monarchs.

The First World War had cut down the last great flowering of European monarchy; the field was now ready for the dictators and the Second World War.

Epilogue

Victors and Vanquished

NOT UNTIL thirty years after the end of the First World War did the last of the embattled monarchs finally disappear from the scene. Those two crowned Balkan patriarchs, Nicholas of Montenegro and Peter of Serbia, both died in 1921. Nicholas, with his old mountain kingdom about to be absorbed into the new state of Yugoslavia, died in exile in the South of France at the age of seventy-nine. Peter, as monarch of this new kingdom, died – an all-but-forgotten recluse – in his villa at Topchider. He was succeeded by his son, as King Alexander I of Yugoslavia.

King Alexander's task, in controlling his polyglot kingdom, was no more successful than Franz Joseph's had been in managing his multi-national empire. The Serbian dream quickly turned into a nightmare. The nine different national groupings, whose determination to be united had sparked off the First World War, were soon at each other's throats. No one co-operated; no one compromised. Parliament was simply a collection of bickering minorities. In the end Alexander, who had started his reign with every intention of making parliamentary democracy work, was obliged to assume dictatorial powers. He was assassinated, by a Croat organisation, in 1934.

In the year of Alexander's accession, 1921, the ex-Emperor Karl of Austria–Hungary made two attempts to regain at least one of his two crowns. In 1920, with the fall of a short-lived communist regime, Hungary was once again declared to be a monarchy, under the regency of Admiral Horthy. With Horthy showing very little sign of keeping his promise to restore the exiled ex-Emperor, Karl twice arrived in Hungary to claim his throne. Both of these quixotic gestures failed. On the second, and very nearly successful occasion, when Karl and Zita landed from a small private aeroplane, Horthy had to get rid of them by force. The imperial family was then banished, on British insistence, to the island of Madeira. Here, in a damp and doleful little villa, on 1 April 1922, the last and almost penniless Habsburg Emperor died of pneumonia. He was thirty-five. The Empress Zita, at the age of ninety-four, is still alive in 1986.

The return of King Constantine of the Hellenes to his kingdom was an altogether more triumphant affair. In October 1920 his second son, who had ascended the throne as King Alexander on Constantine's dethronement, died suddenly of blood poisoning after being bitten by a monkey. To solve the problem of the succession, Venizelos, the Greek prime minister, called an election. In it, his own party was soundly defeated. The disgusted Venizelos left the country. A plebiscite decided, by almost a hundred to one, on the return of King Constantine. So, on 19 December 1920, Constantine and Sophie arrived home to a tumultuous welcome. Constantine was deeply moved by this riotous show of affection; the more cynical Sophie considered it 'too exuberant to last'.

She was right. Against his better judgement, Constantine was obliged to continue a campaign – started by Venizelos in his stubborn pursuit of the Great Idea of Greek aggrandisement – against the Turks. In September 1922 the Greeks were soundly beaten and the largely Greek population of the city of Smyrna savagely massacred. The Greek army revolted and, quite unjustifiably blaming the King for the defeat, demanded his abdication. Constantine agreed. For a second time he and Sophie left Athens. This time there was no frantic crowd to prevent their departure.

Three months later, on 11 January 1923, in a hotel room in Palermo, Sicily, Constantine died of a brain haemorrhage. In his hand was clutched a small leather pouch containing Greek soil. Like the Emperor Karl, his life had been shattered by the war.

Constantine was succeeded by his eldest son as King George II. But in just over a year after Constantine's death, George II was also in exile. In March 1924 the Greek National Assembly passed a resolution abolishing the monarchy and declaring Greece a republic.

Some ten years later the volatile Greeks restored the monarchy. Forty years after that, in 1974, they again abolished it.

The post-war gratification of King Ferdinand of Romania had also turned sour. His last years were clouded by the feckless behaviour of his eldest son, Crown Prince Carol. Carol's scandalous and widely publicised private life culminated in his desertion of his second wife, Princess Helen of Greece, for the more voluptuous charms of Elena Lupescu. The couple fled Romania and Carol renounced his rights to the throne. His position as heir was taken by his only son, the four-year-old Prince Michael. (King Michael went into exile with the fall of the Romanian throne after the Second World War.)

A shared concern over their son Carol's transgressions brought King Ferdinand and Queen Marie closer together. It seemed to them almost inconceivable that their wartime years of sacrifice and suffering, followed by their post-war realisation of the Romanian Dream, should have led to this.

Ferdinand, his spirit broken by this dynastic crisis, died of cancer on 27 July 1927. Marie, a fascinating figure to the end, died in 1938.

King Albert of the Belgians was the next sovereign to die. If the *Union Sacrée* – the wartime co-operation of all the Belgian people – did not long survive the coming of peace, the King at least had the satisfaction of seeing his country become relatively prosperous. And although he suffered from periods of disillusion, Albert remained a dedicated and conscientious monarch. He remained, also, an extremely modest one. Few things embarrassed him more than references to his heroic wartime role. 'I suppose I shall once more be greeted with acclamations as the Warrior-King,' he once muttered before attending a reception. 'I am getting so *bored* with it.' Kaiser Wilhelm II would never have said that.

King Albert was killed, in a rock-climbing accident in the Ardennes on 17 February 1934, at the age of fifty-eight. He was succeeded by his eldest son, as Leopold III. The redoubtable, remarkable and ultimately controversial Queen Elisabeth (the 'Red Queen' they called her because of her visits to various communist countries) outlived him by over thirty years. She died, in her ninetieth year, in 1965.

King George V died, a revered and popular father-figure, on 20 January 1936. By then he had developed into a quintessentially British monarch; the very symbol of the nation. All but forgotten was his German ancestry and his Continental connections: George V, and his dynasty, had become a truly national institution, the embodiment, it was said, of everything that was best in British life.

Strangely enough, George V's cousin and enemy, Wilhelm II, had become increasingly like an English country gentleman with the passing years. This, the Kaiser had once said, was what he would have preferred to have been above all else. Wilhelm's twenty-two-year-long exile, at Doorn in Holland, was as notable for its tranquillity as his reign had been for its turbulence. Relieved of the pressures of his position, his personality mellowed. He became, if no wiser, certainly more relaxed and more benign. With his white beard, his tweed suits and his passion for dogs, gardening and chopping wood, Wilhelm made the perfect country squire.

But he could not resist some self-justification. There was, of course, a great deal to be explained away, particularly with regard to the outbreak of the war. For this Wilhelm persisted in laying the blame on everyone but himself. Chief amongst his host of villains – his advisers, his generals, rival diplomats, foreign rulers – was his uncle, King Edward VII, 'the Encircler'. The 'peace of Europe', argued Wilhelm, 'was never in such danger as when the King of England concerned himself with its maintenance'.

Yet it was to Edward VII's son, George V, that the dethroned sovereigns of the German Reich sent a petition after the peacemakers at Versailles had decided that the Kaiser was to be tried for 'a supreme offence against international morality and the sanctity of treaties'. Reminding the British King, none too tactfully, that his family had originated in Germany, and that to threaten one monarch in this way would be to threaten the sanctity of all monarchs, himself included, the 'German Princes' begged King George to prevent the trial.

Their request threw the King into a quandary. Fortunately, he was saved from having to take any action by the Dutch government's resolute refusal to deliver up the ex-Kaiser.

With the passing years, the Kaiser's attitude towards Britain began to soften. Unlike Germany, Britain was still a monarchy and for this reason alone Wilhelm felt kindly disposed towards it. Compared with Germany during the 1920s and 1930s, it seemed like a haven of stability. Not until two years after George V's death, though, did the Kaiser make direct contact with his British relations. In 1938, after Neville Chamberlain's meeting with Hitler in Munich, Wilhelm wrote a letter to the widowed Queen Mary. The two of them had last met at the Kaiser's daughter's wedding, in Berlin in 1913. The tone of the letter was richly typical of the writer.

'May I with a grateful heart relieved from a sickening anxiety by the intercession of Heaven unite my warmest, sincerest thanks to the Lord with yours and those of the German and British people that He saved us from a most fearful catastrophe by helping the responsible statesmen to preserve peace!' ran the feverish phrases. 'I have not the slightest doubt that Mr N. Chamberlain was inspired by Heaven and guided by God who took pity on his children on Earth by crowning his mission with such relieving success. God bless him. I kiss your hand in respectful devotion as ever.'[1]

A link had once more been forged, and a few months later, on the Kaiser's eightieth birthday, he received several congratulatory telegrams from the British royal family. In 1940, at Winston Churchill's suggestion, George VI offered the Kaiser refuge in England from Hitler's invading army. Wilhelm refused the offer. It would not do for even a rejected monarch to seek protection from his country's enemies.

And although Wilhelm's attitude towards Germany's new master, Adolf Hitler, had been equivocal, he could not resist sending the Führer a telegram of congratulations on the fall of Paris. 'The German war flag over Versailles!' he wrote exultantly to his daughter. 'Thus is the pernicious *entente cordiale* of Uncle Edward VII brought to nought.'[2]

Kaiser Wilhelm II died, a year later, on 4 June 1941.

King Victor Emmanuel III of Italy did not long enjoy the reputation won during the war years. By the end of 1922, the social and political turbulence of post-war Italy had thrown up Mussolini; and the liberal king found himself completely outshone by the fascist dictator. Although *Il Duce* made Victor Emmanuel Emperor of Ethiopia and King of Albania, the little monarch was never more than a cipher in affairs of state. He was treated even more summarily by Hitler and Mussolini than he had been by Wilhelm II and Franz Joseph.

Nor, as in 1915, could he reap any benefits from changing sides. His switch came too late. His dismissal of Mussolini in 1943 could not save him from the stigma of fascism; his subsequent failure to make a clean break with Hitler cost him his throne. In 1944 he withdrew from public affairs; two years later he abdicated in favour of his son, Crown Prince Umberto. The reign of Umberto II lasted for a month. In a closely contested plebiscite, the Italian people opted for a republic.

Victor Emmanuel III spent his exile in a modest villa in Alexandria, Egypt, lent to him by King Farouk. He died there on 28 December 1947 at the age of seventy-eight.

The longest lived of these First World War sovereigns was the most colourful of them all: Tsar Ferdinand of Bulgaria. Like Victor Emmanuel III, Ferdinand lived to see the collapse of everything to which he had devoted his life. Yet his first years of exile were not unpleasant. He had gone to live in Coburg, the cradle of his dynasty; and as – in his astute fashion – Ferdinand had managed to salvage much of his fortune, he was able to live in some style. Always the actor, Ferdinand played the role of what he insisted on calling *le pauvre exilé* with dignity and restraint. Although he allowed himself a little plaintive grumbling from time to time, he was never bitter or vindictive about his change of fortune. The possibility of exile was simply one of the hazards of kingship. He devoted his time to natural history, gardening, the arts, travel and the occult. He could still, with his white beard and his dramatic clothes, impress visitors by his appearance; his *outré* conversation could still shock.

Inevitably, as he moved among the royal families of Europe, exiled or reigning, Ferdinand would come up against reminders of the time when the war had torn many of them so cruelly apart. To the Infanta Eulalia of Spain, he spoke drily of continuing French accusations of treachery because he, whose mother had been a Bourbon-Orleans, had taken up arms against France. 'This I find somewhat amusing,' he said, 'since France herself gave Louis Philippe (his grandfather) his *congé* and would have none of him or his family.'

And at the wedding of his eldest son, by now Tsar Boris III of Bulgaria, to the daughter of Victor Emmanuel III in 1930 Ferdinand came face to face with his grand-niece, Princess Françoise of Orleans. When Ferdinand, in his gracious way, assured her that he felt 'more Orleans than Coburg', she was not impressed. 'So, you have already forgotten the war, my uncle?' she answered sharply.

Another of the wedding guests was the widowed ex-Queen Sophie of Greece. Some seventeen years before, during the Second Balkan War, Sophie's husband Constantine had joined Peter of Serbia in inflicting a crushing defeat on their recent ally, Ferdinand of Bulgaria. But Ferdinand bore no grudge. At luncheon, he and Sophie were inseparable. 'What did you find to talk about?' asked Sophie's brother-in-law, Prince Christopher of Greece. The question astonished her. 'Why old times, of course,' answered Sophie.

Prince Christopher appreciated that both Sophie and Ferdinand belonged to a generation where royal freemasonry transcended any narrow nationalism.

Ferdinand's abiding comfort during much of his exile was that he – alone of all the monarchs defeated in the war – had managed to save his country's monarchy. But he would live to see that disappear as well. Just as the years before the First World War had found Ferdinand caught between the Tsar of Russia on the one hand, and the Emperors of Germany and Austria–Hungary on the other, so did the years before the Second World War find his son Boris trapped between their successors – Stalin and Hitler.

This time there was no saving the monarchy. Boris, having been forced to throw in his lot with Germany, was rumoured to have been murdered, on Hitler's orders, for being less than co-operative. His brother Cyril was murdered by the communist regime that took power in 1945. A year later an inevitable plebiscite decided in favour of a republic and Boris's nine-year-old son, Tsar Simeon, took the road to exile.

Ferdinand, having seen the wholesale fall of thrones at the end of the First World War, had lived through a second royal holocaust – the fall of the thrones of Yugoslavia, Italy, Romania and, of course, Bulgaria – after the Second World War. He died, a barely remembered relic of another age, in Coburg, at the age of eighty-seven, on 10 September 1948.

Ferdinand's words on hearing that his son Cyril had been shot would serve, says his biographer Stephen Constant, as a fitting epitaph for the close of his own life.

'Everything', sighed the old monarch, 'is collapsing around me.'

Notes

PROLOGUE

1 Mayer, *The Persistence*, p 13
2 Rose, *George V*, p 154
3 Gerard, *My Four Years*, p 78
4 Gore, *George V*, pp 263–4
5 Hamilton, *Vanished Pomps*, p 316

CHAPTER ONE

1 Haller, *Kaiser's Friend*, pp 200–1
2 Hamilton, *Vanished Pomps*, p 334
3 Balfour, *The Kaiser*, p 175
4 Palmer, *Gardeners*, p 34

CHAPTER TWO

1 Cammaerts, *Albert*, p 80
2 Cunliffe-Owen, *Elisabeth*, p 71
3 Cammaerts, *Albert*, p 130

CHAPTER THREE

1 Gore, *George V*, pp 247–8
2 Marie of Romania, *Life*, Vol II, p 211
3 Christopher of Greece, *Memoirs*, p 162
4 Rose, *George V*, p 106
5 Nicolson, *George V*, p 248

CHAPTER FOUR

1 Waddington, *Italian Letters*, p 243
2 Bagot, *Italian Year*, p 113
3 Griscom, *Diplomatically*, p 282
4 Muller, *Kaiser and his court*, 25/5/1915

CHAPTER FIVE

1 Vyrubova, *Memories*, p 101
2 Newton, *Lord Lansdowne*, p 199
3 Kokovtsov, *Out of my Past*, p 167

4 Botkin, *Real Romanovs*, p 61
5 Kokovtsov, *Out of my Past*, p 223
6 Moorehead, *Russian Revolution*, p 72

CHAPTER SIX

1 Constant, *Foxy Ferdinand*, p 53
2 Fox, *Lenin*, p. 186
3 Massie, *Nicholas and Alexandra*, p ix
4 Rose, *George V*, p 166
5 Bülow, *Memoirs*, Vol II, p 355

CHAPTER SEVEN

1 Festetics, *Diary*, 28/11/1873
2 Thomson, *Europe*, p 452

CHAPTER EIGHT

1 West, *Black Lamb*, Vol II, p 444
2 *The Times*, 18/6/1903
3 West, *Black Lamb*, Vol I, p 594
4 Balfour, *The Kaiser*, p 336
5 Buchanan, *Victoria's Relations*, p 156

CHAPTER NINE

1 Constant, *Foxy Ferdinand*, p 45
2 Palmer, *The Kaiser*, p 153
3 Paléologue, *Journal*, p 255
4 Constant, *Foxy Ferdinand*, p 288
5 Seton-Watson, *Roumanians*, p 469

CHAPTER TEN

1 Mansergh, *The Coming*, p 219
2 Blücher, *An English Wife*, p 14
3 Marek, *The Eagles Die*, p 441

CHAPTER ELEVEN

1 *New York Times*, 11/9/1914
2 Muller, *Kaiser and his court*, 4/9/1914
3 *Ibid.*, 6/11/1914
4 Cammaerts, *Albert*, p 283
5 Paléologue, *Memoirs*, Vol I, p 147

CHAPTER TWELVE

1 West, *Black Lamb*, Vol I, p 602
2 Katz, *House of Savoy*, p 199
3 Bülow, *Memoirs*, Vol III, p 264
4 Robertson, *Victor Emmanuel*, p 134
5 Muller, *Kaiser and his court*, 16/5/1915
6 Constant, *Foxy Ferdinand*, p 305
7 Graham, *Alexander*, p 90
8 Marie of Romania, *Life*, Vol III, p 25
9 Conv. with Queen Mother
10 Elsberry, *Marie*, p 118
11 Nicolson, *George V*, p 372
12 *Ibid.*

CHAPTER THIRTEEN

1 Fischer, *Germany's Aims*, p 301
2 Manteyer, *Austria's Peace Offer*, p 74
3 Brook-Shepherd, *Last Habsburg*, p 74
4 Viktoria Luise, *Kaiser's Daughter*, pp 102–3
5 Paléologue, *Memoirs*, Vol III, p 157
6 Bulygin, *Murder*, pp 94–5

CHAPTER FOURTEEN

1 Balfour, *The Kaiser*, p 375
2 Boothroyd, *Philip*, p 50
3 Nicolson, *George V*, p 403
4 Rose, *George V*, p 174

5 Bocca, *Uneasy Heads*, p 170
6 Cammaerts, *Albert*, p 227
7 Viktoria Luise, *Kaiser's Daughter*, p 104
8 Lloyd-George, *Memoirs*, p 514

CHAPTER FIFTEEN

1 Katz, *House of Savoy*, p 210
2 Artieri, *Il Diario*, p 67
3 *Daily Mail*, 18/1/1916
4 *The Times*, 15/12/1916

CHAPTER SIXTEEN

1 Brook-Shepherd, *Last Habsburg*, p xi
2 Taylor, *Fall of the Dynasties*, p 343
3 ffoulkes, *All This*, p 80
4 Rose, *George V*, p 216
5 Cammaerts, *Albert*, p 287
6 *Ibid.*, 229
7 Palmer, *The Kaiser*, p 204
8 Muller, *Kaiser and his court*, 11/8/1918

CHAPTER SEVENTEEN

1 Madol, *Ferdinand*, pp 254–9
2 Brook-Shepherd, *Last Habsburg*, p 213
3 *Ibid.*, p 214
4 *Ibid.*, p 224
5 Taylor, *Fall of the Dynasties*, pp 355–6
6 Bentinck, *Ex-Kaiser*, p 15
7 Rodd, *Memories*, p 372
8 Oglander, *Keyes*, p 259

EPILOGUE

1 Pope-Hennessy, *Queen Mary*, p 592
2 Viktoria Luise, *Im Strom*, p 286

Bibliography

Albert I, King of the Belgians, *The War Diaries of Albert I* (ed. by Gen. R. Van Overstraeten), William Kimber, London, 1954

Albertini, I., *The Origins of the War of 1914*, 3 vols, Oxford University Press, 1952–7

Alexander, Grand Duke, *Once a Grand Duke*, Cassell, London, 1932

— *Always a Grand Duke*, Cassell, London, 1933

Alexandra, Tsaritsa, *Letters of the Tsaritsa to the Tsar 1914–1916* (ed. by Sir Bernard Pares), Duckworth, London, 1923

Alice, Countess of Athlone, Princess, *For My Grandchildren*, Evans, London, 1966

Almedingen, E.M., *The Empress Alexandra 1872–1918*, Hutchinson, London, 1961

Anon, *The Royal Family of Greece*, Warwick and Rutter, Toronto, 1914

Anon, *Ferdinand of Bulgaria: The Amazing Career of a Shoddy Czar*, Andrew Melrose, London, 1916

Anon, *Ex-King Nicholas of Montenegro and His Court*, Glas Naroda, Sarajevo, 1919

Anon, *Recollections of Three Kaisers*, Herbert Jenkins, London, 1929

Armstrong, H.C., *Grey Steel*, Arthur Barker, London, 1937

Artieri, Giovanni, *Il Re, i Soldati et il Generale che Vinse*, Cappelli, Rocca San Cassiano, 1952

— *Il diario di Vittorio Emmanuele III*, published in *Epoca*, 14 January–3 March, 1968

Asquith, Margot, *Places and Persons*, Thornton Butterworth, London, 1925

Bagehot, Walter, *The English Constitution*, Kegan, Paul, London, 1898

Bagot, Richard, *My Italian Year*, Tauchnitz, Leipzig, 1912

Balfour, Michael, *The Kaiser and His Times*, Pelican, London, 1975

Barker, Elizabeth, *Macedonia: Its Place in Balkan Power Politics*, Royal Institute of International Affairs, London, 1950

Barnett, Correlli, *The Swordbearers*, Eyre and Spottiswoode, London, 1963

Batcheller, Tryphosa Bates, *Glimpses of Italian Court Life*, Doubleday, New York, 1906

Baumont, M., *The Fall of the Kaiser*, Allen and Unwin, London, 1931

Benson, E.F., *The Kaiser and English Relations*, Longmans, Green, London 1936

Bentinck, Lady Norah, *The Ex-Kaiser in Exile*, Hodder and Stoughton, London, 1921

Bertoldi, S., *Vittorio Emanuele III*, Utet, Turin, 1970

Bibesco, Princess, *Ferdinand de Roumania: Une Victime Royale*, Les Amis d'Edouard, Paris, N.D.

Bierme, Maria, *La Famille Royale de Belgique 1900–1930*, Libraire Albert Denuit, Bruxelles, 1930

Bing, Edward (editor), *The Letters of Tsar Nicholas and Empress Marie*, Ivor Nicholson and Watson, London, 1937

Blücher, Evelyn, Princess, *An English Wife in Berlin*, Constable, London, 1920

Blücher, Prince, *Memoirs*, John Murray, London, 1932

Bocca, Geoffrey, *The Uneasy Heads*, Weidenfeld and Nicolson, London, 1959

Boothroyd, Basil, *Philip: An Informal Biography*, Longman, London, 1971

Borgo, Vittorio Solaro del, *Giornate di Guerra del Re Soldato*, Mondadori, Milan, 1918.

Bosworth, Richard, *Italy, the Least of the Great Powers: Italian Foreign Policy before the First World War*, Cambridge University Press, 1979.

— *Italy and the Approach of the First World War*, Macmillan, London, 1983

Botkin, Glyeb, *The Real Romanovs*, Putnam, London, 1932

Bracalini, Romano, *Il Re 'Vittorioso'*, Feltrinelli, Milan, 1980

Brook-Shepherd, Gordon, *The Last Habsburg*, Weidenfeld and Nicolson, London, 1968

— *Uncle of Europe*, Collins, London, 1975

— *November 1918: The Last Act of the First World War*, Collins, London, 1981

— *Victims at Sarajevo*, Harvill Press, London, 1984

Bruce-Lockhart, R.H., *British Agent*, Putman, London, 1933

Buchanan, Sir George, *My Mission to Russia*, 2 vols, Cassell, London, 1923

Buchanan, Meriel, *Recollections of Imperial Russia*, Hutchinson, London, 1923

— *Diplomacy and Foreign Courts*, Hutchinson, London, 1928

— *The Dissolution of an Empire*, John Murray, London, 1932

— *Queen Victoria's Relations*, Cassell, London, 1958

— *Ambassador's Daughter*, Cassell, London, 1958

Bülow, Prince Bernhard von, *Imperial Germany*, Cassell, London, 1914

— *Memoirs*, 4 vols, Putman, London, 1931

Bulygin, Paul, and Kerensky, Alexander, *The Murder of the Romanovs*, Hutchinson, London, 1935

Bunsen, Marie von, *The World I Used to Know 1860–1912*, Thornton Butter-worth, London, 1933

Burrows, Ronald M., *The Abdication of King Constantine*, Anglo–Hellenic League, London, 1917

Buxhoevden, Baroness Sophie, *The Life and Tragedy of Alexandra Feodorovna, Empress of Russia*, Longman, London, 1928

Cammaerts, Emile, *Albert of Belgium*, Ivor Nicholson and Watson, London, 1935

Carol I, King of Romania, *Reminiscences* (ed. by Sidney Whitman), Harper and Brothers, London, 1899

Carr, William, *A History of Germany 1815–1945*, Edward Arnold, London, 1969

Cecil, Lamar, *Albert Ballin*, Princeton University Press, 1967

Chirol, Sir Valentine, *Fifty Years in a Changing World*, Jonathan Cape, London, 1927

Christmas, Walter, *The Life of King George of Greece*, Eveleigh Nash, London, 1914

Christopher of Greece, Prince, *Memoirs*, The Right Book Club, London, 1938

Churchill, Winston, *The World Crisis*, 6 vols, Butterworth, London, 1929–31

— *Great Contemporaries*, Macmillan, London, 1937

Constant, Stephen, *Foxy Ferdinand, Tsar of Bulgaria*, Sidgwick and Jackson, London, 1979

Constantine I, King of the Hellenes, *A King's Private Letters*, Eveleigh Nash and Grayson, London, 1925

Cooper, Lady Diana, *The Rainbow Comes and Goes*, Rupert Hart-Davis, London, 1958

Corti, Egon Caesar, *The Downfall of Three Dynasties*, Methuen, London, 1934

Cowles, Virginia, *The Kaiser*, Collins, London, 1963

— *1913: The Defiant Swansong*, Weidenfeld and Nicolson, London, 1967

— *The Russian Dagger*, Collins, London, 1969

Crankshaw, Edward, *The Fall of the House of Habsburg*, Longman, London, 1963

Cruttwell, C.R.M.F., *A History of the Great War 1914–1918*, Clarendon Press, Oxford, 1934

Cust, Sir Lionel, *King Edward VII and his Court*, John Murray, London, 1930

Czernin, Count Ottokar, *In the World War*, Cassell, London, 1919

Daggett, Mabel Potter, *Marie of Roumania*, Brentano's, London, 1926

Davis, A.N., *The Kaiser I Knew*, Hodder and Stoughton, London, 1918

Dedijer, Vladimir, *The Beloved Land*, MacGibbon and Kee, London, 1961
— *The Road to Sarajevo*, MacGibbon and Kee, London, 1967
De Flemalle, Gabriel de Liebert, *Fighting with King Albert*, Hodder and Stoughton, London, 1915
Dehn, Lili, *The Real Tsaritsa*, Thornton Butterworth, London, 1922
De Lichtervelde, Louis, le Comte, *La Monarchie en Belgique*, G. van Oest et Cie, Bruxelles, 1921
De Meeus, Adrien, *History of the Belgians*, Thames and Hudson, London, 1962
Devine, A., *Montenegro in History, Politics and War*, Fisher Unwin, London, 1918
De Weindel, Henri, and Sargeant, Philip, *Behind the Scenes at the Court of Vienna*, John Long, London, N.D.
Djilas, Milovan, *Land without Justice*, Methuen, London, 1958
Dugdale, Edgar T.S., *German Diplomatic Documents 1871–1914*, Methuen, London, 1928
— *Maurice de Bunsen*, John Murray, London, 1934

Elsberry, Terence, *Marie of Romania*, Cassell, London, 1973
Erbach-Schönberg, Princess Marie zu, *Reminiscences*, Allen and Unwin, London, 1925
Esher, Reginald, Viscount, *Journals and letters*, 4 vols, Ivor Nicolson and Watson, London, 1934–8
Eulalia, H.R.H. the Infanta, *Court Life from Within*, Cassell, London, 1915
— *Courts and Countries after the War*, Hutchinson, London, 1925
— *Memoirs*, Hutchinson, London, 1936
Eyck, Erich, *Wilhelm II*, Eugen Rentsch Verlag, Zurich, 1948

Falls, Cyril, *Caporetto 1917*, Weidenfeld and Nicolson, London, 1966
Fay, Sidney B., *The Origins of the World War*, 2 vols, Macmillan, London, 1967
Ferro, Marc, *La Grande Guerre 1914–1918*, Gallimard, Paris, 1969
ffoulkes, Maud, *All This Happened to Me*, Grayson and Grayson, London, 1937
Fischer, Fritz, *The War of Illusions*, Chatto and Windus, London, 1975
— *Germany's War Aims in the First World War*, Chatto and Windus, London, 1972
Fischer, H.W., *The Private Lives of William II and His Consort*, Heinemann, London, 1909
Forbes, Rosita, *Gypsy in the Sun*, Cassell, London, 1944
Fox, Ralph, *Lenin*, Gollancz, London, 1933
Fulöp-Miller, René, *Rasputin, the Holy Devil*, Putman, New York, 1928

Galet, E.M., *Albert, King of the Belgians in the Great War,* Putnam, London, 1931

Geiss, I., *July 1914: The Outbreak of the First World War: Selected Documents,* Batsford, London, 1967

Gerard, James E., *My Four Years in Germany,* Hodder and Stoughton, London, 1917

Gerlache, Commandant De Gomery de, *Belgium in Wartime,* G.H. Doran, New York, 1917

Geshev, I.E., *The Balkan League,* John Murray, London, 1915

Gilliard, Pierre, *Thirteen Years at the Russian Court,* Hutchinson, London, 1921

Giolitti, G., *Memoirs of My Life,* Chapman and Dodd, London, 1923

Gooch, G.P., *Recent Revelations of European Diplomacy,* Longman, London, 1940

Gore, John, *King George V,* John Murray, London, 1941

Gottlieb, W.W., *Studies in Secret Diplomacy during the First World War,* Allen and Unwin, London, 1957

Gould-Lee, Arthur S., *The Royal House of Greece,* Ward Lock, London, 1956

— *Helen, Queen Mother of Rumania,* Faber and Faber, London, 1956

Graham, Stephen, *Alexander of Jugoslavia,* Cassell, London, 1938

Gregory, J., *On the Edge of Diplomacy,* Hutchinson, London, 1929

Grey of Fallodon, Lord, *Twenty-five Years,* 2 vols, Hodder and Stoughton, London, 1925

Griscom, Lloyd C., *Diplomatically Speaking,* John Murray, London, 1941

Haller, Johannes Philipp, *The Kaiser's Friend,* 2 vols, Martin Secker, London, 1930

Hamilton, Lord Frederic, *The Vanished Pomps of Yesterday,* Hodder and Stoughton, London, 1920

Hanbury-Williams, Major General Sir John, *The Emperor Nicholas as I Knew Him,* Arthur L. Humphreys, London, 1922

Harden, Maximilian, *Word Portraits,* Blackwoods, London, 1912

Hardinge, Sir Arthur, *A Diplomatist in Europe,* Jonathan Cape, London, 1927

Hardinge of Penshurst, Lord, *Old Diplomacy,* John Murray, London, 1947

Hart, Liddell, *History of the First World War,* Cassell, London, 1970

Helmreich, Ernst, *The Diplomacy of the Balkan Wars,* Harvard University Press, Cambridge, Mass., 1938

Hepp, Alexandre, *Ferdinand de Bulgarie Intime,* Plon, Paris, 1910

Hibben, Paxton, *Constantine I and the Greek People,* Century, New York, 1920

Hindley, Geoffrey, *The Royal Families of Europe,* Lyric Books, London, 1979

Holstein, Friedrich von, *The Holstein Papers,* 4 vols, Cambridge University Press, 1958

Hourmouzios, Stelio, *No Ordinary Crown*, Weidenfeld and Nicolson, London, 1972

Jászi, Oscar, *The Dissolution of the Habsburg Monarchy*, University of Chicago Press, 1961

Joll, James, *Europe since 1870: An International History*, Penguin Books, London, 1980

— *The Origins of the First World War*, Longman, London, 1984

Judd, Denis, *Eclipse of Kings*, Macdonald and Jane, London, 1975

Jullian, Philippe, *Edward and the Edwardians*, Sidgwick and Jackson, London, 1967

— *Dreamers of Decadence*, Pall Mall Press, London, 1971

Katz, Robert, *The Fall of the House of Savoy*, Allen and Unwin, London, 1971

Kennan, George F., *The Fateful Alliance*, Manchester University Press, 1985

Kerensky, Alexander, *The Crucifixion of Liberty*, Day, New York, 1934

— *The Kerensky Memoirs*, Cassell, London, 1966

Knox, Sir Alfred, *With the Russian Army 1914–1917*, Hutchinson, London, 1921

Kokovtsov, Count, *Out of my Past*, Stanford University Press, 1935

Kürenberg, Joachim von, *The Kaiser*, Cassell, London, 1954

Kurth, Peter, *Anastasia: The Life of Anna Anderson*, Jonathan Cape, London, 1983

Kurtz, Harold, *The Second Reich*, Macdonald, London, 1970

Lafore, L., *The Long Fuse*, Weidenfeld and Nicolson, London, 1966

Larish von Moennich, Marie Louise, Countess, *Secrets of a Royal House*, John Long, London, 1935

Laski, Harold J., *Parliamentary Government in England*, Allen and Unwin, London, 1938

Lazarovitch Hrbelianovitch, Prince and Princess, *The Serbian People*, Scribners, New York, 1910

Lee, Sir Sydney, *King Edward VII*, 2 vols, Macmillan, London, 1927

Legge, Edward, *The Public and Private Life of Kaiser Wilhelm II*, Eveleigh Nash, London, 1915

Lister, Roma, *Reminiscences*, Hutchinson, London, N.D.

Lloyd-George, David, *War Memoirs*, Ivor Nicholson and Watson, London, 1933–6

Louise, Princess of Schleswig-Holstein, *Behind the Scenes at the Prussian Court*, John Murray, London, 1939

Longford, Elizabeth, *The Royal House of Windsor*, Weidenfeld and Nicolson, London, 1974

Ludendorff, General Erich, *My War Memoirs 1914–1918*, 2 vols, Hutchinson, London, 1919

Ludwig, Emil, *Kaiser Wilhelm II*, Allen and Unwin, London, 1926
— *July 1914*, Putman, London, 1929

Macartney, C.A., and Palmer, A.W., *Independent Eastern Europe*, Macmillan, London, 1962
— *The Habsburg Empire*, Weidenfeld and Nicolson, London, 1968
MacDonald, John, *Czar Ferdinand and His People*, T.C. and E.C. Jack, London, 1913
Mack Smith, D., *Italy: A Modern History*, University of Michigan Press, 1960
Madol, H.R., *Ferdinand of Bulgaria*, Hurst and Blackett, London, 1933
Magnus, Philip, *King Edward the Seventh*, John Murray, London, 1964
Mann, Golo, *The History of Germany since 1789*, Chatto and Windus, London, 1968
Mansergh, Nicholas, *The Coming of the First World War*, Longman, New York, 1949
Manteyer, G. de, *Austria's Peace Offer 1916–1917*, Constable, London, 1921
Marek, George R., *The Eagles Die*, Hart-Davis, MacGibbon, London, 1975
Marie of Romania, Queen, *The Story of My Life*, 3 vols, Cassell, London, 1934
Marie, Grand Duchess of Russia, *Things I Remember*, Cassell, London, 1930
Marie-Louise, Princess, *My Memories of Six Reigns*, Evans Brothers, London, 1956
Martineau, Mrs Philip, *Roumania and Her Rulers*, Stanley Paul, London, 1927
Massie, Robert, *Nicholas and Alexandra*, Gollancz, London, 1968
May, A.J., *The Habsburg Monarchy 1867–1914*, Oxford University Press, 1961
— *The Passing of the Habsburg Monarchy 1914–1918*, University of Pennsylvania Press, 1966
Mayer, Arno J., *The Persistence of the Old Regime*, Croom Helm, London, 1981
Maximilian, Prince of Baden, *The Memoirs of Prince Max of Baden*, 2 vols, Constable, London, 1928
Melas, George M., *Ex-King Constantine and the War*, Hutchinson, London, 1920
Miller, W., *The Ottoman Empire and Its Successors 1801–1927*, Cambridge University Press, 1927
Miyatovitch, Cheddo, *Serbia of the Serbians*, Pitman, London, 1915
Monroe, Will S., *Bulgaria and Her People*, Page, Boston, 1914
Moorehead, Alan, *The Russian Revolution*, Collins and Hamish Hamilton, London, 1958
Mossolov, A.A., *At the Court of the Last Tsar*, Methuen, London, 1935
Müller, G.A. von, *The Kaiser and His Court: the Diaries, Note Books and Letters of Admiral G.v.M. Chief of the Naval Secretariat 1914–1918*, MacDonald, London, 1961

Napier, H.D., *Experiences of a Military Attaché in the Balkans*, Drane's London, 1924

Nelson, W.H., *The Soldier Kings: The House of Hohenzollern*, Putnam, New York, 1970

Newton, Thomas, Lord, *Lord Lansdowne*, Macmillan, London, 1929

Nicholas II, Tsar, *Journal Intime de Nicholas II*, Payot, Paris, 1925

— *The Letters of the Tsar to the Tsaritsa 1914–1917*, Bodley Head, London, 1929

— *The Secret Letters of the last Tsar*, Longman Green, London, 1938

Nicholas of Greece, Prince, *My Fifty Years*, Hutchinson, London, 1927

— *Political Memoirs 1914–1917*, Hutchinson, London, 1928

Nicolson, Harold, *Sir Arthur Nicolson, Bart, First Lord Carnock*, Constable, London, 1930

— *King George V*, Constable, London, 1952

Nowak, Karl Friedrich, *Kaiser and Chancellor*, Putman, London, 1930

Oglander, Cecil Aspinall, *Roger Keyes*, Hogarth Press, London, 1951

Owen, Sidney Cunliffe, *Elisabeth of the Belgians*, Herbert Jenkins, London, 1954

Paget, Walburga, Lady, *Embassies of Other Days*, 2 vols, Hutchinson, London, 1923

— *The Linings of Life*, 2 vols., Hurst and Blackett, London, 1928

Paléologue, Maurice, *An Ambassador's Memoirs*, 3 vols, Hutchinson, London, 1923–5

— *Journal 1913–1914*, Plon, Paris, 1947

Palmer, Alan, *The Gardeners of Salonika*, Deutsch, London, 1965

— *The Kaiser*, Weidenfeld and Nicolson, London, 1978

Paoli, Xavier, *My Royal Clients*, Hodder and Stoughton, London, N.D.

Pares, Sir Bernard, *The Fall of the Russian Monarchy*, Jonathan Cape, London, 1939

Pauli, Hertha, *The Secret of Sarajevo*, Collins, London, 1966

Petrovich, M.B., *The Emergence of Russian Panslavism*, Columbia University Press, 1956

Pitt, Barrie, *1918: The Last Act*, Cassell, London, 1962

Pless, Daisy, Princess of, *Princess Daisy of Pless* by Herself, John Murray, London, 1928

— *From My Private Diary*, John Murray, London, 1931

— *What I Left Unsaid*, Cassell, London, 1936

Poincaré, Raymond, *Au Service de la France*, Librarie Plon, Paris, 1932

Ponsonby, Frederick, *Recollections of Three Reigns*, Eyre and Spottiswoode, London, 1951

Pope-Hennessy, James, *Queen Mary*, George Allen and Unwin, London, 1959

Radziwill, Princess Catherine, *Germany under Three Emperors*, Cassell, London, 1917
— *The Intimate Life of the Last Tsarina*, Cassell, London, 1929
— *Nicholas II: The Last of the Tsars*, Cassell, London, 1931
Ramm, Agatha, *Germany 1789–1919*, Methuen, London, 1967
Rasputin, Maria, *My Father*, Cassell, London, 1934
Redlich, Joseph, *Emperor Francis Joseph of Austria*, Macmillan, London, 1929
Reed, J., *Ten Days that Shook the World*, Lawrence and Wishart, London, 1962
Reischach, Baron Hugo von, *Under Three Emperors*, Constable, London, 1927
Remak, Joachim, *Sarajevo*, Weidenfeld and Nicolson, London, 1959
Renzi, W.A., *Italy's Neutrality and Entrance into the Great War: A Reexamination*, The American Historical Review, June 1968
Ritter, Gerhard, *The Sword and the Sceptre*, 4 vols, Allen Lane, London, 1972
Roberts, J.M., *Europe 1880–1945*, Longman, London, 1967
Robertson, A., *Victor Emmanuel III, King of Italy*, George Allen and Unwin, London, 1925
Rodd, Sir James Rennell, *Social and Diplomatic Memories 1902–1919*, Edward Arnold, London, 1925
Rodzianko, M.V., *The Reign of Rasputin*, A.M. Philpot, London, 1927
Röhl, John C.G., *Germany without Bismarck*, Batsford, London, 1967
— *From Bismarck to Hitler*, Longman, London, 1970
Rose, Kenneth, *King George V*, Weidenfeld and Nicolson, London, 1983
Roosevelt, Theodore, *Letters* (ed. by E.E. Morison), Harvard University Press, 1951–1954
— *Cowboys and Kings*, Harvard University Press, 1954
Ryder, A.J., *The German Revolution of 1918*, Cambridge University Press, 1967

Salandra, A., *Italy and the Great War*, Arnold, London, 1932
Savinsky, A., *Recollections of a Russian Diplomat*, Hutchinson, London, 1927
Savolea, Charles, *How Belgium Saved Europe*, Heinemann, London, 1915
Sazonov, Serge, *Fateful Years*, Stokes, New York, 1928
Scaroni, S., *Con Vittorio Emanuele III*, Montadori, Milan, 1954
Schepens, Luc, and Vandewoude, Emile, *Albert et Elisabeth 1914–1918: Albums de la Reine, Notes du Roi*, Credit Communal, Bruxelles, 1984
Schmitt, B., *Triple Alliance and Triple Entente*, Holt, Rinehart and Winston, New York, 1934
Schwering, Axel von, *The Berlin Court under William II*, Cassell, London, 1915

Seth, Ronald, *Caporetto*, Macdonald, London, 1965
Seton-Watson, R.W., *The Southern Slav Question and the Habsburg Monarchy*, Constable, London, 1911
— *Sarajevo*, Hutchinson, London, 1926
— *A History of the Roumanians*, Cambridge University Press, 1934
— *The Russian Empire 1801–1917*, Oxford University Press, 1967
Shumway, Harry Irving, *Albert the Soldier-King*, Page, New York, 1934
Sixte de Bourbon, Prince, *l'Offre de Paix Séparée de l'Autriche*, Librarie Plon, Paris, 1920
Stancioff, Anna, *Recollections of a Bulgarian Diplomat's Wife*, Hutchinson, London, 1930
Steed, H.W., *The Habsburg Monarchy*, Constable, London, 1919
Stevenson, F.S., *A History of Montenegro*, Jarrold and Sons, London, 1914
Stone, Norman, *Europe Transformed 1878–1919*, Fontana, London, 1983
Summers, Anthony, and Mangold, Tom, *The Fall of the Tsar*, Gollancz, London, 1976

Taylor, A.J.P., *The Course of German History*, Hamish Hamilton, London, 1945
— *The Habsburg Monarchy*, Hamish Hamilton, London, 1948
— *The Struggle for Mastery in Europe 1848–1918*, Oxford University Press, 1979
— *The First World War*, Oxford University Press, 1979
Taylor, Edmond, *The Fall of the Dynasties*, Doubleday, New York, 1963
Temperley, H.W., *History of Serbia*, G. Bell, London, 1917
Thomson, David, *Europe since Napoleon*, Longman, London, 1957
Tirpitz, Admiral von, *My Memoirs*, 2 vols, Hurst and Backett, London, 1919
Trevelyan, G.M., *Grey of Fallodon*, Longman, London, 1937
Tschuppik, Karl, *The Reign of the Emperor Franz Joseph*, Bell and Sons, London, 1930
T'Serclaes, Baroness Elsie de, *Flanders and Other Fields*, Harrap, London, 1964
Tuchman, Barbara W., *August 1914*, Constable, London, 1962

Vaka, Demetra, *Constantine, King and Traitor*, John Lane, The Bodley Head, London, 1918
Valiani, Leo. *The End of Austria–Hungary*, Secker and Warburg, London, 1973
Varé, Daniele, *Twilight of the Kings*, John Murray, London, 1948
Victoria, Empress of Germany, *Letters of the Empress Frederick*, Macmillan, London, 1928
Viktoria Luise, Duchess of Brunswick and Lüneburg, *Im Strom der Zeit*, Göttingnen, Hanover, 1975

— *The Kaiser's Daughter*, W.H. Allen, London, 1977

Vorres, Ian, *The Last Grand Duchess*, Hutchinson, London, 1964

Vyrubova, Anna, *Memories of the Russian Court*, Macmillan, London, 1923

Waddington, Mary King, *Italian Letters of a Diplomat's Wife*, Smith, Elder and Company, London, 1905

Wallersee-Wittelsbach, Countess Larisch, *Her Majesty Elizabeth*, John Long, London, 1934

Waring, L.F., *Serbia*, Home University Library, 1917

West, Rebecca, *Black Lamb and Grey Falcon*, 2 vols, Macmillan, London, 1967

Wheeler-Bennett, John W., *Hindenburg, The Wooden Titan*, Macmillan, London, 1967

— *King George VI*, Macmillan, London, 1958

Whitlock, Brand, *Belgium under the German Occupation*, Heinemann, London, 1919

Whittle, Tyler, *The Last Kaiser*, Heinemann, London, 1977

Wilhelm II, Kaiser, *The German Emperor's Speeches*, Longman, London, 1904

— *The Kaiser's Letters to the Tsar* (ed. by N.F. Grant), Hodder and Stoughton, London, 1920

— *My Memoirs 1878–1918*, Cassell, London, 1922

Wilhelm, Crown Prince of Germany, *Memoirs*, Thornton Butterworth, London, 1922

Witte, Count Serge, *Memoirs*, Heinemann, London, 1921

Wolff, Robert Lee, *The Balkans in Our Time*, Harvard University Press, 1956

Wolff, T., *The Eve of 1914*, Gollancz, London, 1935

Youssoupov, Prince Felix, *Rasputin*, Cape, London, 1927

Zeman, Z.A.B., *The Break-up of the Habsburg Empire 1914–1918*, Oxford University Press, 1961

Newspapers, Magazines and Reference Books

Daily Mail, Daily Telegraph, New York Times, The Times, Illustrated London News, The Graphic, Burke's Royal Families of the World, History of the First World War (BPC Publishing Ltd, Purnell, London), The Times History of the War 1914–1918 (The Times, London).

Index